Praise for *Proud Parents' Guide to Raising Athletic, Balanced, and Coordinated Kids*

"Karen encourages safe and fun physical activity for kids and parents to share and sets a foundation for a lifetime of good exercise habits."

Dara Hunt; Physical Therapist

"What a great resource for parents! You will have fun, bond with your children, and put them on the path to lifelong physical and mental health!"

Mariaemma Willis; Coauthor, *Discover Your Child's Learning Style*

"An essential read for those parents and educators who truly want to help youngsters of all ages become physically, socially, emotionally, and academically fit."

Pete Saccone; Creator, It's "Funner" to Be a Runner program

"The activities, which help build self-confidence and success in sports and life, are easy to incorporate in any family lifestyle."

D. Ross Campbell, MD; Lecturer & Author, *How to Really Love Your Child*; Associate Professor of Pediatrics and Psychiatry, University of Tennessee College of Medicine

"Very practical, quick, and easy to use. I will recommend this book to my colleagues and to all parents who attend my classes."

Marina Monta; Associate Professor, Parent Education; San Diego Community College District, Continuing Education

"If you want happy, active, healthy, confident, and coordinated children, Karen Ronney will explain what you need to know and show you how to do it. Any parent can coach their children using activities that are light on instruction and heavy on fun."

Kirk R. Anderson; Director, Recreational Coaches and Programs, United States Tennis Association

"Karen has written an excellent volume that provides recommended age-specific activities to help nurture development, growth, and good health. It is a must-read for every new parent!"

Allen D. Schwartz, MD; FAAP; Head of Pediatrics, Scripps Mercy Hospital, San Diego, CA

D1455696

"This book fills a void of parenting information that is not usually available until children are involved in an organized sport. We wish we'd had this book when we were raising our families!"

Karla Holland-Moritz and Glen Campbell; Codirectors, Strings by the Sea; Cellists, San Diego Symphony Orchestra

"As an educator for twenty-one years I've seen the sad faces of children in grades K– 8 who were picked last to participate in a recess game or PE sport. *Proud Parents' Guide* is the first step toward ensuring children are not subjected to this kind of isolation by their peers or lacking confidence when confronted with participating in physical activities."

LaDreda P. Lewis; CEO, 40 Acres and A Mind, Inc.; dba Sylvan Learning, La Mesa, Bonita, and Imperial Beach, CA

"An excellent hands-on book that is practical for every parent and educator. A must-read!"

Jeff Paterson, MA; Educational Administration, Azusa Pacific University; President, California Home School Sports; Athletic Director, Christian Heritage School; Physical Education Teacher, Moreno Valley Unified School District

"Buy this book, use it, and you will see very positive results."

Joseph Nyiri; Artist and Art Instructor, San Diego City Schools, San Diego Zoo

"Refreshingly sane and low-keyed. If you want outlandish sports diets, promises of superstardom or guarantees of future athletic scholarships, this isn't the book for you. Ronney emphasizes the importance of recognizing different learning styles, maintaining realistic expectations, and keeping things fun."

Wayne Wilson; Vice President, Education Services; LA84 Foundation

"Ms. Ronney has created an easy-to-use yet very helpful resource for parents to strengthen the physical health and ability of their young children with activities that are as playful as they are useful."

Christine D'Amico; Author, *The Pregnant Woman's Companion*

"Karen Ronney has written a comprehensive, well-researched, easy-to-read guide that not only covers physical skills but also helps parents understand brain development, learning styles, and gives great suggestions for fun activities."

Dr. Jenn Berman; Marriage, Family and Child Therapist; Author, *The A to Z Guide to Raising Happy, Confident Kids*; Four time USA Rhythmic Gymnastics National Team Member; Mother of two

Kara Ronney

PROUD PARENTS' GUIDE
to Raising Athletic, Balanced, and Coordinated Kids

Karen Ronney

THOMAS NELSON
Since 1798

NASHVILLE   DALLAS   MEXICO CITY   RIO DE JANEIRO   BEIJING

Published in Nashville, Tennessee, by Thomas Nelson. Thomas Nelson is a trademark of Thomas Nelson, Inc.

Thomas Nelson, Inc., titles may be purchased in bulk for educational, business, fund-raising, or sales promotional use. For information, please e-mail SpecialMarkets@ThomasNelson.com.

The Proud Parents' program is meant to be a source of information with suggestions for playing various games and activities that can promote coordination and fine and gross motor skills in children from birth to age six. This plan is not written as medical advice, nor should it be perceived as such. It has, however, been reviewed and edited by pediatricians, occupational and physical therapists, biologists, early education teachers, professional coaches, and parents.

The Proud Parents' program, the author, and Thomas Nelson Publishers do not endorse any particular method of parenting, coaching, teaching, or child development philosophies. In all cases of working with your child, when in doubt, err on the side of caution, and avoid any activity that makes your child feel unhappy or uncomfortable. If you have serious concerns about any issues, seek appropriate medical advice.

Library of Congress Cataloging-in-Publication Data

Ronney, Karen, 1959-
    Proud parents' guide to raising athletic, balanced, and coordinated
kids : a lifetime of benefit in just 10 minutes a day / Karen Ronney.
        p. cm.
    Includes bibliographical references.
    ISBN 978-0-7852-2822-6 (pbk.)
    1. Motor ability in children. 2. Exercise for children. 3. Physical
fitness for children. I. Title.
    RJ133.R66 2008
    613.7'042—dc22

                                                                    2008014053

Printed in the United States of America
08 09 10 11 12 RRD 7 6 5 4 3 2 1

To the memory of my father,
Bob Frawley
September 18, 1917 to May 2, 2008
Thank you for ninety wonderful years and a lifetime of memories.
You were my inspirational Proud Parent, father, and coach, who taught me all
things were possible with love, hope, faith, dreams, and hard work.
God Bless and Safe Home.
Dad, your legacy lives on . . .

To my mother,
Irene Frawley
Thank you for your dedication and eternal support.
You've led by example showing what it means to be a great Mom.

And always to my husband,
Doug
For seventeen wonderful years of marriage and an endless supply of love,
patience, and computer technology magic.

And to my three treasures,
Alexis, Brooke, and Julia
My constant source of inspiration and a reminder that miracles happen daily
by being blessed with children, family, and friends.

Contents

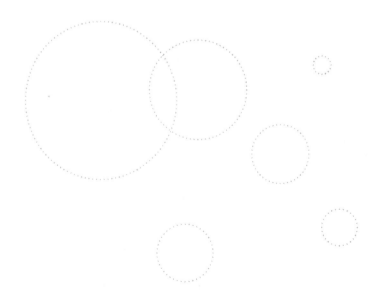

Foreword

When my brother was six, he got a little pudgy—not obese or even significantly overweight, just a little less angular than either he or I had been up until then. Our very progressive pediatrician suggested that my parents limit the bread he ate and cut back on butter. Exercise was never mentioned, but then it didn't need to be. We were Midwestern kids living in farm country in the 1970s.

Our family was active. We played Frisbee and tag, took long bike rides and country walks. On weekends, my brother and I went on grand adventures with the dog, hiking woods and meadows, climbing trees, and fording creeks. Physical education at school was actual *gym*—an hour each day of hot, sweaty, heart-pounding sports that required showers afterward. We had enough time during our lunch break to run and play sports once we were done eating.

My family cut back on carbohydrates and fat, and my brother hit a growth spurt and leaned out pretty quickly. I forgot about that episode until fifteen years later, when I was in medical school and realized just how unusual our pediatrician had been to intervene with a child who had minimal weight gain like my brother's.

Fast-forward another fifteen years. As a pediatrician myself, I now spend roughly a quarter of my time working on weight management with kids. I direct the Healthy Living Program at Children's Healthcare Medical Associates in San Diego, and I serve as part of a coalition addressing weight issues in children. Obesity is one of the most significant health-care problems facing our kids today.

Not long after starting practice as a pediatrician in San Diego, I recognized that obesity and lack of fitness, even in the children of normal weight, were *huge* problems in my patient population. Immunizations and antibiotics have greatly reduced the threat of infectious disease. Parental awareness, laws governing access to hazards such as swimming pools, better protective gear, safer cars, the near-elimination of child labor, and a move away from farming all have helped to decrease the rate of pediatric trauma.

As the world of children gets safer, the incidence and complications of obesity and lack of physical fitness are rapidly on the rise. Nationally 15 to 20 percent of kids are considered to be overweight, and another 15 percent are categorized as being at risk of becoming overweight. This is a huge change over the last four decades.

The reality is that when it comes to obesity and a lack of fitness in children, the most important changes happen at home. A recent longitudinal study looking at pediatric obesity in children of the Pima tribe of Arizona found the single best predictor of obesity at age ten was the presence of obesity by age five. In our practice, we emphasize taking daily walks from the time babies are born and restricting their diets to *only* breast milk or formula for the first six months. Then, slowly, parents can introduce solid foods and water between six and twelve months, placing emphasis on fruits and vegetables and limiting carbohydrate portions. We encourage avoiding all juice, fried foods, fast foods, and foods with refined sugar for at least the first three years, serving children the same healthy foods the rest of the family is eating, rather than making separate dishes for the little ones. We emphasize not exposing babies and toddlers to television at all, limiting preschoolers to no more than a half-hour per day, and school-aged kids to an hour of combined recreational screen time (television, videos, movies, and video games—screen-based and handheld nonhomework computer use), and never allowing televisions or computers in kids' rooms. Finally, we stress not using strollers once toddlers start walking and getting kids into organized sports very early. Many of our local sports programs start T-ball and soccer at age three.

The bottom line is our kids eat too much junk and not enough healthy food, spend too much time sitting passively in front of various sorts of screens, and perhaps most of all, don't get enough exercise. In many ways, the underlying problem really isn't weight—it's living a sedentary lifestyle. As it turns out, today's children don't actually consume any more calories than kids in the 1960s, and they actually eat a lower-fat diet. What our kids do is take in a lot more carbohydrates and get very little exercise. Studies have shown that even one extra hour of moderate exercise a week can reduce the risk of obesity, keeping kids from rising out of their ideal body weight range.

My brother and I were lucky. We didn't grow up in the era of fast food or 6 a.m.-to-6 p.m. after-school daycare programs. We didn't have televisions in our rooms, video games, or computers. Our diet included far more fruits, vegetables, and seafood than that of our meat-and-potatoes neighbors. Healthy living choices are tougher now. It's so easy at the end of a long day to drive through and pick up fast meals, rolled tacos, or a bucket of fried chicken. We work long hours and are exhausted at the end of the day.

The parents of the children in my weight management program love and care for their kids just as much as my parents loved me. They are good parents but live in a more complicated world. Raising physically fit and competent children today is a challenge that requires commitment and lifestyle changes. With the program put forth in this book, it's not only possible but fun and easy. You don't need to pay for classes or buy expensive equipment. These games develop fine and gross motor skills with things you already have around the house.

Karen Ronney's extensive experience as a coach, educator, and mother, and her concern for kids who lack even the most basic physical skills, has led to the development of this program. It's not about raising a superathlete. It's about raising a healthy kid, with good skills and coordination, one who considers physical activity an essential and enjoyable part of daily life.

Children with good motor skills can participate in and enjoy sports that use those skills. Adults who participated in regular physical activity as children are far more likely to get adequate exercise and maintain healthy weights as adults. Fit adults are healthier and feel better. The choices you make for your kids today are likely to influence them for the rest of their lives. So get your kids and start playing!

—Whitney Carr Edwards, MD
Director, The Healthy Living Project
Children's Healthcare Medical Associates
San Diego, California

Author's Note

I have always wondered what it means to be a "naturally coordinated and athletic" kid. Exactly what makes an individual so naturally talented? For many years, I thought it was a gift at birth reserved for a fortunate few. After twenty-five years of coaching and teaching kids in sports, academics, art, and music, however, I know that is simply not true. With timely intervention, kids who might have otherwise struggled can become naturally coordinated individuals who are ready to excel in school, sports, music, art, drama, dance, electronics, computer skills, and many other areas.

COORDINATION IS MULTIFACETED

The definition of a coordinated child might be someone with balance, body awareness, concentration, focus, keen depth perception, spatial skills, and auditory and visual acuity. A coordinated individual must also have excellent fine and gross motor movements, as well as cognitive, psychological, and social development. That may sound like a lot to ask for in a human being—that is, if one were to expect all of those talents to appear instantaneously in a child's life (preferably at birth, if one could select the timeliness of the gift). Given that specific criteria, then yes, there are very few naturally coordinated children born into this world.

Yet, if one considers the possibility of a child gradually developing these traits over a period of years—from birth to age six—it is not such a monumental task. In fact, it's not only very possible but also very realistic and fairly easy to accomplish. There are three critical factors necessary to develop a well-balanced and coordinated kid: early intervention with Proud Parents' games, the consistent use of this program, and a child's desire to engage in these activities.

All three factors are important, but the most critical element is developing coordination as soon as possible. While it is never too late to help kids, the earlier you begin, the greater chance your child has of becoming coordinated and athletic. The second factor is being dedicated to developing your child's natural abilities by *consistently* playing these games three to five times a week. Over a period of months and years, you will be amazed at the ease with which your child performs basic fundamental fine and gross motor skills. The final factor is your ability to keep this program fun so your child will be motivated to continue to participate in these games with you.

MY PERSONAL PROOF

Now that you know the definition of a coordinated child and the criteria it takes to develop overall skills, let's move on to the proof and the reason I wrote this book. As a child, I had average eye-hand coordination with below-average gross motor skills. I needed help with balance, footwork, speed, quickness, agility, and basic running techniques. Honestly, I was clumsy and awkward, and I often tripped over my own two feet.

Through early coaching intervention from my father, a former physical education instructor at Rockefeller Center in New York, I received the right help in that critical window of opportunity of early childhood. By age twelve, he had taught me the fundamentals of various sports, including volleyball, softball, track, tennis, basketball, football, badminton, swimming, and table tennis. My father showed me how to move with balance; throw, catch, and hit a softball; and shoot, dribble, and pass a basketball. I learned to use my wrist in badminton, hit topspin groundstrokes in tennis, and dive with pointed toes. In high school, I excelled in track and held league records in 400- and 800-meter events. I was the number one singles player on the girls' tennis team at Ulysses S. Grant High in Los Angeles. Later I became the top-ranked singles tennis player for California State University, Northridge, and was a finalist in the 1986 Division II National Collegiate Athletic Association (NCAA) team championships. My desire to become a professional athlete was fulfilled after playing four years in women's professional tennis tournaments throughout the United States, Europe, and Australia. I then pursued a college degree and a career in journalism as a sportswriter.

Now that you know my story, you can see that I was not born a naturally gifted child but developed into a coordinated kid with early intervention and a lot of practice. As a result, I know it is possible to develop fine and gross motor coordination, and I believe that potential exists in your child if you are willing to provide the early support and guidance.

THE BIRTH OF THE PROUD PARENTS' PROGRAM

For the past twenty-five years I have developed a collection of more than two hundred games to develop coordination in kids from birth. I know this program works because it was inspired by parenting my three children and has been tested on thousands of other youngsters of all ages and abilities. In almost every circumstance, these games have helped children improve their fine and gross motor skills, eye-hand and eye-foot coordination, ball-throwing skills, manual dexterity, and visual, cognitive, and spatial awareness.

The ten-minute format emerged out of necessity. As a busy mom, coach, and teacher, I realized time was a precious commodity. I wanted to play Proud Parents' games with my kids, but I did not have all day to do it. As it turned out, we learned that the best results are obtained by playing games in ten minutes or less, because that is the limit of a young child's attention span.

Our limited financial resources at the time led to creative uses of basic sports equipment and generic household supplies. That is why the games in this program incorporate everyday items, including buckets, laundry baskets, scarves, rope, tape, towels, pillows, small trash cans, cardboard paper towel rolls, pencils, rulers, empty two-liter soda bottles, tweezers, cotton balls, mixing bowls, rice, flour, and plastic cups. The basic sports supplies include a variety of playground balls, balloons, inflatable beach balls, child-sized rackets, plastic bats, jump ropes, bubbles, and hula hoops. Nothing fancy, nothing expensive. All of the items in this book are available at neighborhood toy, craft, sports, and home improvement stores.

BENEFITS OF THE PROUD PARENTS' PROGRAM

As of this writing, my children are eight, twelve, and fifteen years old. I started playing Proud Parents' games with them from birth. Over the years, they have sampled many activities such as gymnastics, soccer, karate, ballet, volleyball, softball, tennis, baseball, badminton, football, swimming, diving, canoeing, sailing, kayaking, and fishing. To maintain balanced and healthy lifestyles, they eventually narrowed their focus to a few sporting interests each: soccer, tennis, water polo, and swimming. All three kids play tennis about three times a week and are currently ranked in Southern California. Additionally, the younger two compete in club soccer, and my oldest child plays tennis and water polo and is a member of her high-school swim team. That might sound like a crazy over-scheduled family lifestyle, but it works. The activities we seem to have little time for are watching television and playing electronic games, which are reserved for occasional weekend fun. Keep in mind these sports, music, and extracurricular experiences have occurred one at a time over the past eight to fifteen years.

The Proud Parents' games in this book I played with my children not only helped them in sports and coordination, but they had some unexpected benefits. As a result of playing these games, they were physically, socially, and emotionally ready to learn to play music and sports, and to speak a second language early in life. They began playing Suzuki-style violin and cello between ages three and six, and they currently play string instruments in a local youth orchestra. They learned German as a second language by age four and now attend a French lan-guage immersion school. All are fluent in French and English, and the older two girls recently added Spanish to their middle- and high-school curricula.

The Proud Parents' program also helped build stronger relationships within my family. My kids looked forward to playing these fun games, and we integrated them into our normal daily activities, much like eating family meals or reading sto-ries at bedtime. Excursions to the park became obstacle courses filled with visual, tactical, and spatial challenges to enhance fine and gross motor skills. Car rides were ideal for cognitive development by reciting memory games, and the kitchen became an activity center for finger control by writing letters in rice-filled cookie trays. These were all small *parts* that contributed to developing the *whole* child.

PROUD PARENTS' AND SPECIAL-NEEDS KIDS

The Proud Parents' program can benefit special-needs and developmentally chal-lenged children. As a Special Olympics national coaching instructor and regional event director for Special Olympics of Southern California, I have used this program to help many athletes with autism, Down and Asperger syndromes, and other neurological or genetic disorders. Proud Parents' games can help special-needs individuals develop fine and gross motor movements that are helpful to participating in track, soccer, tennis, basketball, volleyball, floor hockey, swimming, and softball. In fact, helping kids with special needs is so important to me, a portion of the royalties earned from the sale of this book are being donated to Special Olympics.

NOW IS THE TIME TO GET STARTED

Proud Parents' can work for you and your child, just as it has for me, my family, and my students. You do not need special coaching credentials or expertise to play basic coordination games and athletic activities with your child. This program leaves nothing to chance, and these purposeful games and activities can empower you to make a difference in your child's life. You and your child have everything to gain. Try it today!

How to Use This Book

The Proud Parents' program is made for busy parents who have a great desire to help their kids but not a lot of time to do it. This user-friendly format is divided into two sections. The first is designed to help you understand how your child develops coordination, handedness, depth perception, sensory integration, fine and gross motor movement, and brain-cell growth. It also explains the windows of learning for your child and defines the skills to emphasize during these critical periods. You could skip to the second section and begin playing Proud Parents' games. However, it is important to read the first part to determine, at least, your child's strongest learning style, whether auditory, visual, or kinesthetic. Then use the suggested methods for ultimate results when playing games with your baby.

The second part of the book is a comprehensive collection of games you can play with your child. It's a reference book of activities conveniently divided into age groups, developmental goals, and levels of difficulty. You can briefly glance at a game and within seconds discover the objective, rules of play, and supplies needed for the activity.

To select a game, find the chapter that corresponds to your child's age. Your child's skills will likely fit into the age-appropriate category in many areas. It is also possible, however, to benefit from games in the younger and older age groups. For example, your three-year-old may excel at fine motor skills and may be advanced in hand manipulation toys, drawing, and craft activities. Start with the fine motor games in "Building Blocks for Three-Year-Olds," but also look for that same skill in the "Golden Years: Four- to Six-Year Olds" chapter. Your youngster might be ready for some advanced activities. On the other hand, your strong fine motor learner may need help with gross motor skills. Maybe you have noticed your child's difficulty balancing or hopping on one foot. Look in the "Athletic Activities for One, Two, and You" chapter for gross motor and eye-foot coordination games. Sample a little bit from each chapter and experiment with the different games. For special needs, consider your child's actual skill developmental level as opposed to his or her chronological age when selecting games.

POSITIVE CHILD'S PLAY

Each activity is designed to last two to ten minutes, depending on your child's age, ability to focus, and the difficulty of the game. Factors for overall success include selecting a playtime when your child is healthy, rested, and well fed. Fatigue, hunger, and illness make it more difficult to concentrate and can be a distraction to both children and adults. For example, when your five-year-old is healthy, he may be very capable of dribbling a ball with ease through a simple obstacle course, but a stomachache can alter eye-hand coordination, giving a false reading on your child's skills.

Other factors to consider for positive parent and child playtime include having the right motivation for using this program. The Proud Parents' plan is written to give you the tools to help your child become a happy, active, confident, and coordinated kid, who will grow up to become a successful adult with a satisfying career and a passion for recreational sports participation and physical fitness. If your child experiences a career in professional athletics along the way, that's a bonus!

LEARNING STYLES

How does your child learn? Your child probably has a preference for one of the three styles of learning. Have you noticed your baby happily responding to music, voices, and noise? Is your child captivated looking at books, watching videos, and observing the world at large? Does your toddler make it a life goal to climb out of a stroller on a regular basis? These are some examples of auditory, visual, and kinesthetic learners, respectively. Included in this chapter are great tips on how to adjust your parenting style to meet your child's needs.

BUILDING BETTER BRAINS

Your child's brain is an amazing neural network. Early visual, auditory, sensory, emotional, and fine- and gross-motor-stimulating games can increase the number of neural connections in your child's brain as well as create new pathways of learning. You will learn about the blooming and pruning periods of the brain and how to expand your child's learning potential in these key periods.

FINE MOTOR DEVELOPMENT

Good eye-hand coordination is one of the basic elements of fine motor skills and the cornerstone of athletics. Chapter 5 describes the gradual development of hand control, from reflexive grasping patterns in newborns to voluntary release skills in babyhood, in-hand manipulation in toddlerhood, and the use of tools and toys in the preschool years when ball-throwing skills begin to emerge. Find out what you can do to help the process. Finally, help your child develop fine motor planning in preparation for sports and school.

RIGHT- OR LEFT-HANDED

Your child's decision to be right- or left-handed happened long before birth. Research shows that kids come neurologically prewired for hand preference. In chapter 8 you will learn when it's typical for your child to be ambidextrous and the age of discovery for selecting a dominant right or left hand. If your child is a left-hander, it is important to understand life as a southpaw in a right-handed world.

GROSS MOTOR DEVELOPMENT

Ages and stages of growth vary greatly among children. Some babies are on the fast track while others are happy to take their time, slowly achieving developmental milestones. This chapter covers many aspects of gross motor movement, which is using the larger muscles and the limbs. You can learn about newborn reflexes and the developmental steps that can lead to rolling, sitting, standing, walking, galloping, skipping, and running. From ages three to six, your child's gross motor function should begin to include coordination, locomotion, and balance, all of which set the stage for future athletics.

COORDINATION AND SIDEDNESS

Coordination is a skill that relates to your child's sidedness, which is a concept of right- and left-brain dominance involving the use of the hands, feet, eyes, and ears. Each of these elements has a direct impact on your child's athleticism and ability to learn. Use the tips in this chapter to test your child's sidedness and check out the games that will reinforce the appropriate skills.

SUPER SENSORY INTEGRATION

Key elements of the sensory system are defined in chapter 9, involving the senses of hearing, vision, touch, taste, and smell. All contribute to the development of the total child, regarding speech, language, balance, eye-hand and eye-foot coordination, movement in space, motor planning, and bilateral limb use, which is the simultaneous control of both arms and legs while performing tasks. Other areas of sensory integration help with your child's ability to remain upright and balanced while in action as well as directing the flow of information between the senses, muscles, and the brain.

RULES OF PLAY AND PRAISE

Kids are motivated by positive words and actions. In chapter 10, you will discover the best ways to insure success on every level and how to encourage with compliments. Use a cheerful and upbeat tone of voice and shower your child with affection. Reward all types of effort with the top one hundred phrases of praise, and try the sandwich technique when directing behavior. Build your child's self confidence when applying the rules of praise for successful communication. Positive support makes a huge difference.

HELPING KIDS WITH DISABILITIES

If your child has special needs or developmental delays, there are a variety of games in all age groups that can be helpful. For example, in toss-and-catch games, instead of using large balls, substitute beanbags, wadded-up washcloths, knotted socks, or scarves. Try inflated beach balls for soccer or volleyball instead of playground balls. Each game is perfect for all types of kids with all types of needs.

DESIGN A BALANCED, PERSONALIZED PROGRAM

The games section of this book provides a wide variety of activities that promote the development of fine and gross motor skills; intellectual, cognitive, and spatial awareness; and overall physical coordination. Be sure to try each game several times to solidify your baby's neurological and muscle memory. Kids love familiarity and learn by repetition.

The process of developing coordination is gradual. Have patience—the learning curve for kids is much slower than you might imagine. It could take hundreds of repetitions for a child to understand, imitate, and then produce skills at will. There is no way to predict if your youngster will get it on the third or the ninety-third attempt. When that magical moment of learning kicks in, you'll know it was worth the effort.

GIVE YOUR CHILD A FUN AND POSITIVE EXPERIENCE

The mission of this book is for you to have fun with your child, playing purposeful games that will develop coordination and athleticism in later life. Remember, the Proud Parents' philosophy is to give your child a fun and positive experience through parent and child play. The more success your infant, toddler, or preschooler experiences in the first six years, the more success your child can expect in later life. Positive playtime awaits!

PART ONE

How Your Child Develops Coordination

What Is Physical Fitness?

Raising athletic kids is not an easy job. Often it's a mystery. Doing the right thing at the right time requires desire, good instincts, and sometimes just plain luck.

When my three children were babies, my desire to find information on how to raise athletic kids produced a big zero. I found plenty of parenting books offering advice on how to coach older children once they were established athletes. There was nothing in print, however, that could help me teach kids the fundamental skills used in all sports geared toward little ones from birth to preschool.

As a result, I used my coaching background and parenting instincts to create my own program to develop coordination and athleticism. It was playtime with a purpose. The games were fun, and my kids gradually developed balance, strength, flexibility, and overall coordination. By age seven, they were skilled and ready to participate in youth sports, school, music, and art, and to learn a second language. Fifteen years later, this powerful parenting program is available to you and your family or other loved ones.

AN UNFIT GENERATION

After seeing positive results from this program within my own family, I began to observe other children in the community—at schools, playgrounds, pools, and amusement parks. Too many were unfit or uncoordinated, and only a few moved like athletes, with balance, skill, and body control. I wondered what causes kids to lag in physical fitness and development. Could it be poor nutrition, a lack of exercise, or maybe too much television? Perhaps it is all of the above.

In the past twenty-five years, the number of overweight children from birth to age eleven has more than doubled, from 7 to 16 percent, according to the Centers for Disease Control and Prevention. Kids are at risk for diabetes, heart disease, stroke, high blood pressure, sleep apnea, and asthma. This is a disturbing trend that can be easily reversed. Recent studies from the Medical College of Georgia and the National Institutes of Health show that vigorous exercise performed for twenty to forty minutes at least three times a week made a huge difference in two hundred overweight and inactive kids. Physical activities included running, jumping, and playing with hula hoops. At the end of three months, all of the participants improved fitness levels by up to 21 percent. Other benefits included reduced body fat, increased bone density, and a decreased risk of developing type 2 diabetes. Also, kids who exercised longer showed greater improvement in cognitive and math skills. One final catch: the results of the study indicated that if a participant stopped exercising, all benefits would be lost.[1]

FOUR COMPONENTS OF PHYSICAL FITNESS

Physical fitness is defined as a state of well-being in which the body is ready and able to meet the physical challenges of everyday life. According to the National

Association for Sport and Physical Education, there are four components of physical fitness. They are as follows:

THE COMPONENTS OF PHYSICAL FITNESS

Area of Development	Definition
The Cardio-Respiratory (Aerobic) System	Elements are the heart, blood, and lungs, which in combination can provide the stamina a child needs to participate in physical activities for long periods of time.
Muscular Strength and Endurance	This type of fitness involves the use of muscles in performing skills such as running, hitting balls with bats or clubs, and hammering a nail. Endurance is the ability to continue in motion without getting tired.
Flexibility	Your child's ability to bend and stretch easily is called flexibility. This is critical to the prevention of injuries to the muscles and tendons.
Body Composition	The concept of body composition refers to your child's weight and body fat. Excess fat can stress ligaments, tendons, and bones.

Source: National Association for Sport and Physical Education, 2002

WHAT HAPPENED TO OUR PHYSICAL FITNESS?

Physical fitness was once a necessity and part of daily life. Before the advent of the automobile, people walked as a means of transportation. Pedestrians logged miles each day. Now people walk to and from their cars, and exercise is measured by counting steps. Children do the same, walking from their bedrooms to the couch for television viewing. Another destination is the computer for playing games.

Today's kids are taking huge leaps forward with technology and bigger steps backward in fitness. Children under age six are watching television programs or videos almost two hours each day, according to a 2003 study by the Kaiser Family Foundation. Also, one in four kids in that same age group is proficient on a computer, spending an average of one hour per day e-mailing, instant messaging, and playing computer games—often without adult supervision. One might conclude that when children are spending two to three hours a day after school, or up to twenty-one hours a week in passive or sedentary activities rather than outdoor play, exercise and family recreation have diminished to dangerously low levels. The Proud Parents' program strives to reverse this trend, which is not entirely a child's fault but a reflection of today's culture.

For better or worse, gone are the days of neighborhood pick-up sports games until dark without parental supervision. Child safety is a priority. Kids can be in danger on unsupervised bike rides to parks or school playgrounds. It seems the only chance a child has for exercise is when a parent, caregiver, or responsible adult takes the time to help with sports or other activities. In addition, adults are working longer hours and many children are being raised in single-parent homes. As a result, it's safer for kids to hang out inside their homes and engage in solitary and sedentary activities after school and on weekends. In other words, it is easy to become couch potatoes or technology junkies.

FITNESS AND EDUCATION ARE NATURAL PARTNERS

Years ago, children had about one hour of intense physical education (PE) instruction in schools every day. Now PE has been reduced to one or two classes a week. In addition, kids often exercise at a leisurely pace as opposed to the high aerobic standards necessary to develop fitness. This is not enough to keep kids fit.

Thankfully, the nation's educators are beginning to wake up and acknowledge the gap between our kids' current fitness levels and healthful standards. However, decades ago there were educators who created groundbreaking fitness programs with stunning results.

In 1985, the Cajon Valley Union School District in San Diego County published the results of a five-year study on a children's fitness program called F.A.S.T., or Fitness, Academics, and Self-Esteem Training. Pete Saccone, a fifth-grade teacher, created a program that encouraged children to walk, jog, or run for the first forty-five minutes of each school day. The goal was to promote cardiovascular fitness and respiratory efficiency while improving mental, emotional, and social health. The F.A.S.T. results dazzled school district leaders. After ten months of running, the students logged thousands of miles and surpassed preset physical fitness goals.

Saccone's program was one of the first to make the critical connection between fitness and improved academics. Two groups of fourth and fifth graders participated in this program as well as sedentary students from the normal school population. In one school year, the F.A.S.T. fourth graders who ran each morning raised their academic test scores by over 16 percent in reading, language, and math compared to a .5 percent gain for a control group of non-running students. A similar group of F.A.S.T. fifth graders showed an academic improvement of over 12 percent while control group peers logged a mere 2.8 percent academic gain. Additionally, the F.A.S.T. participants experienced lower blood pressure, a decreased body-fat percentage, and lower resting heart rates along with improved oxygen consumption. The study also noted improvements in nutrition, school attendance, and discipline problems among participants.

EXERCISE IS A MIND-BODY EXPERIENCE

More than twenty years have passed since the F.A.S.T. program hit the schools, and researchers continue to find additional benefits for active kids. Antronette Yancy, a professor from the University of California, Los Angeles (UCLA), has said that kids who regularly exercise are better able to focus in school and to develop positive self-esteem. They are also less likely to fidget and be disruptive in the classroom. Other benefits of exercise on students include higher test scores and less depression and anxiety. Children who exercise perform better in language, reading, and a basic battery of tests.

The bottom line is that exercise is food for the brain as well as the body, according to Harvard professor John Ratey. He says exercise stimulates cell growth in an area of the brain called the hippocampus, which improves memory and learning capacity.[2]

Here is a brief look at the benefits of physical fitness and exercise:

- Improves self-esteem
- Improves concentration
- Reduces anxiety and depression
- Stimulates brain growth
- Builds bone density
- Produces higher test scores and improved academics
- Creates coordination
- Creates less-disruptive kids in the classroom
- Makes it easier to excel in language, reading, and math

- Increases overall learning capacity
- Reduces kids' fidgety behavior and improves their focus
- Stimulates the creation of new neurons
- Improves cardiovascular fitness
- Increases muscle strength and flexibility
- Improves memory and the ability to retain information
- Promotes more oxygen to the body
- Increases the flow of oxygen-rich blood to the brain
- Results in faster thinking
- Promotes brain plasticity
- Reduces the risk of diabetes
- Controls blood sugar levels
- Lowers body fat percentage
- Improves respiratory efficiency

ATHLETICISM BEGINS AT BIRTH

Kids need to get hooked on physical exercise within the first years of life for the best chance of becoming coordinated and athletic and in order to maintain a lifestyle of fitness. Why? The process of developing visual, cognitive, auditory, sensory, fine, and gross motor coordination unfolds over years of practice. As a result, children can become quicker, stronger, and faster at much earlier ages. They also can develop a love of exercise and a positive self-image.

The basis of the California Children and Families Act of 1998 was the springboard for the California First 5 program, which recognizes that all children prenatal to age five need early child-development educational and medical services as a foundation to be ready to learn and realize the potential to become productive, well-adjusted members of society. It was based on current research in brain development, which clearly indicates that the emotional, physical, and intellectual environment that a child is exposed to in the early years of life has a profound impact on how the brain is organized.

To gain maximum long-term benefits of physical activity, it is essential to exercise or play Proud Parents' games at least three times a week because building coordination is a gradual process that takes years. (Optimum results will come from daily exercise.) However, playing active games just twice a week can help your child as long as they are performed on a consistent basis over a period of years.

Start your baby with visual, cognitive, and tactile stimulation along with basic gross motor arm and leg movements. Your toddler will love playing games with his hands and fingers to improve fine motor control. Preschoolers have a world of opportunities in which to grow in every area of life. If you provide ample mind and body stimulation starting from birth, your preschooler will likely be able to run, skip, jump, slide, leap, hop, swim, read, draw, dance, climb, and throw a ball with ease. Early exposure is best, but because children are always growing and learning, it is never too late to start.

A BOOK IN BITE-SIZED PIECES

Proud Parents' Guide to Raising Athletic, Balanced, and Coordinated Kids can be read from cover to cover the first time and at intervals afterward as a refresher. It can also function as an instructional reference book for guidance in selecting quick and easy games because it is written in a simple format. This program is a recipe for success that can give your child the skills and confidence to be prepared for future athletics.

2

Positive Child's Play

By reading this book, you have taken an important first step toward helping your child, grandchild, or favorite youngster start on a path toward physical fitness and overall coordination. Kids will learn to use their minds and bodies in effective ways to achieve amazing milestones. Balance, flexibility, strength, and visual, cognitive, and spatial skills will gradually emerge along with a blossoming sense of achievement. Playing Proud Parents' games will start you on a journey of purposeful play that will help you enjoy your child's baby, toddler, and preschool years.

CHILD'S PLAY WITHOUT PRESSURE

Before you begin, there are a few words of caution. This program must be played without any pressure to perform or unrealistic expectations placed upon your child. Kids need to be free to learn just for the joy of learning, without any strings attached or negative consequences. Children are intuitive about many things. They know when an experience has transitioned from fun into forced learning. They also catch on when an adult loses perspective, such as expecting a hesitant four-year-old female soccer player with beginning foot skills to immediately turn into a skilled goal scorer in her first season. Young boys might also feel stress in youth baseball when parents project visions of all-star performances on their inexperienced young athletes who are just learning to catch, throw, and hit a baseball. Chances are these children will need years of fundamental skill development to reach the top echelon in their sports. So try to keep the fun in playing physical activities and be realistic about your child's progress.

WHY ARE YOU INTERESTED IN USING THIS PROGRAM?

Before you begin, ask yourself this question: *Why am I interested in using this program?* If your answer is to raise a coordinated child who will be ready to participate in physical activities, school, sports, music, drama, and hobbies of all kinds, then you are right on track. Fit, balanced, and coordinated kids are often better prepared to develop the strength, confidence, and physical skills that will most likely lead to success in later life.

If your answer to the above question is to prepare your child for a college scholarship or a career in professional athletics, carefully read the following sentence: *you have a greater chance of winning the lottery than you do of ensuring your child a spot among the elite ranks of professional athletes.* The odds are not in your favor. It is exceedingly rare for someone to attain the fame, fortune, and recognition of soccer's David Beckham or Mia Hamm, basketball's LeBron James or Cheryl Miller, football's Peyton Manning, Olympic gold medal gymnasts Mary Lou Retton or Bart Conner, Olympic gold medal ice skaters Kristi Yamaguchi or

Scott Hamilton, tennis stars Roger Federer or Maria Sharapova, swimming's Matt Biondi or Janet Evans, or track Olympians Gail Devers or Carl Lewis. Millions of people try, but only handfuls ever reach that pinnacle of athletic success.

THE ODDS OF PLAYING HIGH SCHOOL SPORTS

Let's look at the facts. There are currently an estimated twenty-five million American youngsters ages four to twenty involved in youth sports. After receiving up to ten years of various levels of coaching and training, approximately seven million boys and girls will qualify for U.S. high school athletics in about forty-eight sports, according to a 2006–2007 survey by the National Federation of State High School Association.

THE ODDS OF GETTING A COLLEGE SCHOLARSHIP

Now fast-forward four years, when only 5 percent or four hundred thousand out of seven million male and female high school athletes will be handpicked for NCAA Division I, II, and III sports teams, according to a recent NCAA Sports Participation Survey. A further wake-up call comes when the average number of athletes who are selected to represent a college or university sports team is considered. Among thousands of students at each school, coaches will accept an average of eleven student athletes each for the men's and women's golf and tennis teams. There are about fourteen spots each for volleyball and basketball, cross country racing, and skiing. There are sixteen openings per team in gymnastics, eighteen in softball, twenty-two in water polo and swimming, and twenty-three in soccer and wrestling. On average, only thirty athletes per team make it in track and baseball, thirty-six in college lacrosse, forty-eight in rowing, and about ninety-nine in football. That's a very competitive situation for aspiring college athletes. Bear in mind that few of the students who play intercollegiate sports do so on sports scholarships.

THE ODDS OF BECOMING A PROFESSIONAL ATHLETE

Many of those fortunate enough to play college sports may dream about entering the professional ranks. That can be a good thing, as long as they also have academic and career goals. Consider that the average professional sports career lasts just three to five years, and much depends on an individual remaining injury free. Many hardworking and gifted pros have been sidelined for health or physical reasons and have been forced out of their sports long before their time. They suddenly find themselves out of a job and in search of a new profession. In this case, a college degree and a backup career goal would come in handy.

For example, Michael is a gifted six-year-old athlete who lives, eats, sleeps, and dreams about playing professional baseball. He is one of over two million children who registered for youth teams across the country last year. Michael is doing all of the right things. He practices up to three hours each afternoon, gets professional coaching, and has full family support. He appears to be on course to climb the ladder to the top.

The fact is only 1.9 percent of the two million kids like Michael will advance to play for an NCAA Division I, II, or III baseball team. If Michael beats those odds and plays up to four years of college ball, he then has less than a .06 percent chance of being considered for one of thirty Major League Baseball teams. Michael is lucky because his parents have also nurtured him in math, and he likes playing with numbers. Now he talks about becoming a baseball-playing accountant. The idea of a double goal in sports and academics can plant the seeds for a well-rounded future without crushing a child's dreams.

Maybe you're thinking the odds are only tough in baseball and it is easier to break into other professional sports. Think again. In youth flag and tackle football, the odds shrink dramatically. Almost three million U.S. kids play the sport prior to high school, and there is only room for seventeen hundred professional athletes in the National Football League. That translates to less than a 2 percent success rate of becoming a professional football player in the United States, a career that lasts an average of about four years. There are a few fortunate individuals who manage to exceed that time, but those results are not typical.

Perhaps your child doesn't play football or baseball. Let's glance at some other possibilities. Over five million kids in the United States will train their entire lives to compete for six spots each on the men's and women's U.S. Olympic gymnastics teams. The odds are .0001 percent of achieving that goal. Millions of kids take lessons and compete in ice skating, but approximately eight men and women will be considered for each of the Olympic squads. In youth softball, there are over 1.5 million girls who play the sport each year, but only twelve to twenty athletes will be named to the U.S. National team. The story is much the same for soccer. Untold millions of kids play the game in recreational leagues and private clubs, but there are only about fifteen to twenty each on the U.S. Olympic men's and women's soccer teams.

THE FACTS ABOUT EARNING POTENTIAL FOR PROFESSIONAL ATHLETES

If you prefer individual sports, maybe you are thinking about training your child for golf or tennis. The lure of prize money is very attractive because

Professional Golf Association (PGA) and Ladies Professional Golf Association (LPGA) prize money leaders make millions of dollars annually. In a twelve-month period ending in June 2007, golfing legend Tiger Woods earned $100 million. The breakdown was $13 million in prize money and $87 million in endorsements.[1] He was the highest paid athlete in the world for that year. Annika Sorenstam, the highest paid female golfer in 2007, earned over $20 million.

On the opposite end of the spectrum, male pro golfers ranked below number 534 earned career totals of about $19,000 or less, according to PGA Tour statistics. Female pro golfers ranked at number 185 and below have earned career prize totals of $2,000 or less, according to the LPGA. These are gross earnings before deducting expenses and taxes.

It is obvious there is a great deal of money to be made by professional athletes in sports, but the buck stops somewhere near the top. Simple math speaks volumes, and the message is clear: the dream of major financial success as a professional athlete works only for a small handful of people. It is more fantasy than reality.

THE ROCKY ROAD TO PROFESSIONAL ATHLETICS

Those determined to encourage their children to pursue a career in professional sports would be wise to consider the emotional, social, and financial costs of reaching that level of proficiency. Formal sports training involves more than a basic introduction to the fundamentals very early in life. It means your child will need years of expensive professional coaching, supervised practice sessions, frequent opportunities for competition, and total focus on the goal. Most or all of your free time and your youngster's precious childhood will be dedicated to this mission.

FIVE IMPORTANT QUESTIONS AND ANSWERS TO CONSIDER

Start by asking yourself a few questions:

- "Does my child honestly have what it takes to be a pro athlete?"
- "At what emotional, physical, and financial costs am I pursuing this?"
- "How much does my child really want to be a pro?"
- "What kind of impact will it have on my family?"
- "Can my child really handle the road to professional athletics?"

"Does my child honestly have what it takes to be a pro athlete?"

Let's assume your child has some athletic talent, or you probably wouldn't be entertaining the idea of a long-term sports goal. But is it enough? There are many levels of skill in the sports world. You might start with a grassroots recreational youth program that last two to three months each year. The next step is to transition into a year-round competitive club commitment, which is much deeper in talent. The cream of the crop might be recruited by traveling teams or Olympic development programs, which compete in state, regional, national, and international events. Even if your child were to be selected to compete at the highest level, only one or two top international stars ever develop into world-class professionals. So regardless of where your child stands in this hierarchy of talent, try to keep in mind your kid is still just a kid. If he or she is destined to become a sports legend, let it happen naturally.

"At what emotional, physical, and financial costs am I pursuing this?"

Over the next ten to twenty years, chasing this goal will require untold thousands of dollars to pay for good coaching, equipment, travel, and competition.

That is your hard-earned money that could have been used for family vacations, purchasing a home, your child's college savings plan, or your retirement fund. The chances are likely that the pursuit of professional athletics will become a financial strain. Factor in the value of time, and say good-bye to free afternoons and weekends. Maybe that's a price you're willing to pay, but is it one that your kid has agreed to as well? Often, this is the place where the theory "sports is just for fun" consciously or unconsciously gets thrown out the window. It's also the place where kids begin to feel the pressure of their parents' expectations, which is not a good thing. If you are at this point, perhaps it might be time to take a break and gain some perspective. Put the "fun" back into playing "fundamental" activities with your child.

"How much does my child really want to be a pro?"

For a few weeks, try to observe your child's behavior. Notice if your budding tennis star is constantly hitting a ball against the garage, or your young basketball sensation is always dribbling a ball in the house. Does your talented athlete get excited about practicing swimming, gymnastics, ice skating, hockey, tennis, running, or golf? Or do you have to provide the daily reminders to prompt your child to get ready for sports activities? Do you have to drag your child to games? Check out how much effort your child puts into each day's sports play and look for the smile signaling enjoyment. Reflect upon how well your child thrives under the pressure of competition. Finally, look for your child's reaction when the end of practice is near. Is he or she relieved, or is it hard to drag this athlete off the field or court? These are all clues that will tell you who wants this college or professional sports career more. Is it you or your child?

"What kind of impact will it have on my family?"

The serious pursuit of an athletic commitment for a child of any age is hard on the entire family. Siblings can get lost in the shuffle, and parents spend a lot of time apart. While this setup appears to benefit the talented athlete, it might slowly and quietly split up the family. Be aware of this emotional and psychological strain because it is very difficult to repair the damage. You can't take back years of doting on one child and neglecting the rest. These experiences, for better or worse, make a permanent mark on the psyche of all involved. Think carefully before you embark on this path. Strive for a healthy, balanced, and loving family environment that meets the needs of all.

"Can my child really handle the road to professional athletics?"

When embarking on the road to professional athletics, consider your child's emotional, mental, psychological, and physical makeup. The easiest place to start is to honestly assess your child's talent. If you're not sure, consult objective professional coaches and ask for critiques. Be open-minded and really listen to their answers.

An intense structured practice schedule for a toddler or preschooler can be quite stressful. Kids under the age of six are just beginning to develop muscle strength and physical control. Repetitive movements such as running and throwing, hitting, or kicking balls for a couple of hours a day can potentially cause injury and do long-term damage to a young child's growing body. Be on the lookout for signs of fatigue, and listen to your athlete when something hurts. Perhaps your child needs a physical or mental rest.

The emotional pressure of an intense practice schedule can be overwhelming. Kids play sports because they are fun, but five days a week of training can become a grind. It might be better to take the intensity down a notch and reevaluate your commitment to this goal.

Psychological stress begins when kids do not properly grasp the idea of winning and losing in a competitive environment. They take it personally, and self-esteem suffers. Parents are inadvertently pushing their children as if those they were miniature adults, possibly causing harmful consequences that might take years of counseling or therapy to mend. Kids often crave normal childhood experiences, such as playing with their toys, pets, and neighborhood friends.

A SECOND LOOK AT WHY YOU
ARE INTERESTED IN USING THIS PROGRAM

So going back to the original question, *Why are you interested in using this program?* Be sure the answer is to help your child become a happy, active, healthy, confident, and coordinated kid who will grow up to be a happy, active, healthy, confident, and coordinated adult—with a great education, a thriving career and a lifelong passion for sports and physical fitness. If your child attains success in athletics at a various levels along the way, that's a bonus!

3

Learning Styles

If you observe a roomful of preschoolers at play, you might notice they experience their world in a variety of ways. Some might be sitting at a table quietly drawing or stringing beads while others are dressing for an impromptu dramatic performance as warriors, princesses, dragons, teachers, shopkeepers, or chefs in a fine restaurant. A few young architects are creating towering skyscrapers out of large colorful plastic blocks, while still more are climbing on an outside play structure. All of the children are doing what comes naturally, and each type of play results in learning. They are absorbing new information, processing it, and building a foundation of knowledge that will serve them well throughout life.

Kids are genetically wired at birth to interpret their environments in three basic learning styles: visual, auditory, and kinesthetic. Each is a very successful style of learning. In the previously described preschool setting, the visual learners would be the young artists because they are adept at using their "looking" skills to develop fine motor control and spatial awareness. The auditory children are the young actors who have used their listening skills to hear language and develop an impressive ability to speak with passion and clarity. They can recite lines, memorize stories, and easily sing nursery rhymes. The kinesthetic kids are the architects who use gross motor movement to lift colorful blocks and build imaginary skyscrapers. They are often balanced and coordinated kids, who excel in physical activities. They love to run, hop, skip, jump, and climb on playground equipment. Their lives are defined by moving, doing, touching, feeling and, being in constant motion.

All of the learning styles are conducive to learning and experiencing success in later life. In this chapter, you will discover your child's strongest mode of learning and the characteristics attributed to each style. If you are aware of how your child learns best, you can create situations that help your child feel comfortable and most receptive to learning.

LEARNING STYLES AT PLAY

Here is a common scenario for infants and toddlers. Have you ever noticed parents casually pushing their babies in strollers at a park? There are some very telling responses if you look closely at the kids. Visual babies will be content to sit and observe the trees, birds, dogs, and flowers. They will often communicate their thoughts by verbal and nonverbal gestures such as pointing at colorful objects. Auditory kids will be the first to hear planes flying overhead and chirping birds in the trees. They will point in the direction of the sound and vocalize questions. Both visual and auditory children often enjoy these explorations outside of the house. Kinesthetic kids, however, are not as content to sit, look, and listen. In fact, these children consider a stroller experience much like a miniprison. This mover will twist, turn, squirm, flip, flop, and strain to get out of the stroller as soon as possible. The kinesthetic kid would rather push an empty stroller than ride in one.

The stroll through the park shows three children with totally different learning styles at play. The parents of the visual learner might point out objects and name them to teach language and vocabulary. The auditory family would gravitate toward things that make noise, such as birds, rushing water, crunching gravel, slippery sand, squeaky swings, or the swooshing sound when one glides down a slide. The kinesthetic movers might go on a hunt to collect interesting leaves, rocks, bugs, or twigs, swing on the monkey bars or create an obstacle course with playground equipment. All activities are fun, educational, and designed to pique your child's interests based on learning styles.

Now that you understand the obvious differences in the way kids experience the world, let's talk about your family. How does your child learn? There are many clues that give you insight into your child's learning style, starting from birth. Begin paying attention to what stimuli your kids positively respond to, as well as the type of games they enjoy playing and the physical skills that are in place at each age and stage. Visual babies are attracted to vivid color, bright pictures, familiar faces, and items with black-and-white contrast. They are often able to concentrate on a task for an extended length of time, and they love face-to-face interactions with familiar people. Visual infants also easily make eye-hand contact with close-dangling objects. Auditory babies are entertained by language, sound, music, and soothing familiar voices. They usually vocalize cooing and babbling sounds as infants and become early talkers. Since they are sensitive to noise, they are often overwhelmed by booming voices and loud environments—noisy classrooms, fireworks, bustling shopping malls, and sporting events with intermittent clapping and cheering. Kinesthetic babies are often wiggly infants who develop physical strength, coordination, and reach milestones early—rolling, crawling, and walking, for instance.

VISUAL LEARNERS

As babies grow into toddlers, they will expand their physical, mental, and emotional awareness. Visual learners will continue to rely on sight and will develop the ability to process first impressions. They might get a mental *picture* of an environment or room and immediately know if it is a fun, happy place. Have you ever wondered why a baby or toddler cries with emotional discomfort in certain settings? It just might be that intangible element that gives some babies a sixth sense based on this learning style. Visual preschoolers will unconsciously notice the color, shape, and use of space in a room. Is the area cluttered, bland, or unorganized? If so, this can be stressful for the visual child.

Characteristics of Visual Learners

The visual child often has well-developed fine motor skills and excellent eye-hand coordination and small finger movement, such as the kind of joint control needed for holding a crayon or cutting with scissors. Kids with this learning style also excel in puzzles, arts and crafts, board games, writing, drawing, cutting, and pasting paper. They also notice details in picture books. Visual kids are the best at finding lost toys or clothing because they remember *seeing* the last location of the missing objects. Finally, keep in mind while this type of child might excel in a lot of areas, you might have to help the looker become a better listener through music, reading stories out loud, and conversation. Also, it's possible the visual learner could use support developing gross motor skills, eye-foot and total body coordination.

AUDITORY LEARNERS

The world can be an easy place for auditory kids since most people use this mode of communication. This style of learning gives kids an advantage with spoken language, reading skills, musical talent, memory retention, drama, and role-play. Using words and sounds tends to be the norm; therefore, kids who learn best by listening get first crack at processing information. The auditory child's brain is often stimulated in the womb. Babies have been known to hear music or their parents' voices before birth and recognize them when they are newborns.

Characteristics of Auditory Learners

Auditory kids are calmed and inspired by music, and they are often the best at following directions. This learner is often bilingual or multilingual because they are wired for language development. They are often creative when it comes to finding solutions because they think outside the box. The auditory child is usually an independent thinker with a clear sense of purpose. With all of those skills, however, the listener can still struggle with visual tasks like art, drawing, writing, and fine motor skills. Also, the listener may need help with balance, coordination, eye-foot, gross motor, and total body development. They prefer structure and guidelines and can complete multistep tasks. The adept auditory child usually only needs to hear instructions or information once and feels repetition is akin to nagging or punishment.

KINESTHETIC LEARNERS

It is not always easy to parent the active child who learns best by moving, touching, doing, and feeling. This means your child picks up information through body movement and tactile stimulation rather than listening skills or visual information. This kid-on-the-go needs to be in motion the majority of the time and is very strong in gross motor skills. While this may seem overwhelming for some, the good news is there are positive ways to help a kinesthetic child succeed in school, sports, and life. Once you learn new ways to parent the active child, it will become a way of life. Kinesthetic kids need a safe, hands-on learning atmosphere in the house and yard. If you have a kinesthetic learner, pack up the delicate knickknacks and say good-bye to Grandma's antique china for about the next fifteen years.

Characteristics of the Kinesthetic Learner

The first clue is when you notice your kinesthetic baby wiggle and strain in your arms to break free or frequently change positions. This child is *not* content to calmly observe the world while being held in adult arms. The mover infant often becomes an early crawler and a competent walker. They are often very strong, athletic, and bright, but they do not necessarily excel in a structured and sedentary school environment, which is typically designed to teach auditory children first and visual learners second. Active kids prefer hands-on projects, games, and activities and dislike pencil-and-paper tasks. They might have difficulty memorizing information and could find it overwhelming to count without manipulative objects like beads, blocks, or small toys.

COMBINATION LEARNERS

Most kids are combination learners, with one strongly developed style and a second mode that closely complements the first. A third learning style might need extra attention to develop. The goal of this program is to help children become well-balanced learners. There are a few kids who are naturally strong in all three styles, and this program will help them improve their overall skills.

Try to use the clues and suggestions in this chapter as a guide to figure out your child's learning-style strengths. For primarily visual learners, the possible combinations are visual-auditory-kinesthetic or visual-kinesthetic-auditory. For primarily auditory learners, the orders of modes are auditory-kinesthetic-visual or auditory-visual-kinesthetic. Finally, for primarily kinesthetic learners, a child might be kinesthetic-auditory-visual or kinesthetic-visual-auditory.

How is this information helpful? You might apply this knowledge by initially appealing to your child's strongest learning style to captivate attention. This is the most direct path because you are tapping into the way your child's brain is neurologically wired. Next, consider your child's second strongest mode of learning and use it to complement the primary style. Also include the third learning style to encourage the development of a well-rounded child. For example, if you are showing a visual-auditory-kinesthetic learner how to throw and catch a ball, you must first slowly and accurately demonstrate those skills several times so your child will *see* them. Support the visual instruction with a verbal description and allow your child to *listen* to the information. The third step is for your child to slowly practice throwing and catching balls.

If your child is a visual-kinesthetic-auditory learner, you would start the same way by giving your child a visual picture of the skill. Then quickly move to the kinesthetic style and have your child experience what it feels like to actually throw and catch the ball. Keep the talking to a minimum, using ten words or less. Your parenting challenge is to figure out your child's learning preferences; use this combination one-two-three approach to encourage interest and motivate your child to play Proud Parents' games with you.

LEARNING STYLES CHART

Skill	Visual Learner	Auditory Learner	Kinesthetic Learner
General Characteristics of Learning Styles	Learns by seeing and looking at demonstrations.	Learns by hearing information.	Learns by doing, feeling, moving, and touching.
Babies to Age 3: Communication	Uses simple sentences. Might have trouble pronouncing some words. Could leave out articles and prepositions.	Very vocal. Babbles, coos, and quickly learns words. Uses phrases early, and loves to imitate others.	Quiet, uses nonverbal gestures like pointing, late to speak. Might slur or mumble words, can be difficult to understand.
Preschoolers Ages 4 to 6: Communication	Moderate language skills, quiet by nature, uses simple language. Often needs encouragement to speak. Uses words sparingly.	Speaks very much like an adult with excellent sentence structure. Can recite rhymes and tell stories. Has excellent change of tone, volume, and pitch.	Can be slow to speak, slurs or mumbles, and can be difficult to understand. Often uses nonverbal gestures like pointing. Jumps for joy, stomps, or hits when frustrated or angry.
Babies to Age 3: Toys and tendencies	Colorful blocks, books, hanging mobiles, beads, watching videos and television, and drawing.	Loves music, listening to stories read aloud, talking with others, and forming social relationships.	Loves outdoor play, moving in open spaces, and climbing on playground structures. Good at athletic movements and activities.

Skill	Visual Learner	Auditory Learner	Kinesthetic Learner
Preschoolers Ages 4 to 6: Toys and tendencies	Loves puzzles, books, arts and crafts, cutting and pasting, computer games, TV, electronics, and basic board games.	Enjoys computer games with verbal feedback in music or words, good prereading skills. Likes to play with others. Loves verbal games.	Outdoor activities, sports, walking, hiking, skipping, climbing on playground equipment, and riding bicycles with or without training wheels. Adept at group sports play.
Babies to Age 3: Drawing and writing	Holds a pencil with some skill and can draw moderately straight lines.	Might have difficulty manipulating a pencil. More into talking than writing.	Good hand control, can scribble with purpose, but has a short attention span for writing, drawing, and coloring.
Preschoolers Ages 4 to 6: Drawing and writing	Good base of letter recognition, possibly reading, can write own name clearly. Enjoys drawing, coloring, and painting.	Tends to write with light pressure, recognizes name, and can write it with some skill. Can copy basic shapes.	Writes own name well in large spaces. Has trouble writing in small spaces. Prefers not to color inside the lines, might prefer freehand drawing.
Babies to Age 3: Moving and playtime	Uses hands and fingers in play, likes to look around, can sit for an activity with ease, loves puzzles and television, and shows emotions easily.	Concentrates on language, likes social and dramatic play, might struggle with some physical skills, very expressive verbally.	Very busy moving, crawling, and climbing on baby and toddler toys. Likes push-and-pull toys such as strollers and wagons. Kicks balls and thrives in open group play. Likes to take toys apart to see how things work.

Skill	Visual Learner	Auditory Learner	Kinesthetic Learner
Preschoolers Ages 4 to 6: Moving and playtime	Cuts, colors, and prints with ease, enjoys crafts, can draw a recognizable person, enjoys some physical movement.	Prefers activities that allow talking, tends to be a leader, and speaks with adult-like inflection and comprehension.	Runs, skips, hops, and jumps well. Prefers one-on-one social situations. Takes toys off of shelves, plays for a short time, then moves on.
Babies to Age 3: Social and emotional skills	Uses facial expressions to show emotions. Enjoys being with people. Responds to physical touch as positive feedback.	Vocalizes feelings of happiness, sadness, or frustration. Likes to hear words for positive feedback.	Responds physically to feelings. May hit or strike out when sad or frustrated. Enjoys physical touch for positive feedback.
Preschoolers Ages 4 to 6: Social and emotional skills	Socially advanced. Likes group activities and shows emotions easily to others. Likes to be in charge when possible. A natural leader. Shows emotions on face and with nonverbal gestures.	Enjoys some group interaction and leads with verbal skills. Likes to recite the rules and share knowledge. Tries to keep the peace by talking things out. Sometimes bossy. Shows joy and sadness through sound and words.	A very social person who enjoys small-group interactions. Shows feelings through body language. Can have difficulty finding words to express emotions. Relates physically to environment and people through sense of touch in hugs, pats on the back, high fives, or handshakes. Can be a charming child.

Skill	Visual Learner	Auditory Learner	Kinesthetic Learner
Babies to Age 3: Memory retention	Easily remembers familiar people and toys. Might need some repetition to retain information. Sometimes needs to see an object to talk about it.	Remembers names and forgets faces. Likes to talk about objects, movies, toys, and anything that pops into the mind. Does not need a visual cue to remember things.	Remembers what was done or physically experienced. Descriptions help, but learning is best in an active hands-on environment. Learns best when moving, or when touching objects.
Preschoolers Ages 4 to 6: Memory retention	Remembers faces, forgets names. Likes to write things down in words or pictures. Sees visual images in the mind to remember things.	Recalls information easily. Only needs to hear things once. Can quote favorite TV shows or characters from movies. Loves trivia.	Remembers skills, activities, and information best after trying them out. Is very attentive when able to get physically involved in the learning situation. Gets bored when sitting too long.
Babies to Age 3: Group settings or school	Needs time to look at a setting to get comfortable. Takes awhile to get involved.	Listens and follows directions well. Likes to obey the rules. Likes to stand up and talk in front of people.	Is restless in controlled-group settings. Squirms during sitting activities. Tries to exit group situations too soon. If forced to stay, might distract others.

Skill	Visual Learner	Auditory Learner	Kinesthetic Learner
Preschoolers Ages 4 to 6: Group settings or school	Likes to do individual tasks like cutting and pasting. Prefers to watch how things are done before getting involved.	Gets involved in groups and likes to take charge. Verbally becomes the boss. Answers the teacher's questions.	Cooperates in active group games. Tends not to follow directions in passive social situations that involve sitting, looking, and listening.
Babies to Age 3: Response to periods of inactivity	Looks around and finds something to watch.	Verbalizes and makes sounds.	Touches things in close proximity.
Preschoolers Ages 4 to 6: Response to periods of inactivity	Stares at people, doodles on paper. Likes to watch the action in an environment. A quiet atmosphere is most comfortable.	Sings, hums, and talks to self and others. Needs to be verbalizing or listening to noise or music at all times. Silence is uncomfortable.	Squirms and tends to fidget. Some body part is in constant movement. Needs to be playing with something to be content.
Babies to Age 3: Response to new situations	Looks around. Needs the comfort of someone or something familiar.	Vocalizes questions for information. Needs verbal feedback.	Gets involved and tries things out. Does not wait. Likes to know how things work by touching.

Skill	Visual Learner	Auditory Learner	Kinesthetic Learner
Preschoolers Ages 4 to 6: Response to new situations	Stands on the outside of an activity at first. Watches to see how things work. Prefers to see how others deal with situations and learns from their mistakes.	Asks questions about new information. Needs guidelines, background, and structure. Listens to advice and rules, and likes to follow instructions.	Understands by moving, touching, feeling, and playing in a new situation to discover likes and dislikes. Tends not to listen to advice or safety warnings. Has to learn by experience.
Babies to Age 3: Reading and spelling	Recognizes and remembers letters by looking at them.	Remembers letters better if they are verbally pointed out and identified.	Remembers letters if they can write them in sand, the air, or on paper.
Preschoolers Ages 4 to 6: Reading and spelling	Reads well and can recognize words by sight. Usually very good in reading and spelling.	Prefers to read aloud and spells words the way they sound. Often an excellent reader.	Good with big print and books with fewer words. A lot of text becomes visually confusing. Gradually increases reading skills.
Babies to Age 3: Attitude toward appearance	Likes to have some part in deciding on clothing early in life. Likes to self-dress.	Prefers to make decisions and likes to discuss them. Accepts help easily when dressing.	Clothes are not an important part of life. Anything will work. Colors are not an issue either. Is skilled at self-dressing and changes often.

Skill	Visual Learner	Auditory Learner	Kinesthetic Learner
Preschoolers Ages 4 to 6: Attitude toward appearance	Very neat, prefers clothes that are well-matched. A strong opinion on colors or styles.	Clothes might be matching, but it is not an important decision. Likes to talk about it.	Likes to dress neatly but doesn't stay that way long. Might have trouble keeping clothes clean. Also tends to lose clothing like jackets and shoes. Colors are often mismatched.
Babies to Age 3: Logic and problem solving	Looks and thinks about things for a while before acting on a solution. Tends to be quiet when processing information.	Verbalizes while trying out solutions. Older infants begin to use language early while discovering how things work.	Attacks problems with physical solutions, banging, swatting, and throwing as infants.
Preschoolers Ages 4 to 6: Logic and problem solving	Visualizes solutions. Sees the possibilities in puzzles and spatial issues and takes care before starting to solve the dilemma.	Talks about all of the options. Asks questions to discover the possibilities.	Physically starts solving the problem without much discussion. Right or wrong, this child will take immediate action.

4

Building Better Brains

At birth, your baby's brain is blessed with untold trillions of brain cells. They are genetically wired and ready to make connections with other brain cells. The brain is an extraordinary and complex organ made up of different regions, each designed to perform specific functions. This introductory network will undergo a great deal of change, growth, and pruning in the first decade of life. There are critical periods of development windows of learning—for physical coordination, vision, hearing, language, emotional attachment, math and music, and reading and writing. During these windows of time, certain parenting input can forever give your baby an advantage that will pave the road for future success. This chapter will explain how and why brain development occurs and what you can do to maximize your child's potential in sports, school, music, math, and other creative activities.

ANATOMY OF THE BRAIN

It is important to grasp a brief overview of the structure and function of the brain. This amazing organ, which weighs about three pounds and has the consistency of jelly, is part of the central nervous system. It consists of two halves or hemispheres, with four lobes in each half that are in charge of various skills. People use the total brain for processing information on a daily basis. There are also distinct preferences of right- or left-hemispheric dominance based on an individual's genetic wiring of the brain and spinal cord that appear early in life.

The right half of the brain controls the muscles on the left side of the body and the ability to think conceptually and grasp ideas as whole concepts. This hemisphere can generate visual images of sight, enhance emotional development, and help with senses such as sound, touch, taste, and smell. Right-brained thinking can analyze the relationship between objects and aid in spatial perception, creativity, musical ability, and artistic intelligence.

The left half of the brain controls the muscles on the right side. Left-brain thinkers tend to deal well with abstract symbols of language and numbers. This hemisphere helps people develop logical, linear, and sequential thinking by following a step-by-step progression from the small parts to the whole picture. The left brain also specializes in comprehending math and writing and reading skills, as well as verbal and nonverbal cues.

NIFTY NEURONS

The brain consists of basic building materials; called *neurons*, these cells send and receive information within areas of the brain and to the rest of the body. At birth, your baby starts with billions of neurons, about twice as many as is needed to become a fully functioning adult. No new cells are created after birth, but intellectual development occurs by creating new connections or pathways between these existing neurons.

FRIENDLY HELPERS: DENDRITES AND AXONS

The miracle of neurons (or brain cells) is that they direct the flow of information in your child's brain with help from two partners: dendrites and axons. Dendrites are the short fibers that extend out from the cells like bushy trees whose job is to collect information from other neurons. The other part is the axon, which consists of one long fiber per cell that extends out to other neurons like a telephone line. An axon's role is to send signals or messages along the line to other neurons, which also have dendrites ready to receive the impulse.

SENSATIONAL SYNAPSES

The meeting of axons and dendrites occurs along electrochemical pathways called *synapses*. At birth, an infant might have twenty-five hundred synapses per neuron. By age three, there is a tremendous expansion of the neural network to include up to fifteen thousand synapses per neuron, which is about twice the amount that exists in the average adult brain. Other important factors that influence the development of new synapses are an individual's age and learning environment. [1]

NEURON TRAFFIC CONTROL

Your child's brain has billions of neurons and thousands of synapses per neuron, and they are brilliantly wired to avoid collisions. How? Each neuron has preprogrammed instructions that control its function as well as the direction and flow of messages or impulses. For example, sensory nerves carry information from the body to the brain. If your child touches something hot like an iron, nerve impulses can leap from neuron to neuron, up to two hundred miles per hour, on the way to the spinal cord or brain where information is stored for future reference.[2]

The brain has the ability to prioritize this type of critical impulse like a computer. The burnt finger message is sent out as an emergency response telling your child to pull the hand away from the hot surface. Meanwhile, other impulses or thought processes are automatically silenced until the crisis is over. Then the normal neural network function kicks in to continue the business of learning.

USE IT OR LOSE IT

As the brain cells grow bigger, kids become smarter. And the opposite is also true. Brain cells that are ignored or not stimulated for various reasons will weaken from neglect. That's because the brain and many muscles of the body live by the use-it-or-lose-it theory of development. Neurological connections that receive frequent stimulation have a greater chance of surviving into adulthood. The weak cells with fewer synapses will be eliminated by a paring back process also called *pruning*. In this way, neurons compete for survival, and only those that receive enough attention or stimulation will grow strong enough to survive the pruning cut.

BLOOMING AND PRUNING

Another factor in this natural blooming and pruning process is the necessity to eliminate nonessential neurons to create an efficient and sturdy brain. Cells

that are targeted for extinction are identified by those that did not receive suf-
ficient life-sustaining support. This is similar to a gardener who prunes a tree
to eliminate dead branches and encourage growth along stronger lines, and as
a result controls the overall shape of the tree.

Your child's neural pruning process occurs throughout life, and it takes
place at different times and in specific areas of the brain. For example, this may
explain why kids raised in bilingual homes from birth can become fluent in two
languages: the neural pathways are hardwired to do so. The neurological blooming period for language development is from birth to ten years. If one of a child's
languages is eliminated from daily use in the first decade, it is highly likely that
the child will lose the ability to naturally speak or understand that language as
an adult. Why? The neurological pathways for that second language were not
significantly reinforced long enough to retain the knowledge past puberty and
into adulthood.

EFFECTS OF OVERPRUNING

The downside to the pruning process is sometimes the brain will use excessive
force to overprune needed yet neglected areas. This can happen when children
are deprived of necessary attention, love, or stimulation. It's also the case when
kids are exposed to severe neglect, abuse, domestic violence, drugs, or trauma.
Studies show abnormal or traumatic experiences can cause kids to end up with
smaller brains and reduced cognitive or motor function as adults.

In 1989, thousands of children were discovered in Romanian state orphan-
ages after the fall of the Nicolae Ceaușescu regime. In many cases, they were
inhumanely institutionalized with little food, attention, or physical or mental
stimulation. A great number of the malnourished and neglected Romanian
orphans were adopted by families worldwide. Canadian researchers from Simon

Fraser University tracked a group of adopted orphans for a period of ten years after being placed with new families. All of the children received intervention and intensive rehabilitation. The kids who were institutionalized from birth to eight months made excellent progress on post adoption checks at eleven months, four and a half years, and ten and a half years. However, the children who were exposed to neglect from eight months to several years still showed indications of the following disabilities: lower IQ, stunted growth, dwarfism, behavior and attachment problems, and delays in cognitive and social development.[3] The research team at Simon Fraser continues to observe these children and document their remarkable recovery. The incredible resilience of the brain is evident in this study, whether the kids were able to reach normal or partial developmental milestones.

BRAIN GROWTH AND PLASTICITY

A child's brain has a tremendous capacity to achieve intellectual excellence, become multilingual, develop athletic and musical talent, or recover from neurological deprivation or injury. It is due to a characteristic called *plasticity*, which allows the brain to reorganize neural pathways based on new experiences. For example, if you wanted to make an imprint of a large coin in clay, you must press the coin down on the clay hard enough to make an impression. This is similar to the development of new neural networks in children. Involved parents who provide a plethora of positive feedback and stimulating information to their kids are solidifying new pathways or imprints in their youngster's brains. The end result is long-term potential for developing advanced intellect, athleticism, memory and language acquisition, and analytical thinking, as well as mathematical, writing, and reading skills in young children.

EXERCISE AND THE BRAIN

For years, researchers have been promoting exercise as beneficial to the body. Today that still holds true, but there is additional evidence that exercise also builds the brain. Literally. Studies at the Salk Institute in San Diego, California, have shown that exercise may stimulate new brain cell growth by increased blood flow, in the hippocampus, frontal, and prefrontal regions of the brain. As a result, the studies showed there were improvements in memory, executing functioning, attention span, concentration, and psychomotor speed.

WINDOWS OF LEARNING

Current research in child development indicates kids have prime times of learning when their brains are highly receptive, based on the characteristic of neural plasticity. These key growth phases or windows of learning can open and close in a matter of months or last a few years.

VISUAL DEVELOPMENT: BIRTH TO AGE FOUR

Visual development takes place from birth to age four, when your child's brain is open to seeing new sights, colors, and images. The eyes learn to focus at varying distances and begin to develop visual acuity and depth perception. The brain also becomes adept at organizing and classifying images to be recalled for future use. It is critical that your child have clear and accurate vision in this phase. Check with your child's pediatrician if you have concerns.

LANGUAGE ACQUISITION: BIRTH TO AGE TEN

The door to learning language is wide open in the first decade of life. Babies are born with the ability to learn any language, and conceivably multiple languages, if the process is started from birth and continued through adulthood. The dominant sounds your child hears will be the ones most likely repeated in later life. Swiss psychologist Jean Piaget, who pioneered theories of language acquisition in children, believed kids need to hear the spoken word early and frequently in conversation and dialogue. The more you talk to your child, the greater chance he or she has of becoming fluent in one or more languages. This includes developing native accents, language structure, grammar, vocabulary, and syntax, or the way words are put together.

For example, a three-month-old infant can distinguish the difference between hundreds of different spoken sounds used in languages around the world. If the infant were raised to speak Japanese, after about twelve months the brain would hone in on sounds relevant to that language and gradually prune out the rest. By toddlerhood, that child would not recognize that *ra* is different from *la* because the latter is not used in Japanese.

LANGUAGE FLUENCY: BIRTH TO AGE THREE

Early on, Korean children learn to hear the subtleties of their spoken language by miniscule differences in the pronunciation of similar words. A sound that is a shade off may indicate a totally different meaning. The language center of the brain also allows Spanish speakers to easily roll their *r*'s, French-speaking kids to learn guttural throaty sounds, and German children to hear the sound of *v* for the English pronunciation of *w*. The magical window for language allows for brain plasticity in this area until about the age of ten. After that, most have a more difficult time developing fluency in foreign languages. While they may become proficient, it is unlikely they will speak as well as a native.

MUSIC AND MATH: BIRTH TO AGE FIVE

The perfect partnership exists between music and math. Children who excel in one area will likely do so in the other. The part of the brain that is geared to hear music also deals with numbers and regulates analytical thinking and mathematical calculations. Listening to classical music by Wolfgang Amadeus Mozart, Ludwig van Beethoven, Antonio Vivaldi, and Johann Sebastian Bach can help kids develop spatial skills, the ability to reason, and memory retention. The earlier a child is exposed to learning a musical instrument, the greater chance of developing the cortex.

EMOTIONAL SECURITY: BIRTH TO AGE TWO

Research shows that a measure of an individual's success in life involves having emotional security. The part of the brain that regulates emotional control is developed in early childhood when a baby's needs are consistently met in the first two years. If parents can provide consistent comfort, security, and love by quickly answering a child's cries, then the emotional wiring of the brain becomes firmly established in a positive manner. This can set a child's temperament and attitude toward life based on feelings of happiness, joy, and hopefulness. Providing emotional security in this critical window is the basis for experiencing future trusting relationships, building self-esteem, and developing self-confidence to meet new challenges.

AUDITORY DEVELOPMENT: BIRTH TO AGE TWO

The brain has to learn to hear. It is an active process that requires neurological development and proper functioning of the mechanics of the ear. The auditory window of opportunity is in the first two years of life, because that's when the wiring or pathways are making critical connections. Good hearing sets the stage for speech development and auditory processing skills that link both hemispheres of the brain.

FINE MOTOR SKILLS: BIRTH TO AGE FIVE

In the first two years, babies learn to control their fingers, hands, wrists, and arms to perform basic functions like holding on to small objects, picking up tiny pieces of food, and grasping and stacking blocks. They also learn to use both hands when playing with toys and manipulating objects in their environment. Other critical steps in this window are being able to voluntarily grasp and release objects, as well as using one hand to purposefully cross the center or midline of the body when performing tasks.

The second window for fine motor development happens from ages two to five when complex skills emerge, including writing with pencils, self-care activities with buttons and zippers, cutting with scissors, and throwing and catching balls.

HANDEDNESS: BIRTH TO AGE FOUR

Right- or left-handedness happens in the first few years of life. It is not something that a child chooses but is more of a realization of one's natural tendencies.

In the first two years, children will use both hands indiscriminately for various tasks; but by about age four, parents may start to see one hand being used most often. Usually it is the hand in which a child chooses to hold a pencil for writing or drawing.

SIDEDNESS: BIRTH TO AGE SEVEN

Sidedness is determined by your child's dominant hand, foot, eye, and ear. Left- or right-side dominance has neurological roots and is something one becomes aware of through activities in life. Some people are often solidly right- or left-side dominant in the hand, foot, eye, and ear, but some people can be mixed-dominant. These tendencies can easily be identified by about age seven. (See chapter 8 on coordination and sidedness.) There might be learning or coordination issues with mixed-dominant kids. If parents have a strong need to alter an aspect of their child's eye, ear, hand, or foot dominance, it is best to make changes early in this window of learning.

GROSS MOTOR SKILLS: BIRTH TO AGE TEN

If your child has good tactile development, then chances are likely for excellent gross motor skills and muscle tone. This window is open throughout the first decade because gross motor development is a gradual process. Kids need to go through the steps of rolling, crawling, standing, walking, skipping, and running. This involves developing muscle strength, range of motion for limbs, balance, coordination, flexibility, and spatial awareness. A strong gross motor foundation sets the stage for potential excellence in athletics.

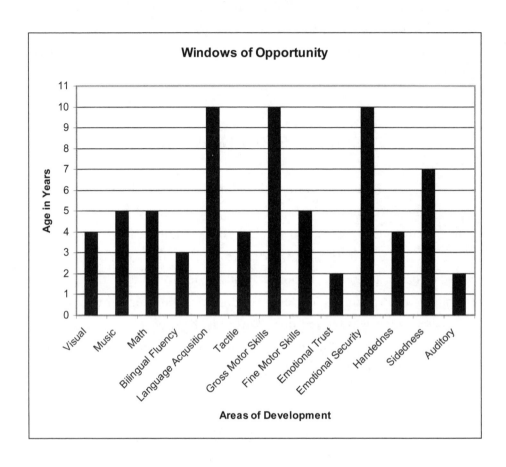

Windows of Opportunity

Age in Years

Visual · Music · Math · Bilingual Fluency · Language Acqusition · Tactile · Gross Motor Skills · Fine Motor Skills · Emotional Trust · Emotional Security · Handednss · Sidedness · Auditory

Areas of Development

5

Fine Motor Development

Great things can come from small muscle movement, and that's exactly what fine motor development is all about. It boils down to your child's ability to move tiny muscles in the individual body parts such as hands, fingers, feet, and toes, and also the use of vocal cords and organs required for singing or speaking. For the purpose of this chapter, let's take a closer look at motor skills as they pertain to hand and finger coordination used for reaching, grasping, self-care, ball skills, early sports fundamentals, and manipulating toys and tools. We will also investigate spatial awareness, timing, balance, and moving individual muscle groups in sequence. These elements are some of the pieces of the puzzle of fine motor development, which can give your child an exceptional foundation for the future.

EYE-HAND COORDINATION PROMOTES LIFE SKILLS

Why is it important to develop excellent eye-hand coordination? There are life benefits that emerge from being coordinated in areas such as language and literacy, academics, math concepts, athletics, musical talent, and exploring art and science. (See the Fine Motor Development Areas and Their Practical Applications chart that follows.) There are also functional, creative, and expressive ways kids use their eye-hand coordination, ranging from manipulating a computer mouse and drawing pictures to skillfully playing physical activities with peers. When kids know they can trust their bodies to accomplish these fine motor tasks, they feel confident to participate in group activities that build self-esteem and positive self-images. This process does not happen overnight or even in a matter of a few months. It takes years of trial and error and experimentation to develop the muscle control, hand strength, and sensory awareness. This is where parent-guided play is essential to providing kids plenty of eye-hand experiences that can contribute to overall coordination and intelligence.

FINE MOTOR DEVELOPMENT AREAS AND THEIR PRACTICAL APPLICATIONS

Fine Motor Development Areas	Practical Application
Academics	Handwriting skills, concentration, amount of work completed, attention span, drawing, understanding of educational materials presented, visual perception, self-esteem, social skills, and confidence for self-care needs.

Fine Motor Development Areas	Practical Application
Art	Crafts, cutting, pasting and gluing, drawing, painting, and sculpting.
Athletics	Eye-hand coordination; spatial skills; visual acuity; depth perception; use of arms, hands and fingers; hand strength; hand grasping skills in throwing and catching balls; hitting balls with rackets, clubs, and other objects; perception of moving objects like balls coming toward and away from the athlete, which is critical to most sports
Communication (Verbal and Nonverbal)	Listening skills, oral development, vocabulary, positional language (*on*, *under*, *over*, *above*, and so forth), understanding visual cues in social conversation, and social development in peer situations.
Drama	Dramatic play, reciting language, dressing up, and making props.
Language	Recognition of letters, reading words, listening skills to hear pronunciation, speaking skills, and applying language in social situations.
Literacy	Reading and holding books, writing the alphabet, learning the shapes of letters word recognition, drawing skills, and holding paper.

Fine Motor Development Areas	Practical Application
Math Concepts	Counting, adding, subtracting, multiplying, dividing, sorting, manipulating objects, drawing and understanding shapes, pouring and measuring liquids, stringing beads, stacking cubes, and fractions, parts, and whole concepts.
Musical Talent	Learning and playing musical instruments of all kinds, clapping hands, rhythmic activities, making noise with drums, sticks, and other objects. Crafts, cutting, pasting and gluing, drawing, painting, sculpting, dramatic play, props, and dress-up clothes.
Science Investigation	Measuring liquids and other objects, calculating numbers, pouring liquids into containers, visual skill in using microscopes, manipulating magnets, magnifying glasses, and controlling experiments.
Social Benefits	Self-care in doing simple tasks such as tying laces and using zippers and buttons, handling utensils, and other independent actions give a child confidence to interact in peer and other social situations.
Vocational Applications	Fine motor skills are needed in most jobs whether in using computers or in medicine, dentistry, secretarial work, building, construction, engineering, architecture, clothing design, art, music, or teaching.

THE *EYES* HAVE IT

The term eye-hand coordination begins with the eyes, and there's a good reason for it. It's because your child must first *see* to be able to coordinate voluntary fine motor movement with the hands. There are two types of vision that contribute to the development of overall eye-hand coordination. The first is visual-motor skills, which include your child's ability to see and coordinate voluntary movements with the hands. The second is visual-perceptual skills, which help kids recognize and compare information like size, shape, form, color, and distance. The eyes pick up data and send it through the central nervous system. This process contributes to the development of your child's depth perception, which is needed to cut lines on paper, manipulate toys, color, paint, and tie shoes. Children also use depth perception to comb hair, put toothpaste on a toothbrush, use computers, electronic toys, play games and sports, dress, fold clothes, read, and write. Many of these activities require processing and understanding multiple amounts and types of information all at once.

For example, Melanie is an active six-year-old who loves to walk and play with her parents by the shore of a nearby lake. She often gravitates near the water's edge, which is lined with rocks of all sizes. She likes to pick up small stones and throw them so they skip atop the surface of the water many times before submerging. She visually discriminates the difference between the size, shape, and texture of rocks. She prefers small, lightweight, oval-shaped rocks with smooth textures. She also likes to find thin rocks because they move through the air like flying discs. Another game is to find rocks that make the biggest splash. Large boulders might work for that game, but they provide a different challenge. Melanie knows from experience that she can't pick up or throw a three-foot boulder. By experimentation over the years, she has learned it is too heavy. That knowledge is the accumulation of years of sensory stimulation and muscle development that started from birth.

HAND ACTIVITY IN NEWBORNS

In the first few months of life, your child will have a hand grip that might appear to be an indicator of power and athletic potential. Your baby can squeeze your finger and hold on with seemingly incredible strength, which could be great later for gripping a baseball bat, tennis racket, or golf club. The fact is your newborn's hand strength is an involuntary reflex controlled by the brain and spinal cord. It is called the *palmar reflex* and is an instinctive reaction that kicks in at birth. Notice when you try to pull your finger back, your infant may try to hold on tighter and stronger. This reflex lasts for approximately the first six months.

There are some fun games you can play with your child using the palmar grasping reflex. Try placing a washcloth over your arm and encourage your baby to use this grasp to pull it off. The texture of terrycloth makes this a fun activity. Also place a rattle into the palm of your infant's hand. Your child will initially just hold it. Use this grasping instinct to move your child's hand up and down to teach the motion of shaking something to make noise.

GREAT GRASPING

The world of grasping can open up dramatically for babies from six months old to one year. Your child will begin to develop the critical hand sequence of *reach, grasp, carry,* and *voluntary release.* These patterns of developmental hand control are the foundation for your child to learn about objects, people, nature, toys, animals, and overall sensory stimulation.

The first phase is your child's ability to *reach* the hand and arm toward a desired object with purpose and intent. Good visual skills play a part by helping kids determine the distance to the object. For example, a sitting baby might see a toy block about twelve inches away. The child's trunk or torso must be strong and stable enough to lean forward with balance while simultaneously extending an arm. Initially it might be a one-handed reach, but by the end of the first year, kids might use both hands together to reach for objects. When one or both hands are above the block, your child might *grasp* it by placing the whole hand as a unit around the top. Seeing and feeling the toy provides sensory information that it is time to curl the fingers around it for the grasp. If the intent is to *carry* the block, then your child will hold on to it and move it to another position or location. Perhaps you have asked your baby to place the block in the palm of your hand. To successfully carry out this request, your child would need to *voluntarily release* it into your hand. This skill is the first step of being able to build block towers, to self-feed with crackers, and later to push, pull, and carry things.

Children learn to use a variety of grasps to explore their world. The *power* grasp is one that allows the thumb and fingers of the hand to hold a knife to cut a piece of bread. The *hook* grasp allows a child to hang onto the handle of a lunch box. The *pincer* grasp with the thumb and index finger helps preschoolers pick up beads to string them. The *spherical* grasp is used to hold a tennis ball in the palm of the hand and marks the beginning of ball-throwing skills. The *cylindrical* grasp, which includes the thumb and finger pads, allows a child to open a lid on a jar. These hand skills are essential movements that adults use to work, play, drive a car, garden, cook, clean, use a computer, play sports, and succeed in school.

HAND GRASPING PATTERNS IN THE FIRST YEAR

Grasping Patterns	Description and Application
Non-prehensile	Pushing or lifting an object with the entire hand and palm as a unit, such as when picking up a block.
Prehensile	Grasping an object with purpose, power, or precision. The thumb can be opposable, meaning working separately and opposite of the fingers.
Precision	The thumb and fingers hold on to an object.
Power	When one uses the entire hand to force a motion on the object; for example, when using a hammer, playing the drums, or cutting with a knife.
Hook	This is the type of grasp needed to carry objects such as the handle of a lunch box, backpack, or suitcase.
Tip Pinch and Pincer Grasp	Moving the thumb and tip of index finger so the fingers form a circle or an oval. This is for picking up tiny objects like beads, cereal, and small toys.

Grasping Patterns	Description and Application
Tripod Grasp	The thumb, index, and middle fingers are used to pick up and manipulate objects like pens, pencils, or drinking straws.
Spherical grasp	This hold is used to throw a tennis ball, which rests in the palm of the hand.
Cylindrical Grasp	The fingers and thumb cup around a flat object like the circular lid on a jar. It requires force to turn the lid to open it. Only the pads of the fingers hold the object as it is turned.

IN-HAND MANIPULATION

Once your child has mastered the different grasping skills, it is important to develop intricate in-hand movements. For example, a preschooler has a ball of soft clay about two inches in diameter in the palm of one hand. Good in-hand manipulation skills would allow that child to use only the fingers of the hand to roll the clay up to the fingertips. This move requires wrist strength and stability, thumb control, and finger-joint dexterity. Another scenario might be when a child has two or more pieces of cereal in the palm of his hand but only picks up one to pop into his mouth. Finally, kids with good hand skills can easily pick up a drinking straw, properly grip a pencil, and slide the thumb and fingers back and forth to separate pieces of paper that are stuck together.

Parents can try this experiment to understand a child's learning process.

Use one hand to pick up three or more coins off a flat surface and immediately drop them into the palm of that same hand. Using your fingertips, try to select one coin and bring it back up to the thumb and index fingertips. Imagine that you intend to place it into a vending machine change slot. Repeat it several times and notice how your fingers are able to perform that skill. This is an example of fine motor skills that adults take for granted and kids have to work hard to master.

IN-HAND SKILLS IN THE FIRST TWO YEARS

In-Hand Manipulation Skills	Description and Application
Finger to Palm	The object stays in contact with the thumb and fingers, and then it is transferred to the palm, such as when picking up a coin or bead with the fingers and moving it into the palm of the hand.
Palm to Finger	This is the opposite of the finger-to-palm movement. While the coin or bead is in the palm of the hand, it is moved to the fingers. Then you might put the coin into a vending machine slot or place the bead on a string.
Shifting	The thumb and pad of the fingers can separate two pieces of paper when they are stuck together. This is also used to adjust a pen or pencil after the initial grasp so you can move closer to the writing end.

In-Hand Manipulation Skills	Description and Application
Simple Rotation	The fingers turn or roll an object in the hand at the finger pads and the thumb. One example of this is unscrewing a small bottle cap or picking up a small peg from a flat surface and placing it vertically into a hole. Another example is when playing with a puzzle piece; kids rotate the piece to find the correct fit.
Complex Rotation	This movement includes turning an object 180 to 360 degrees one or more times using the fingers and the thumb. This action happens when a child turns a pencil over to use the eraser.

BILATERAL HAND USE

The use of two hands can be better than one when it comes to banging blocks, clapping hands, cutting paper with scissors, and playing catch with your child. The journey to this stage of development takes years of progressing through many fine-motor milestones. This is a three-step process. From birth to about three months, your child will likely reach for a desired object with one hand. You may see this as your baby tries to grab your nose with one hand while you are holding him. From three months to about ten months, your baby may use a bilateral motion of both arms and hands to simultaneously reach and grasp for objects. From about ten months on, your child may be able to hold an object in each hand and bang them together. Fast-forward a bit, and your two-year-old might catch a ten-inch ball with two hands. Then by about age three, your toddler could possibly throw and catch an eight-inch ball.

To accomplish these skills, your child must be able to disassociate the two sides of the body and use them for different functions. Other factors are torso strength, shoulder stabilization, and elbow and wrist control. Progress will continue as long as your child practices the reach, grasp, carry, and voluntary release pattern with both arms and hands. The average four- to six-year-old will likely perform these skills with ease along with the age-appropriate development of cognitive, eye-hand, and fine and gross motor development. You may see the results of this integrated coordination as your child learns to read, write, self-dress, tie shoes, play a musical instrument, turn pages of a book, play sports, use construction tools, cut paper, pour liquids, and eat with utensils.

BALL-THROWING SKILLS

Some parents believe it is never too early to teach your child to throw a ball. But is that true? There are two sides to every story, and this is an excellent example of such. In some instances, developing skills early in life might be better; however, there is such a thing as too early when it comes to childhood development. In the first year of life, babies are busy learning to use their eyes and hands and figuring out how to voluntarily release a ball with some control. By about thirteen months, kids might hold a tennis ball and fling it with minimal control, but they are still not ready to play catch. At about sixteen months, a sitting baby can often throw a small ball underhand in a forward direction with some control but still with a random result.

The age of readiness for ball-throwing skills could begin around eighteen months. A balanced, standing child might be able to throw overhand in a forward direction a distance of about three feet. At two years old, a toddler can stand and throw a ball at a target that is three feet away with some accuracy. The concept of playing catch could become a strong possibility for children ages three to six, because they may have integrated fine and gross motor movements. Throwing distances with moderate accuracy can range between five and twelve feet. Further refinement of ball-throwing skills in distance and accuracy happens over the next few years, but much depends on exposure to the skill and practice with parents, friends, and coaches.

USE OF TOYS AND TOOLS

For kids, it might be said that play is work and work is play. Learning to use their hands and fingers to voluntarily release objects and practice in-hand manipulation skills takes work. These hand-motor abilities enable a child to use tools as an extension of the limbs. For example, tools can help a child perform in school, excel in sports, explore creative arts, play musical instruments, build small projects, and take care of oneself. School activities include writing with pencils and cutting with scissors while some sports use rackets, bats, and clubs. Creative arts involve drawing with pencils, markers, and pens, while painters use brushes with oils, acrylics, or watercolors. Sculptors and potters work in clay. Kids' building projects require the use of hammers, saws, levels, and all different kinds of hardware. Musical instruments need agile fingers for plucking or strumming strings, banging drumsticks, bowing string instruments, and manipulating keyboards and wind instruments. Taking care of oneself requires using tools like combs and brushes. (For more on self-care, read further in this chapter.)

Ask yourself, what does my child want to do with the tool and how can this task be accomplished? There are gradual stages of development. Initially, kids are learning the skills, and they gradually improve with trial and error. In the first year, kids are learning how to use their hands. In the second year, they can apply that knowledge to the use of tools along with more advanced cognitive thinking.

Children must also know what they want to do with the tools and have a plan to accomplish the task. For example, a six-month-old may learn to hold a spoon in his hand and can have great fun banging that tool on a food tray. It will take another year for that child to realize the spoon is a tool used for self-feeding. At about two and a half years old, that same child may be eating with a fork, and it may take until four to six years old before he is using a dull knife for cutting or spreading. This last skill takes longer because it also requires the use of the other hand to hold the food while the dominant hand is cutting or spreading.

The use of tools expands to cutting paper with scissors and drawing or writing with pens, pencils, or markers. Many kids are able to use scissors at about age two, when they can place their fingers in the scissor handles. They may be able to open and close the scissors to cut little snips one movement at a time. Repetitive hand movements are yet to come. A great game for this level is cutting snips off of dough snakes. (For more on this activity, see the games for three-year-olds in chapter 15.) The ability to continuously cut across a six-inch paper can emerge at about four years old, and one year later, kids can cut various shapes like circles and squares. This is a perfect time to have your child practice cutting out coupons in the newspaper. Other factors to consider in cutting skills are the width of the line and the size and complexity of the design.

CUTTING WITH SCISSORS AND DEVELOPMENTAL PROGRESS

Age	Cutting with Scissors
0 to 2 years	Developing grasps, fine motor skills, and in-hand muscle manipulation.
2 to 2.5 years	Can snip small paper corners with scissors or cut through dough.

Age	Cutting with Scissors
3 to 3.5 years	Able to cut across a two- to four-inch piece of paper.
4 to 4.5 years	Cuts various shapes like circles and squares.
5 to 6 years	Skilled with scissors and can cut complex designs and intricate lines.

AGES AND STAGES OF WRITING

Babies in the first fourteen months can pick up a chunky crayon or pencil soon after developing hand-grasping skills. They usually grab it with their whole hand and move the instrument by shifting their entire arm and shoulder. Kids display writing readiness at different ages based on maturity and physical development. The prerequisites are fine motor development, eye-hand coordination, the ability to use tools, the capacity to form basic strokes like a vertical line, letter recognition and perception, and right and left discrimination. The sequence of prewriting strokes and shapes your child may learn include: a vertical line (l), a horizontal line (—), a cross (+), a forward slash (/), a backslash (\), and finally, a circle (o). A great skill to practice is the infinity mark (∞) as well as the above-mentioned strokes. These are all of the shapes and lines your child will need in order to print every letter of the alphabet.

THE DEVELOPMENT OF HANDWRITING SKILLS

Age	Task	Developmental Games
Birth to 12 months	Scribbles on paper.	Crayons on a large piece of paper in free-form drawing.
2 years	Attempts horizontal and vertical lines, and semi-open circles.	Roll ¼-inch balls of dough or clay. Pick up small objects like cereal. Draw dotted horizontal and vertical lines for your child to trace.
3 years	Copies horizontal and vertical lines and can possibly draw a closed circle.	Use tweezers to pick up small objects like raisins. Pinch and seal a zipper-type sandwich bag open and closed. Draw dotted shapes for your child to copy.
4 to 5 years	Draws diagonal lines, a cross, circles, possibly some letters, and maybe can write own name.	Practice twisting toothpaste caps open and closed with the thumb and index finger, while holding the tube with the ring and pinky fingers. Write letters in trays of shaving cream.

Age	Task	Developmental Games
5 to 6 years	Copies a triangle, prints own name, may be able to write all of the letters in both upper- and lowercase forms.	Give your child dot-to-dot activities and mazes, draw letters in trays of rice, do guided drawing, in which kids draw animals, shapes, and objects based on verbal instruction.

HAND USE IN SELF-CARE

The ability to use your hands effectively is critical to self-dressing. Kids need to learn to put on and remove shorts, pants, shirts, dresses, jackets, sweatshirts, underclothing, socks, and shoes. Hand control is needed to grasp tools like toothbrushes, unscrew small toothpaste caps, squeeze shampoo bottles, and glide a hairbrush down the head. These skills are performed with help from the shoulders, arms, and elbows, which provide the right amount of pressure and movement to accomplish these tasks.

For more information on fine-motor milestones, see the American Academy of Pediatrics developmental ages and stages charts found in Recommended Resources in the back of the book.

6

Right- or Left-Handed

We live in a right-handed world. Our tools, school supplies, cutting implements, eating utensils, clothing fasteners, musical instruments, and industrial equipment are usually designed to accommodate right-handed people. The tendency to move toward the right side also extends to the design and use of space, the flow of pedestrian sidewalk movement, and automobile traffic. Most languages are written to be read directionally from left to right. Numbered keypads on telephones, computers, and calculators are strategically placed from one to nine in a right-facing direction. The definition of *clockwise* means to rotate in a circle to the right, and wrist watches are adjusted by little knobs placed on the right side of the timepiece. These are just a few ways life is easier for right-handers, but more challenging for left-handed kids.

Why does this preference for right-handers exist in most countries? It is because approximately 90 percent of the population is believed to be predominantly right-handed. The remaining 10 percent, therefore, are either left-handed or ambidextrous, having equal strength and ability in both hands. No one knows for sure how handedness occurs in children, but it does indicate a need for understanding how kids learn to live with their individual tendencies.[1]

HANDEDNESS AT BIRTH

When babies are born, they are like blank canvases ready to become priceless masterpieces. It is normal for your newborn to show no hand preferences. Both arms and hands should move equally well prompted by strong primitive reflexes, which you can read about in the chapters on fine and gross motor development. Your newborn's hands should be free to move in any direction. You may notice, however, that one hand is fisted more often than the other. You may also notice the head is turned to one side more frequently and one arm may move more vigorously. This has very little to do with your baby's being right- or left-handed. More often it is attributed to your child's natural primitive reflexes, and occasionally to strained neck or shoulder muscles resulting from the birthing process.[2]

Researchers say that up to 70 percent of babies will turn their heads to the right for unknown reasons, and there is a strong likelihood that those children may turn out right-handed. Studies also show that kids who frequently turn to the left are more likely to become left-handers. These observations may still be indications of developmental phases as children switch back and forth between left to right, because handedness is not completely determined until the preschool years.

HAND PREFERENCE IN THE FIRST TWO YEARS

In the first four to six months, the majority of babies may start holding toys in their right hands a little bit longer than their left. By six to nine months, a few might show a clear preference for the right but will still use both sides at least some of the time. You might begin to see some tendencies emerge by twelve to eighteen months, as kids learn to use both hands to manipulate an object. For example, begin to notice when your child holds a toy with moving parts. One hand will support the toy while the other tries to twist or turn an interesting feature. A potentially right-handed baby might hold the toy with the left hand to enable manipulation with the right. About one in seven possible left-handed or ambidextrous kids will hold the toy with the right to manipulate it with the left.

By eighteen months to two years, fine motor muscle control improves and hand skills become more intricate and specific. Grasping patterns are often advanced to allow a child to hold, carry, and voluntarily release objects. A fun game to play with your child is to stack toy blocks and notice which hand takes control during the activity. You might see a dominant hand emerge at this point, but there are still many kids who regularly flip back and forth. In many cases, babies will select the hand most convenient for the task. A typical scenario is when your child is sitting on the floor and the blocks are placed all around within his reach. You might see the left hand pick up the blocks on the left side of the body and the right hand pick up the blocks on the right. An interesting observation might be to note which hand reaches for blocks in the middle or center of the body. This may be a clue regarding hand preference, but then again, maybe not.

The preschool years are a playful paradise of opportunities for hand use in active three-year-olds. Observing your child in this environment may begin to provide solid right- or left-handed clues. You may see your child predominantly use one hand for some activities while others switch back when playing, drawing, dressing, cutting, and eating. The critical age for determining handedness is about four years old because at that point many neurological pathways are set. If your child has not indicated any hand preference by this age, it might be beneficial to get an assessment by an occupational therapist to build coordination and confidence in writing, cutting, and using a pencil. By the end of the preschool time at ages three or six, it will most likely be clear whether you are raising a righty, a lefty, or an ambidextrous child.[3] Here is a look at some clues to determine your child's hand preference.[4]

TESTS FOR HANDEDNESS IN PRESCHOOLERS

Skill	Right Hand	Left Hand	Age
Picks up a toy that is directly in the middle of the body.			
Sucks thumb or finger(s) of the hand.			
Scribbles, writes, or draws with a pencil or crayon.			
Pushes a peg into a hole.			
Snaps blocks together (note the hand that uses force to interlock the blocks).			

Skill	Right Hand	Left Hand	Age
Paints on an easel.			
Uses a toy hammer or bangs the ground with a stick.			
Waters flowers with a cup or watering can.			
Throws dice when playing games.			
Brushes teeth.			
Throws a ball.			
Combs or brushes hair.			
Turns on and off light switches.			
Cuts with scissors.			
Opens a door or window.			

Skill	Right Hand	Left Hand	Age
Makes a tower of blocks (note the stacking or balancing hand).			
Opens or closes a zipper on clothing.			
Snaps puzzle pieces together (note the hand that turns and twists the piece to make the fit).			
Drinks from a cup that is directly in front of the child.			
Strikes a hand or arm out in frustration (note the first hand that reacts).			
Eats with a spoon.			
Strings beads (note the hand holding the string).			
Total			

Gross Motor Development

Each child grows at different rates and develops new skills at various ages and stages of life. For some, "normal" can mean speeding along the fast track of skill discovery. So-called late bloomers arrive at important milestones when they are good and ready. Both rates of growth are completely healthy. For example, there are nine-month-old babies who are not only walking but also moving at a fast clip. There are also fifteen-month-old children just taking their first steps. Both ends of the spectrum are considered healthy, and a child's developmental timeline is not an indicator of coordination or future athletic ability. By the preschool years, most kids will master these skills when they are physically, emotionally, and neurologically ready.

THE AMAZING NEWBORN

A child goes through a tremendous amount of growth and development during the first six years of life, but none is greater than the prenatal period. Most of this growth is in preparation for life outside the womb, and this growth period is critical for your baby to be ready to survive in this world. Your newborn infant must learn how to breathe, master internal temperature control, begin to self-regulate the circulatory system, and eat and digest food.

Your child's behavior in the first month of life includes deep and restful sleep, light sleep, and being mildly or fully alert. Your baby's moods swing from happy and content to unhappy, crying, and fussy. Many of these behaviors are affected by the external environment, which is dependent upon your child's physical and emotional needs of hunger, warmth, love, security, human touch, dry diapers, and sound sleep being met.

STAGES OF GROWTH

The rate of physical growth for each child is dependent upon various factors and influences, such as genetics, culture, environment, nutrition, gender, disabilities, and access to health care. In all circumstances, however, the same general principles will dictate the *direction* and the *sequence* of physical development.

For example, the *direction* of a child's muscle development will begin with moving the head as a newborn. By about twelve months to two years, muscle development will reach the feet and toes as most kids learn to walk. Children start to lift and turn their heads as babies, then raise their torsos, discover the use of arms and hands, and finally begin to stand with or without support.

The *sequence* of muscle development starts closest to the center of the body and extends to the extremities such as the hands, fingers, feet, and toes. Most children will learn to crawl before they can pick up small objects with the pincer grasp, which is using the thumb and index finger. As a result, kids typically develop their gross motor movements before they establish control of the fine motor muscles such as manipulating buttons on clothing or turning pages in a book. Young kids enjoy discovering all of these stages as they explore their abilities and figure out the magic of motor development.

Let's explore an overview of fine and gross motor skills, hand control, cognitive, speech communication, and social behaviors from birth to age six.

GROSS MOTOR REFLEXES IN THE NEWBORN

Your child's gross motor skills have been in place long before birth. Many of your newborn's muscular movements are not controlled actions but instinctive or primitive reflexes triggered by the spinal cord and brain. There are two gross motor reflexes that are critical to a newborn's survival: *rooting* and *sucking*. Rooting is a physical reaction that causes your baby to turn his head toward a source of physical touch on the mouth or cheek for breast-or bottle-feeding. This can last throughout the first year. The sucking reflex occurs when an object like a nipple, bottle, or pacifier touches the roof of your baby's mouth and he starts sucking for nutrition, comfort, or reassurance.

The *startling* reflex is your baby's reaction to a sudden loud noise. You might notice your child quickly tilt his head backward or change its position. Other physical cues are arms and legs briefly extending outward and then returning to the body. In addition, your baby might cry as a result of this reflex because it can be a shock to the nervous system. This reflex usually disappears by about three to six months.

Other important involuntary gross motor movements that should appear in the first twelve months include the *plantar, walking,* and *standing* reflexes. The plantar reflex occurs when you lightly touch the bottom of an infant's foot, which might make the toes curl inward. This appears to be a ticklish reaction, but it's neurological in nature and lasts the first nine through twelve months. The walking reflex is a reaction that makes it appear your child is ready to take steps. Don't be disappointed when this reflex disappears after the first three months; it will reappear between ten to eighteen months when your child is physically and neurologically ready to walk.

The standing reflex is similar to the walking response because it appears your infant will be able to stand alone very early in life. While you are holding your child's head and neck and supporting the body securely under the armpits, your baby will try to straighten his legs for about thirty seconds. After that brief time, your baby will collapse his legs into a sitting or bending position. This reflex usually disappears by about four months and shows up again at approximately six to eight months when your child is physiologically ready to stand and possibly begin to take steps.

Please keep in mind it is very normal to show some but not all of the reflexes on any given day. However, the absence of any of these in the first year might be cause for concern and further investigation, as is the continued persistence of a reflex that should have disappeared or been replaced by the redevelopment of other skills in an older infant or young preschooler. The best approach is to look at your child's overall development to see that everything is progressing normally. Your child's pediatrician can help with that assessment.

POSTURAL REACTIONS

Infants also have reflexive *postural reactions,* which are simple gross motor movements that lead to major developmental milestones. At about four months, your child may display the *derotational righting* response, which involves turning the body to follow the direction of a head turn. It is a prerequisite to being able to roll over with purpose and control. At about six months, the *parachute response* kicks in when your baby extends his arms out to catch or prevent a fall. Also, the *propping responses* help your child learn to sit by extending his arms forward, sideways, and backward for balance. It is critical that your child show these responses on the right and left sides of the body for normal development. If only one side is responding, that could be an indication of a muscular weakness, and it might be wise to consult your pediatrician.

GROSS MOTOR SKILLS IN THE FIRST TWO YEARS

With each passing month, your child will begin to improve gross motor skills, starting with head control, rolling over, and then moving on to sitting, creeping, possibly crawling, standing, and finally walking. Accomplishing simple movements builds the foundation for performing complex skills.

MOVEMENT FROM THE PRONE POSITION

The first area of your baby's development is from the prone position, in which your child is facedown and lying on the abdomen. Infants can begin to lift and hold up their heads for a few seconds, turn their heads side to side, and bend at the hips with their bottoms pushed up into the air. These new movements allow for more visual stimulation, and your child will be able to see toys and brightly colored objects at the sides of the crib or play areas. Also, it becomes a tactile experience for the baby to feel the softness of the fabric against the cheek when turning his head side to side. A four-month-old might be able to hold up his head about 45 degrees while rotating it to look around. As upper torso strength develops, your baby can prop his body up by putting weight on the forearms and hands. Between six and eight months, your child can remain in the prone position for long periods and begin to shift body weight forward on the forearms for precrawling skills.

MOVEMENT FROM THE SUPINE POSITION

From a supine position, where the baby is lying on the back and facing up, the world becomes a visual paradise with a 180-degree view of life. This panoramic view is an important source of sensory information. Babies can see, hear, smell, and touch their immediate surroundings. There is freedom of movement for the arms and legs, and the hands become a source of wonder. Your child might be mesmerized by opening and closing the fingers, grabbing toys, and clapping hands. By six months, babies discover that their hands can grab their feet. It then becomes great fun for them to put hands, feet, and toys into their mouth.

ROLLING OVER

The emergence of head, torso, limb, and upper-body control triggers the ability to roll from a prone (facedown) to a supine (faceup) position in the first six months. This is the start of locomotion for an infant. When babies learn to use the head, lower body, or legs to trigger the rolling motion, it becomes a means to move from a few inches to a few feet across the floor. Watch out because your child is officially on the go as he voluntarily rolls from front to back and back to front. This milestone can happen anywhere from about six to fourteen months.

SITTING SKILLS

As your baby gradually develops head control and a strong back, sitting with help becomes easier. For example, a seven-week-old has a rounded spine and would have great difficulty sitting upright. According to the American Academy of Pediatrics, a seven-month-old might be physically and neurologically ready to sit with some support or possibly without help. At eight to ten months, a baby might sit unsupported for a short length of time. At one year, that same infant could sit for about five minutes, rotate the upper body, maintain balance, and successfully reach for toys or objects. By ages two to four, kids are skilled at sitting for longer periods of time, typically about ten minutes.

READY, SET, CRAWL

If you thought rounding up a rolling baby kept you busy, you might be in for a surprise because the crawling infant knows no boundaries. Creeping or crawling is a reference to four-point or four-limbed mobility, such as moving with the hands and knees or feet. It requires coordinating two sides of the body to move in an opposite arm and leg sequence with balance, flexibility, torso strength, trunk rotation, and excellent shoulder and pelvic stability. This is the point where all the building blocks of physical, mental, and neurological growth merge into controlled mobility. Research shows that by nine months babies use independent locomotion, such as crawling exhibit more flexible memory retrieval or recall in the first year of life.[1] Studies also show that kids who were skilled and early crawlers are likely to develop strong gross motor skills in later preschool years.[2] According to the American Academy of Pediatrics, at twelve months babies might get into sitting positions and crawl forward without help using the arms and legs. This may be a result of improved balance, core strength, and cross-limb muscle coordination. It will likely be a short time before your motocross-crawler moves into the next phase of gross muscle development of standing and cruising.

SUPERIOR STANDING

A child's ability to stand evolves when there is overall stability in the head, neck, torso, back, hips, pelvis, and legs. The preparation for a weight-bearing and upright posture begins in the first few weeks of life with the positive support reflex mentioned earlier in the newborn skills segment. By four to six months, children can bear some weight on the legs if they are holding on to someone or something for support. However, the pelvis and hips are often behind the shoulders. The legs are apart and the feet are turned, which helps a child bounce up and down in a standing position. At six to twelve months, kids often begin to stand independently without help.

WONDERFUL WALKING

A child's early attempts at walking are often short and erratic steps, but they are a source of pride to parents. There is great joy seeing your baby reach that important milestone, and balance is a big factor. The process begins at about twelve months when your baby cruises while holding on to furniture. After a few weeks, children gain confidence. They usually master the skill by an average age of eighteen months. This newly discovered autonomy gives kids another way to explore their environment, but it also requires a great deal of supervision from parents. By age two, children begin to walk up and down steps, and over the next two years, they gain the confidence to run with balance and moderate speed.

THE COMPETENT PRESCHOOLER

After the first two years, children gradually exhibit more independence. They can communicate effectively with good language skills, develop body control, and are socially aware of their school and home environments. They often move with confidence and a sense of purpose. Their physical coordination has probably developed to allow dressing without help, self-feeding, and mastering buttons, zippers, bows, drinking from cups, and using utensils. Preschoolers are steadily maturing with each accomplishment.

GROSS MOTOR DEVELOPMENT: AGES THREE TO SIX

Kids learn to control their bodies through three different types of gross motor skills: locomotion, coordination, and movements that balance on an internal axis. All three are realized by a step-by-step progression and are dependent upon one another to develop the total child.

Locomotion is a collection of controlled motor movements that include rolling, standing, sitting, and walking. The rate, speed, and rhythm of these locomotive skills emerge in conjunction with your child's neurological, physical, and psychological development. Babies will roll, stand, sit, and walk when they are ready.

The second gross motor skill is *coordination*, which can have an impact on future athletic talent. This includes throwing and catching balls, and hitting balls with bats, clubs, rackets, and sticks. An other activity that requires a great deal of coordination is mastering toys with wheels, such as tricycles, bicycles, roller and in-line skates, skateboards, and scooters.

The third gross motor skill involves *total body movement* that is regulated by and balanced on an internal axis. That means kids need to find their core of stability that extends through the head, neck, torso, and spine. It enables them to perform activities with their extremities along with sudden starting and stopping action such as skipping, running, sliding side to side, cartwheels, somersaults, dancing, twirling, gymnastics, surfing, rock climbing, skiing, snowboarding, and most sports. These activities can challenge a child's equilibrium, visual awareness, flexibility, fitness, strength, and depth perception.

Body maturation plays a role in motor development. Research indicates that kids who are exposed to appropriate activities through the critical toddler and early-preschool years from one and a half to four years old will show normal neurological advances in shoulder movement, trunk mobility, and age-appropriate fine and gross motor skills involving grasping, sitting, crawling, standing, and walking. The most drastic advances occur between ages two and three, when preschoolers who may be at risk might show early signs of neurological impairment.[3] If you have questions or suspect your child falls into this last category, consult a family doctor. Early intervention for your child can make a huge difference.

GOOD SITTING POSTURE FOR PRESCHOOLERS

One of the requirements for school readiness includes being able to sit quietly and listen to a teacher. The ideal length of sitting time for an average three- to six-year-old would be about ten minutes. That can be challenging because kids want to move freely in their environment, a very natural and healthy instinct. Children are constantly adjusting their bodies to suit their needs by doing things such as bending, crouching, skipping, and walking. Regular movement eliminates unnecessary muscular stress. It's not natural to expect a child to sit at a desk or chair for hours each day, but that's the way most schools work. Kids get tired of sitting, and this encourages poor posture as seen when they slouch, slump, prop up their heads on one arm, collapse their heads on a desk, or awkwardly lean over papers to write with a pen. A child's head, neck, back, and shoulders usually retain so much muscular tension that this strain can begin to affect their entire bodies. These movements often become unconscious habits that could likely cause fatigue by the end of the day.

Since kids must be trained to sit for longer lengths of time, let's highlight a few tips on good sitting posture. (If you are interested in reading about better balance and posture, look into the Alexander Method of movement for kids and adults.)

- *The head should be balanced on the neck.* The human head weighs about nine pounds, and it is important to carry that weight with ease. Look at the position of your child's head. You might notice how it rests on the spine by observing the angle of the chin. There could be neck strain if the nose is a bit skyward. On the other end of the spectrum, the chin should not be too close to the chest. Find a relaxed midpoint.
- *The back or spine is comfortably tall but not rigidly straight.* Your child should be sitting with the back, shoulders, and hips in alignment. The key is to look at the position of the shoulders. If your child is leaning forward toward the knees or backward beyond the buttocks, there could be a great deal of muscular stress on the lower back and neck.
- *The legs should be extended directly in front of the body and the heels flat on the floor.* Your child's thighs should be lined up with the hips to make the shape of the letter *L*. (The torso is the vertical line and the thighs are the horizontal line.) The heels of the feet are flat on the floor and directly under the knees. Positions to avoid are crossed legs at the knees and ankles, and straightened legs that force the pelvis too far forward.

CROSS-LEGGED SITTING

Kids love to sit cross-legged on the floor while playing games or watching television. The proper way to sit in this style is to bend both legs and knees inward toward the center of the body. The best way to describe good cross-legged sitting is to turn your legs into a sitting pretzel. The heel of the right foot is bent under the left thigh. The reverse is also true. The outsides of both ankles are resting on the floor. The incorrect way to sit on the floor is with the legs bent outward in the shape of the letter *W*. (This is when your child's buttocks are on the floor and the legs and knees are hyperextended at an awkward angle away from the center of the body. The arches of the feet are flat on the floor. Your child's legs will form the shape of the letter *W*.)

THE END OF WOBBLY WALKING

The preschool child has overcome the wobbly toddler walk and moves with a gait similar to that of an adult. By ages four to six, most kids have improved their balance and coordination enough to walk uphill, downhill, or on a flat surface. They might be able to walk a straight line, use a balance beam, and perform heel-to-toe movement, where the heel of one foot makes direct contact with the toes of the other. Your child also might be able to quickly walk backward, which requires the ability to balance while lifting the knees and feet high off the ground. Other milestones based on walking skills are marching, moving side to side, and sliding the feet in a nonlinear direction needed for games such as ring-around-the-rosy, where children hold hands and walk in a circle.

CROSS-LIMB COORDINATION DURING LOCOMOTION

Maintaining different rhythms in movement are controlled by the way a child uses the hands and feet during locomotion. For example, when walking, marching, running, skipping, and climbing, the right arm and hand should swing in a forward direction with the left knee and foot. The opposite also holds true.

This internal right-and-left cross-limb coordination should remain intact when the length, pace, speed, and direction of movement are changed.

HAPPY HOPPING

The ability to stand on one leg for up to ten seconds is a critical gross motor skill for preschoolers, according to the American Academy of Pediatrics. It can set the foundation for single- and double-footed hopping. The active four- to six-year-old will need a great deal of balance, torso strength, and coordination to master this skill. It is essential to do so because this movement is a precursor to performing gross motor skills of stair-climbing, marching, skipping, and running.

STAIR- AND LADDER-CLIMBING

Walking on uneven surfaces such as stairs and ladders requires a great deal of strength, balance, and control while bending the knees. It is easier to go upstairs first using a two-footed climbing method: each foot is placed on the same stair before progressing upward. Children later learn to walk downstairs while holding on to a rail for support. Eventually they develop the ability to ascend or descend steps using alternate feet. Exceptionally coordinated kids might enjoy the challenge of manipulating two or more steps at a time.

GALLOPING AND SKIPPING

Some of the most difficult gross motor patterns for kids to learn are galloping and skipping, because these actions involve patterns of sequential stepping and hopping. These physical skills require cross-limb coordination, which is present at some level in most sports activities. Both hemispheres of the brain are engaged, and kids need to be physically and neurologically ready to perform this activity.

When galloping, a four- to six-year-old child might hop and step forward with the same foot. Most kids will reach this milestone using their dominant foot, and this is a good time to notice if your child is right- or left-footed. Sometime before age six, children often become coordinated skippers, which requires a sequential hop-and-step movement using alternate arms and legs. Here is a description of gross motor skipping. Take a look at the Step-by-Step Skipping chart that follows to see how the arms and legs move. To coordinate the limbs, try to remember this phrase: "Hands move from the hip pocket to the eye socket."

STEP-BY-STEP SKIPPING

Action	Feet	Arms and Hands
The starting position is standing upright and balanced on both feet.	On the floor, balanced, and shoulder-width apart.	Both arms are resting at the sides and bent at the elbow. The hands are forward. The arms are shaped in the letter *L*.
Movement 1	Start by lifting your right knee and keep it up.	Hold the arms in the *L*.

Action	Feet	Arms and Hands
Movement 2	Lead with your right knee to hop forward on the left foot.	Pump your left arm forward as you lift your right knee to trigger the hop.
Movement 3	Step forward with the right foot.	Arms stay in the L, similar to the start position.
Movement 4	Now lift your left knee and keep it up. With your left knee raised, hop on your right foot.	Pump your right arm forward as you lift the left knee to trigger the hop.
Movement 5	Step forward with the left foot.	Arms stay in the L, similar to the start position.

RUNNING

Someone once said that every journey begins with a single step, and the same holds true for running. The act of running is very similar to skipping and galloping. They all require cross-limb use of the arms and legs, use both hemispheres of the brain, and require excellent coordination. Kids need to be physically and mentally ready to perform the skill, which usually happens between the ages of two to four. Kids usually become proficient at running at different ages, but you may notice the ability to run, gallop, and skip often emerge around the same time in the early preschool years.

Running requires starting from a balanced position (see the Step-by-Step Running chart below), and the action is triggered by a forward upper-body lean. A moment later, one knee lifts upward at the hip level. The standing or balancing leg then pulls up and initiates the forward hopping action. Running is best described by *forward lean and hop* using alternating feet.

STEP-BY-STEP RUNNING

Step	Body, Legs, or Feet	Arms and Hands
Starting position	The body is balanced and the feet are directly under the hips.	The arms are in the *L* position at the sides, and your hands are relaxed.
Movement 1	Lift your right knee up to the hip level. You are balancing on your left leg and foot.	Arms stay in the *L* position.
Movement 2	Lean the torso and upper body forward.	Arms are still in the *L* position.

Step	Body, Legs, or Feet	Arms and Hands
Movement 3	While you're still leaning forward, pull your left or supporting foot up from the ground and hop forward.	Your right arm swings forward when the left leg pulls up and hops. (Your left arm swings backward.)
Movement 4	Your bent or right leg catches the fall, while your left knee simultaneously lifts to the hip-high position.	Now swing the right arm forward and the left arm backward.
Movement 5	Lean forward again and repeat the lift, lean, and pull action.	Alternate: the right arm swings forward with the left leg. The left arm swings forward with the right leg.

8

Coordination and Sidedness

Moving with coordination can be a total body experience. This happens when either the right or left side of the brain takes charge of receiving, processing, and sending information to all the correct body parts. When a child's coordination appears effortless and smooth, it is most likely because the brain and body parts are working together. This process begins with the brain and ends with the eyes, ears, hands, and feet. When all of these functions are controlled by one side of the body, right or left, this is called *laterality* or *sidedness*.

WHAT DOES SIDEDNESS HAVE TO DO WITH COORDINATION?

Many kids have one dominant side that controls the body, meaning they are right-handed, right-footed, right-eyed, and right-eared. That's a good thing, because all of the critical parts are working together in a linear fashion led primarily by one dominant side. In this case, the right side of the body is controlled by the left half of the brain. The converse is also true for left-handed kids, who might find it easier to also be left-footed, left-eyed, and left-eared. Research shows roughly 10 percent of the population is left-handed, and many are linear left-side dominant with hands, feet, eyes, and ears.[1] That's also a good thing. The reasons for a child's right- or left-sidedness are not completely understood because they are influenced by the complexity of the brain.

WHAT IS SIDEDNESS?

In this chapter, you will learn how to identify many aspects of your child's sidedness, why they are important, and how they influence coordination, balance, learning, and athleticism.

Sidedness is a biological mystery that scientists and neurologists have only begun to understand. Research supports the fact that most societies, past and present, have been predominantly right-handed. In the current culture, statistics reveal that kids have about an 88.2 percent chance of being right-handed, and an 81 percent likelihood of being right-footed.[2] It is possible that eight out of ten kids will likely be laterally right-sided with both the hands and feet. This makes life easier for kids to plan their fine and gross motor movement because the same side of the brain is in charge of both functions.

RIGHT-SIDE USE IN MEN AND WOMEN[2]

Function	Men	Women
Hand	86%	90%
Foot	77%	86%

Function	Men	Women
Ear	55%	65%
Eye	73%	69%

MIXED-SIDEDNESS IN KIDS

Statistics also show that two out of ten kids could have mixed-sidedness, meaning they could be right-handed and left-footed. This can cause some confusion for children while developing balance, footwork, mobility, quickness, and physical skills. It is also essential for parents, educators, and coaches to be aware of a child's tendency to experience the world as a right-hander, and move, step, learn, think, and balance as a left-footer. Sometimes in sports, being left-footed is called "goofy-footed" because it requires different footwork and preparation to perform fundamental skills.

LEFT-HANDED KIDS AND SIDEDNESS

Lefties account for approximately 10 percent of the population, and about eight out of ten left-handed kids will be laterally balanced using the same hand and foot. This means the majority of left-handed kids will also be left-footed, but one or two might likely turn out mixed-dominant, using the left hand and the right foot.[3] The same type of left-right hand and foot confusion is also a factor to consider when raising kids.

SIDEDNESS WITH EYES AND EARS

If you thought hand-and-foot sidedness was confusing, be prepared because the concept of sidedness is even more challenging. The human body and brain is also designed for right- and left-side dominance in hearing and vision. People are born with a stronger right or left eye that takes control of focusing on an object. The same holds true for the sense of hearing. One ear is clearly the boss. (Keep in mind this is assuming your child does not have special needs or suffer from unusual vision or hearing loss that can alter sensory input.) For right-handed kids, approximately 71 percent are right-eye dominant and about 59 percent are right-ear dominant.[4] That indicates about six or seven out of ten kids could be wired to use their eyes, ears, and limbs efficiently on the same side of the body. However, that also implies up to four out of ten kids have a chance of being mixed-sided with their hands, feet, eyes, and ears.

MIXED-SIDEDNESS IS A MIXED BAG

Kids generally receive information through their senses by seeing, hearing, tasting, smelling, and touching, and they process that data through the brain. This requires understanding and analyzing information to be applied to different situations. Examples of this multistep processing include moving specific body parts, learning complex physical skills, acquiring language, reading for comprehension, learning vocabulary, phonetically sounding out words, writing essays, remembering and applying math equations, and storing facts for future use. These cognitive processes are also used when acquiring athletic, social, intellectual, conversational, and educational knowledge.

The most efficient way of learning is done in a linear fashion. For example, in a total right-side dominant child, where the left hemisphere of the brain is in control, information is accepted and stored similarly to an organized filing system. Data can be held for long periods and later retrieved when needed for specific situations. A child with mixed-dominance (see the Variations of Sidedness chart for examples) has a filing system that stores information randomly in both hemispheres of the brain, depending on the unique complexity of the child's neurological wiring. It could take extra time and effort for a mixed-dominant brain to access the stored knowledge before applying it, hence the emergence of cognitive delays.

VARIATIONS OF SIDEDNESS

Function	Hands (Writing)	Feet (Kicking)	Eyes (Seeing)	Ears (Hearing)
Right-Side Dominant	Right	Right	Right	Right
Left-Side Dominant	Left	Left	Left	Left
Common Mixed Dominant	Right	Right	Left	Left
Common Mixed Dominant	Left	Left	Right	Right
Mixed Dominant	Right	Left	Right	Right
Mixed Dominant	Right	Left	Right	Left
Mixed Dominant	Right	Left	Left	Right
Mixed Dominant	Right	Left	Left	Left

Function	Hands (Writing)	Feet (Kicking)	Eyes (Seeing)	Ears (Hearing)
Mixed Dominant	Left	Right	Left	Left
Mixed Dominant	Left	Right	Right	Right
Mixed Dominant	Left	Left	Right	Left
Mixed Dominant	Left	Left	Left	Right

CHALLENGES ASSOCIATED WITH MIXED-SIDEDNESS

It is not uncommon for some kids to show signs of mixed-sidedness or dominance. If you suspect your child falls into that category, it does not mean he or she will grow up to be less intelligent or athletic. (In fact, some mixed-dominant individuals throughout history have made brilliant contributions to society in all walks of life.) The reason for figuring out your child's dominant style is to be able to teach to his or her strengths. It also helps to improve areas that might require some assistance in developing a well-balanced child.

Researchers have found that as many as 20 percent of children today might have varying degrees of mixed right- and left-brain control with the hands, feet, eyes, and ears. (See the Variations of Sidedness chart above.) Possible symptoms of mixed-sidedness can include cognitive delays, compromised long- or short-term memory recall, and difficulty organizing and classifying information. This is because visual or auditory information is going into the nondominant hemisphere of the brain and coming out of the other half. The bottom line is mixed-sidedness might be a cause of neurological confusion in kids. Your child may experience one or several of these symptoms. If so, it is not cause for alarm. It is merely information to use in helping your child grow. There are activities listed later in the chapter that may be of help with mixed-dominance kids.

Here are potential areas to clue you into whether your child may be mixed-dominance:

- Experiences forgetfulness
- Has a tendency to scatter belongings in personal space
- Displays poor test-taking skills
- Mixes up right and left visually or verbally
- Has the tendency to shut down under pressure
- Exhibits inconsistent retrieval of information
- Has difficulty learning right- and left-sided letters such as *b* and *d*, *p* and *q*
- Struggles to make decisions
- Is uncertain about personal right and left sides of the body
- Experiences emotional mood swings that can range from very high to low
- Is easily upset and difficult to calm down
- Has trouble accepting a change when a new rule is in place or a decision is made

TESTS FOR SIDEDNESS

It is clear when you see a coordinated, talented, and intelligent kid in action, whether it is in athletics, academics, music, or other creative pursuits. All body parts and cognitive skills seem to be in perfect unison. Coordinated kids make things look easy. Why? Chances are those talented kids are probably right- or left-side dominant. In the same vein, it is also evident if something seems to be a little bit off when a child performs a physical skill awkwardly or struggles in school. In many cases, it is possible to trace the roots of an issue to mixed-sidedness in the four important functions of using the eyes, ears, hands, and feet. There are a few clues to help determine your child's sidedness.

WHICH HAND DOES YOUR CHILD USE?

There are many ways to test for handedness. The most popular method is to observe the hand your child uses to write, draw, or color. Try not to be anxious, because some children switch hands before settling on the most comfortable side by approximately age six. It is also important to check out several other skills to eliminate a mixed-handed evaluation. Some kids may write with one hand and use the other in various situations such as cutting paper, eating, and throwing a ball. These are only clues but they can be helpful in determining if your child might be mixed-handed or ambidextrous.

As your child grows from birth to age six, occasionally retest about every six months. Be sure to write down results and dates of each test. It might be a good idea to photocopy these charts to retest the same child at intervals or test multiple children.

TEST FOR HAND DOMINANCE

Function	Right Hand	Left Hand	Date
Writes name.			
Uses scissors to cut paper.			
Throws a ball.			
Uses a spoon or fork.			
Cuts with a knife.			
Brushes teeth.			

Function	Right Hand	Left Hand	Date
Combs or brushes hair.			
Hammers an object.			
Manipulates a screwdriver.			
Puts pegs in holes.			
Threads string through beads.			
Puts thread through a needle.			
Flips the lid off a container.			
Unscrews the lid off a jar.			
Pours liquid from a measuring cup.			
Uses a watering can.			
Dresses dolls. (The hand that holds the doll is usually nondominant while the hand that manipulates the clothes is the dominant hand.)			
Uses construction toys (see instruction above).			
Sweeps with a long broom. (The hand that is on top is dominant.)			
Scoops sand with a handheld shovel. Marks which hand is holding the shovel.			
Stacks blocks to make a tower.			

Function	Right Hand	Left Hand	Date
Deals cards from a deck.			
Bangs objects with a stick.			
Picks up a racket or club in sports.			
Zips up clothing.			
Pushes buttons through holes.			
Uses keys to open doors.			
Picks up a straw and places it in a glass. (Also note which hand holds the straw when drinking.)			
Writes on a white- or chalkboard.			
Points to an object.			
Uses an eraser.			
Stirs with a spoon.			
Grasps an object.			
Flips a light switch.			
Rings a small bell.			
Uses a hand puppet.			

WHICH IS YOUR CHILD'S STRONGER FOOT?

Sometimes it appears your child's feet are independently operated. They can be light or heavy, slow or fast, and large or small. Kids' feet come in all shapes and sizes. Many times there is a genetic predisposition for size, quickness, and agility. Either way, your child will have a preference for a favorite foot. It is either all right or all left. Kids who are mixed-sided might be a little more balanced, meaning they have good skills with both feet. One foot, however, will always be more dominant. Here are a few ways to test your child's footedness.

TESTS FOR FOOT DOMINANCE

Function	Right Foot	Left Foot	Date
Kicks a ball.			
Hops on one foot for thirty seconds.			
Steps up to walk up stairs.			
Stomps on top of an object on the ground.			
Uses this foot to stop falling forward or face-planting.			
Stands on one leg like a stork with balance for thirty seconds.			
Pirouettes or twirls on one foot.			
Kicks a door open.			

Function	Right Foot	Left Foot	Date
Plants foot to make a very long jump.			
Takes first step to walk down stairs.			

WHICH IS YOUR CHILD'S STRONGER EYE?

In sports, school, and life, one eye is always in charge of determining clarity of vision. That is the way the human brain is wired. While both eyes may have sight, excluding injury and special circumstances, one eye will dictate how well your child processes information, gauges depth perception, classifies data, and guides the body to move in relation to other objects.

Some kids, who are probably laterally balanced on one side, naturally move with grace and fluidity. Others—most often mixed-sided individuals—have literally crashed into permanent stationary objects. As a coach, I have watched athletes accidentally walk into walls, doors, fences, fire hydrants, and tall poles, and I wondered, *Didn't that child see the object?* Well, obviously not, because if so, the athlete would have walked around the impending permanent structure. This type of behavior, however, does provoke a reason to investigate that child's left- and right-brain dominance.

Eye dominance is a critical factor in developing coordination. A child's stronger eye should be on the same side of the body as the stronger hand and foot. For example, it is best if a right-hander is also right-footed and right-eyed. The converse is true for lefties. What happens when the eye strength is controlled by a different half of the brain than the hands and feet? The child might show faulty depth perception, awkward gross motor movements, and clumsiness in handling items. A kid may have difficulty moving in space in lateral, free-form, or nonlinear directions. For example, mixed-sided children (eyes and hands or feet) might have trouble playing racket sports with moving balls and the need to gauge the distance of objects coming toward them. This is evident when playing sports like baseball, football, tennis, soccer, volleyball, badminton, table tennis, hockey, water polo, lacrosse, cricket, and field hockey. Additional difficulties may show up in activities that require aiming with the eyes, such as archery. Sports that require hitting stationary balls, such as golf, might be easier for the mixed-dominant child. Also consider introducing your child to sports that do not require hitting balls, pucks, or birdies with bats, sticks, rackets, and clubs. Consider exposing a child with mixed-dominance to activities such as gymnastics, swimming, skiing, skateboarding, diving, and dance.

TESTS FOR EYE DOMINANCE

Step	Action
1	Extend your arm and hand while using your finger to point at an object at a spot directly in front of you.
2	Keep looking at the spot. Be sure to look at the spot and not at your finger.
3	Now close one eye and keep looking at the spot. It doesn't matter which eye you choose. Are you still pointing exactly at the spot, or did it move?
4	Open your eye and use both eyes to once again stare at the spot.
5	Now close the other eye and keep it shut. Are you still pointing to the spot, or did it move?
6	If you are not sure about the results, repeat the test several times.

RESULTS FOR EYE DOMINANCE

Your dominant eye is the one that will still see your finger pointing to the object when you close your nondominant eye. Conversely, it might have appeared that your finger moved away from the object when looking through your nondominant eye. For example, if you closed your left eye, and you were still pointing to the object looking through your right eye, then you are right-eye dominant. The opposite is true for left-eye dominance.

ADDITIONAL TESTS FOR EYE DOMINANCE

Function	Right Eye	Left Eye	Date
Looks through a camera lens.			
Looks through a telescope.			
Looks through a microscope.			
Threads a needle.			
Peeks through a fence with one eye.			
Aims with a bow and arrow.			
Peeks through a barely open door.			
Strains to see a road or street sign ahead. (Which eye goes a little more forward to increase vision acuity?)			

Function	Right Eye	Left Eye	Date
Looks down into a bottle or jar of food to see if it is empty.			
Looks through the peephole of a door.			
Looks through a paper towel cardboard tube.			

WHICH IS YOUR CHILD'S STRONGER EAR?

Kids will show a preference for hearing through either the right or left ear, depending on the hemispheric dominance. (This is assuming there is no hearing loss or genetic predisposition for ear problems.) The listening process also depends on age-appropriate auditory development, which means your child can hear, analyze, and understand information to be used immediately or stored for later situations. There are a few ways to determine your child's stronger ear. Keep in mind it may take a few different testing methods to figure it out.

TESTS FOR HEARING DOMINANCE

Function	Right Ear	Left Ear	Date
When using a telephone, which ear is used for listening?			
When someone wants to whisper a secret in your ear, which side leans forward to listen?			

Function	Right Ear	Left Ear	Date
Which ear listens to a wristwatch?			
Which ear listens to a seashell?			
Which ear is pressed against a door when trying to overhear a conversation on the other side?			
In a noisy room, which ear leans forward to hear a speaker?			
When listening to music through earphones, if you had only one working earpiece, which ear would you put it in?			

SOLUTIONS FOR MIXED-SIDEDNESS

Now that you may have determined your child's right- and left-sidedness, as well as hemispheric tendencies, you may be wondering what to do with the information. If your child is laterally balanced using a predominant side with hands, feet, eyes, and ears, then play Proud Parents' games for fun and overall development. If you have discovered your child is mixed-sided, there are a few things you can do. Before you try anything, however, observe your child's overall progress. If your youngster is functioning well within normal range, then it might not be necessary to make any changes. However, if you see cognitive, coordination, or learning challenges in your child, and you feel it would be of great benefit to make some adjustments, you could try a few of the games listed below. Before you begin, please once again read this disclaimer:

The Proud Parents' program is meant to be a source of information with suggestions for playing various games and activities that can promote coordination and fine and gross motor skills in children from birth to age six. This plan is not written as medical advice, nor should it be perceived as such.

The Proud Parents' program, the author, and Thomas Nelson Publishers do not endorse any particular method of parenting, coaching, teaching, or child development philosophies.

GAMES TO ADJUST MIXED-SIDEDNESS IN KIDS

Function	Game
Hand Dominance	Toss and catch a ball with the hand that should be dominant, indicated by the hand that appears more skilled.
Hand	Throw stuffed animals or balls into laundry baskets using the hand that should be dominant. Place the other hand behind the back.
Hand	Play close-up catch with a tennis ball using the hand that should be dominant. You are almost sliding the ball into your child's hand.
Hand	Tape a large piece of construction paper on a wall. Have your child stand and draw, using one hand at a time, the infinity sign (∞) with a washable marker. This activity encourages midline (center-of-the-body) development.

Function	Game
Hand	Play pat-a-cake with your child using the hand that should be dominant. Include patting other body parts like knees, shoulders, ankles, and feet.
Hand	Snap fingers to the rhythm of festive music using the hand that should be dominant.
Foot Dominance	Hop on the foot that should be dominant for ten to thirty seconds. Count the number of hops.
Foot	Sit on a chair and draw the alphabet on the floor with the foot that should be dominant.
Foot	Lay on the floor with your back on the ground. Your feet should be able to easily reach a door or a blank wall. Use the foot that should be dominant to write the alphabet or numbers until the leg gets tired.
Foot	Kick a ball against a wall with the foot that should be dominant. Another option is to pass the ball back and forth using only the correct foot.
Foot	Practice juggling a ball with the foot that should be dominant. Use the shoelaces or knees to keep momentum.
Foot	Lay on your back. Your feet should be able to easily reach a door or a blank wall. Use the foot that should be dominant to roll a ball on the wall and make shapes such as circles, squares, and rectangles.

Function	Game
Foot	Draw letters and/or numbers on the cement with chalk. Have your child hop on the letter or number that is called out using the foot that should be dominant.
Eye Dominance: (In place of closing the eye, your child can wear an eye patch to play some of these games.)	Use the eye that should be dominant and close the other eye while drawing, writing, or coloring. Usually, this means aligning hand and eye dominance, such as right hand with right eye.
Eye	Using chalk or masking tape, draw a target on a wall. Using only the eye and hand that should be dominant, practice throwing a ball at the target.
Eye	Play magnetic child-safe darts using the eye and hand that should be dominant. Practice aiming with the correct eye. (Close the other eye.)
Eye	Drop pencils into a can or empty milk carton from a standing position. Open the eye that should be dominant and close the other eye.
Eye	Find a cardboard paper towel roll and use it as a telescope to play a game of I Spy with the eye that should be dominant. Close the other eye. You can also use child-sized binoculars to do the same, but make sure to close the appropriate eye.
Eye	Read an easy large-print book only with the eye that should be dominant. Close the other eye or cover it with your hand.

Function	Game
Eye	Build block towers by using only the eye and hand that should be dominant. (Close the other eye.) The majority of the blocks should be placed on the side opposite the hand that is being worked. It is critical for kids to cross the midline or center of the body to pick up blocks.
Eye	String child-safe beads using the eye that should be dominant. Close the other eye.
Eye	Play golf, providing your child with an appropriate size putter. Practice putting balls into a large, empty can. Use the eye that should be dominant for aiming; close or patch the other eye.
Ear Dominance:	Place one side of a headset on the ear that should be your child's dominant side, and have your child listen to music by Mozart.
Ear	Place one earphone in the ear that should be dominant and have your child listen to stories or audiobooks at night before sleep.
Ear	Whisper secrets into your child's ear that should be dominant.
Ear	Play the game "operator" behind closed doors. Have one person stand alone inside a room with the door closed. Your child must place the ear that should be dominant against the door to try to hear the message. Repeat and play with other people.

Function	Game
Ear	Watch television with a moldable earplug (like the type used for swimming) inside the ear that should *not* be dominant. Your child should be listening with the side you are trying to reinforce.

OTHER ASPECTS OF BODY-SIDEDNESS

Are you a right-side leaner? How about a left-leg crosser? It might sounds crazy, but there are many body movements people perform on a daily basis that can result in right or left tendencies. They are interesting to note, but not necessarily related to sidedness. A few fun examples include the angle or degree of head tilt when writing on paper or listening to others speak in conversation. The side of the mouth one uses predominantly to chew is a habit. Think about the way you cross your arms. Are you left over right, or is it right over left? Try reversing your arm-crossing habit and see how that feels. It is definitely different. Try sitting in a chair and sit with your legs crossed over the knees. Do you place your left knee over your right, or is it the reverse? Also while sitting, cross your legs at the ankles and notice which ankle is on top. Is it your right or left? When you interlace your fingers and hands, which thumb is on top? Finally, when standing for long periods of time, do you lean on your right or left foot? The dominant standing leg is the side that would be weight-bearing the majority of the time. Have fun discovering your right and left tendencies; they are part of what makes each of us unique and special.

9

Sensory Integration

Kids need a strong sensory foundation to correctly process information for success in sports, academics, and life in general. This foundation is built by using the senses of hearing, sight, touch, taste, and smell. Here's how it works. The brain receives a sensory input and organizes the information to help your child function in different environments. In this chapter, the key elements of the sensory system will be explored along with tips to enhance each function. You will also learn why each part is critical to raising a high-functioning and sensory healthy child.

HIP, HIP, HOORAY FOR HEARING

Good hearing is critical for language development and auditory processing. In the first two years, your child's brain is ready to learn any language and repeat the sounds most frequently heard. Babies enjoy listening to human voices and can easily recognize the sounds of parents and familiar loved ones.

At eighteen months, your child might use between five and twenty words. A two-year-old might be able to say three-word phrases and know one hundred fifty to three hundred words. A three-year-old could expand to up to one thousand words, and within the next two years, your child might be able to hold complete conversations. If you are interested in raising a bilingual child, introduce the two languages at birth and provide ample opportunities to use both languages. These early neurological pathways start with the ability to hear and can pave the road to language fluency and bilingual potential.

BABY COMMUNICATION AND SIGN LANGUAGE

Infants often know what they want to say but have trouble communicating it to their parents. When language is developing in the first few years, your child can supplement learning by using basic baby sign language. It is simple to teach gestures to indicate desires such as *more, eat, drink, please,* and *thank you.* Learning sign language does not delay the spoken word. In fact, it has been known to enhance the process of language acquisition. Studies show that preschoolers who began signing as babies have higher IQs and do better in language skills and on vocabulary tests in later years.

VISION

At birth, babies have limited sight and can see basic shapes but very little detail. Kids gradually fine-tune their vision to take in greater amounts of data. The eyes learn to track objects first horizontally and then vertically. Within the first year, your child's brain learns to control these functions and the eyes begin to work together.

It is important for parents to provide their babies with stimulating sights and colors to help them recognize the sizes and shapes of objects. The first twelve months is also the time when children start to develop depth perception, which is critical to coordination and athletics. Visual development is improved by doing puzzles, hidden pictures, and dot-to-dot activities, stringing beads, and sorting objects by similarity or color.

THE SENSE OF TOUCH

The sense of touch is one of the first systems to be developed in a newborn. Nerves under the skin's surface send information to the brain that includes pain, light touch, temperature, and pressure. These sensations are important for safety and survival. As children grow, they begin to consider other details such as size, shape, and texture. Some parts of the body are more sensitive to touch, such as the fingertips, which can provide the brain with a majority of its tactile information. Less sensitive areas are the back and the soles of the feet.

TASTE AND SMELL

The senses of taste and smell work together to allow children to sample and process thousands of different flavors. The sense of taste helps your child distinguish the difference between salty, sweet, sour, and bitter. The ability to taste food is experienced by the approximately five thousand to ten thousand taste buds located on the tongue. These buds stimulate sensory cells that carry information to the brain and register the flavor. The ability to smell is due to small receptors inside the nose that respond to odors. Through a network of cell communication, the "scent" message is relayed to the brain. The sense of smell heightens the sense of taste by providing complete feedback to the brain.

SENSORY INTEGRATION
WITH BALANCE AND MOVEMENT

The additional types of sensory input that develop coordination in your child are the vestibular and proprioceptive systems. From birth to age seven, these areas are highly receptive to the games and activities found in this book. The vestibular system refers to structures in your child's inner ear that help with maintaining balance, standing upright, and moving in space. It coordinates information between the inner ear, eyes, muscles, limbs, joints, fingertips, palms of the hands, soles of the feet, gravity receptors, emotional controls, heart rate, blood pressure, muscle tone, and immune responses. It also contributes to your child's sense of equilibrium, depth perception, spatial skills, and ability to function while in motion—a requirement to play most sports. Your child's vestibular system can be improved by walking up and down ramps, curbs, and balance beams and by navigating obstacle courses.

PROPRIOCEPTIVE POWERS

The proprioceptive system receives input from the muscles and joints of the body, telling your child how and where the limbs and other parts are moving. When it is working at peak performance, the body knows how to successfully function in school, home, and outside environments. It also tells you when your head is in an upright position, which is helpful when changing elevation such as sitting in chairs, stepping up onto curbs, and walking downhill. This proprioceptive system also allows your child to establish fine motor control necessary for writing with a pencil, cutting with scissors, and using utensils to eat. Other functions aided by this system include manipulating buttons, zippers, and snaps for self-dressing, and playing sports that involve kicking or hitting moving balls, such as soccer, baseball, all racket sports, volleyball, and much more. Kids might improve their proprioceptive powers by bouncing on a trampoline or a large ball, crawling, hanging from bars by the hands and arms, rocking in a rocking chair, or drawing on a vertical chalkboard.

MOVEMENT

Good athletes move with grace because they are able to integrate the vestibular and proprioceptive systems by keeping their bodies balanced while changing position. For example, skilled soccer players, gymnasts, dancers, and ice skaters frequently change the position, direction, and angle of their bodies, and they generally remain upright to give some amazing performances. An example of this skill in daily activities is the action of walking down escalators and stairs. To improve the vestibular and proprioceptive function, try wheelbarrow walking with your child, doing push-ups on the floor or against walls, crawling, and moving slowly down a playground slide.

BILATERAL COORDINATION AND MIDLINE CROSSING

One of the elements of fine motor function is called bilateral coordination, which is the ability to use both sides of the body at the same time. For instance, using both hands in the same manner, such as with a rolling pin, or using both legs in an alternating fashion to walk up stairs. Another example of bilateral movement is using each side of the body for a different type of action, such as holding a jar with one hand and twisting the lid with the other.

A related issue is midline or center crossing, which requires good bilateral skills. This skill enables a child to use one side of the body to reach across and work with the other. For example, a child might use the right hand to reach over to the left side of the body to pick up a toy. Other examples of midline crossing include when children sit cross-legged or when they reach over to draw a diagonal line across a piece of paper without switching hands.

Bilateral use of the sides and strong midline crossing skills are key elements of balance and coordination. Kids who are bilaterally efficient will have fluid body movements common to all great athletes, performers, and musicians. They will also have great eye-hand coordination and the ability to track moving targets. These skills can be enhanced by pulling apart cotton balls, blowing bubbles with one hand and popping them with the other, stringing beads to make necklaces, skipping, crawling, swimming, performing jumping jacks, opening jars with both hands, and spreading peanut butter on toast or crackers. Playing musical instruments can also aid in developing these skills, especially playing the piano, guitar, or drums, and all other instruments that require two hands moving simultaneously while performing different actions.

MOTOR PLANNING

This is a task that requires all areas of the brain to work together. Motor planning uses sensory information to think of an idea, plan an action to accomplish that goal, and then execute the plan. For example, your adventurous toddler might be hungry and knows there is cereal in the pantry. The plan of action might be to open the door, grab the box, open the cardboard flap, and eat the cereal by hand. The final step is the successful completion of the task. If the box of cereal was on a high shelf out of reach, the new motor plan would be to drag a chair to the pantry, stand on it, and then reach for the box. Motor planning can be challenging, because your child needs to focus on the immediate task while unconsciously processing stored information and body sensations. This skill can be improved by negotiating mazes, obstacle courses, and indoor play gyms with large tubes for crawling. Gross motor games for motor planning include playing Simon says, red light–green light, and tag, with backward and sideways movements.

10

Rules of Play and Praise

Play is the foundation for a happy childhood and the cornerstone of the Proud Parents' program. Play is the most important and effective way for kids to learn about life by interacting with parents, siblings, extended family, teachers, and all kinds of caring people. From birth, kids explore their environments through play in cribs, bedrooms, homes, and in their communities. Children develop sensory perception by interpreting visual, auditory, tactile, olfactory, and vocal sounds through play. They gather knowledge about their pets, preschools, nature, music, museums, libraries, zoos, and amusement parks. Through play, all of this data can be integrated and processed in a child's mind to develop neurological, physical, social, emotional, sensory, psychological, and cognitive skills. Child's play is a magical phenomenon that can help kids grow into amazing adults.

The Proud Parents' plan suggests ten rules of praise that apply to kids of all ages. This program also has ten rules of play for children from birth to age two, and a set of suggestions for games that parents can play with kids ages three to six. The goal is for both parents and children to have a happy, healthy, and successful parent-and-child experience. Here are some suggested guidelines.

TOP TEN RULES OF PRAISE

Words are powerful tools that can create confident kids. The right words can motivate children to achieve greatness in athletics, academics, social skills, music, friendships, and family life. Here are ten tips to developing positive communication with your child:

1. *Praise is perfect communication.* Positive communication works wonders because it is uplifting, instructional, and sends a message with respect and love. Kids are motivated by sincere compliments, which can lead to the development of self-confidence and a positive self-image. Praising your child's efforts and good deeds can lay the foundation for nurturing relationships.

2. *Praise your child's efforts.* Today's culture tends to focus on results, whether it is winning in sports, getting good grades in school, or performing musical skills to perfection. Instead of looking for results, praise your child's efforts and outstanding personal characteristics. Compliment intangible traits such as good attitude, focus, concentration, listening skills, determination, memory, and attention to detail.

3. *Capture your child's attention.* Kids learn best when they focus on one thing at a time. When you praise your child, be sure you are not competing with toys, television, or other distractions. To capture your child's attention, call out his name and then state your compliment. For example, "Julia, I like the way you used your fork to eat your food. You

did an outstanding job." Then complete the compliment with words of encouragement, such as, "Keep up the good work."

4. *Be specific with praise.* Find reasons to compliment your child clearly in ten words or less. That is the average attention span for kids under age ten. Be specific and state the exact reason for the words of praise. A great way to start a compliment is, "(Your child's name), I like the way you (fill in the reason)." Possible suggestions to finish that statement include "wrote your name," "practiced your letters," "ate your lunch," "listened to Mommy," and "helped Daddy." There are an infinite number of possibilities. Be creative and observant.

5. *Get eye to eye.* Reassurance comes in many forms, and one of them is talking to your child at eye level. Kneel or bend down to get eye to eye, or pick up your baby when praising good behavior. Your compliment will have a greater impact if it is delivered on equal eye-level terms.

6. *Use the Top One Hundred Phrases of Praise.* Variety is the spice of life, and this also applies to compliments. Select any of the Top One Hundred Phrases of Praise from the following list, and use some of them each day. You can encourage your child with one-word praises such as *great, excellent,* and *superb,* or with more detailed expressions like "You're learning fast" and "That's better than ever." Make a copy of the list and keep it with you, or hang it on the refrigerator as a reference.

THE TOP ONE HUNDRED PHRASES OF PRAISE

1. You're on the right track.
2. You're doing a good job.
3. That's the way.
4. That's right.
5. Great!
6. Now you've got the hang of it.
7. Looks like you really understand.
8. Fantastic!
9. You did it that time.
10. That's coming along nicely.
11. Terrific!
12. That's great.
13. That's a good boy/girl.
14. You make a difference.
15. Tremendous!
16. Good job, (name of child).
17. Nicely done.
18. Wow!
19. Much better.
20. I appreciate your help.
21. Stupendous!
22. Thanks for being here.
23. Excellent!
24. You outdid yourself today.
25. Good for you.
26. Keep it up.
27. That's really nice.
28. Exactly right.
29. That was a complete effort.
30. Great concentration.
31. You make it look easy.
32. That's what I call a fine job.
33. Way to go.
34. Nice going.
35. I've never seen anyone do it better.
36. Thanks for finishing the job.
37. Excellent focus.
38. You are getting better every day.
39. Wonderful!
40. I knew you could do it.
41. Keep on working; you're getting better.
42. You're doing beautifully.
43. You are working really hard today.
44. That's the way to do it.
45. Amazing!
46. Keep on trying.
47. You're the best.
48. Nothing can stop you now.
49. Incredible!
50. Thank you for helping.
51. You've got it made.
52. You're very good at that.
53. You certainly did well today.
54. I'm very proud of you.
55. You're learning fast.
56. You've just about got it.
57. That's good.
58. Great effort.
59. Super.
60. That's the right way to do it.
61. You are really learning a lot.
62. Marvelous!
63. That's better than ever.
64. What an improvement!
65. That deserves a high five.
66. Perfect!
67. That's a superb response.
68. Keep up the effort.
69. That's it.
70. You figured it out fast.
71. You remembered.
72. I think you've got it now.
73. Well, look at you go.
74. You've got that part down fast.
75. Good work.
76. Outstanding!
77. I like that.
78. Great listening.
79. Couldn't have done better myself.
80. You are a pleasure to be with.
81. That was first-class work.
82. Way to pay attention.
83. Sensational!
84. That's the best I've seen you do.
85. Good remembering.
86. You haven't missed a thing.
87. I like the way you pay attention.
88. Unbelievable!
89. Superb!
90. One more time and you'll have it.
91. You make my job really fun.
92. Excellent effort.
93. You've just about mastered that.
94. You must have been practicing.
95. Great idea.
96. Good thinking.
97. You are amazing.
98. Thank you for caring.
99. What a great helper!
100. That's 100 percent effort.

7. *Practice the sandwich technique.* Use positive redirection to correct negative behavior. Instead of listing all of the things your child recently has done wrong, try using the *sandwich technique* to suggest a new and positive course of action. For example, if your child forgets to put toys away after playing, try this method:

THE SANDWICH TECHNIQUE

Step	Behavior	Communication
1. Identify the behavior.	Your child leaves toys out after playtime and often forgets to put them away.	Meet your child in the same room as the toys. Capture your child's attention and calmly state the situation. "(Name of your child), I see you played with your toys very nicely, but they are still on the floor."
2. Make the correction.	The toys need to be returned to their boxes, tubs, or containers.	"Please help the toys find their homes." (Bend down to your child's level and look eye to eye when you make this correction.)
3. Close with encouragement.	Reinforce the desired behavior and close with a compliment.	"(Name of your child), thank you for showing me how well you can do this. I believe you will do an extraordinary job."

8. *Be a good listener.* Good communication is based on being a good listener. To effectively understand how to talk to your child, it is important to be ready to listen, because communication is a two-way street. This process includes asking key questions in a calm and informational manner. Instead of asking why something happened, it is better to question what led up to your child's decision. Other positive communication strategies are to restate your child's answers for clarification or restate the question.

Here is a classic example extracted from my family life. My three-year-old daughter colored her hands and arms with a red permanent marker, and no amount of hand-washing or bathing would remove it. My first instinct was to express a great deal of frustration followed by a reprimand, but I held off and asked a critical question: "What were you trying to do?" The answer was a complete surprise, and it had an immediate calming effect. My daughter replied, "I wanted to make you a card with handprints just like we did for Daddy." The card-making craft had been a recent preschool activity for Father's Day. That activity used non-toxic and washable paint, but my daughter did not have access to those supplies. In her mind, the next best thing was to use the first marker she could find around the house. So my parenting communication quickly changed from frustration to explaining the differences between art supplies and the importance of asking for help.

9. *Ask the three praise questions.* It is easy to find reasons to praise your children once you get into the habit. Look for desire, effort, enthusiasm, participation, cooperation, thoughtful acts, generous gestures, kind words, and helpful behavior. The timing of your compliment is critical because kids usually have an attention span of ten seconds or less. There are three important questions to ask with positive parenting:

THE THREE PRAISE QUESTIONS

Key Praise Questions	Explanation
What should you praise?	Almost everything is praiseworthy. Look for positive actions, thoughts, words, and deeds.
When should you praise?	Compliment immediately or as soon as possible. The most effective window of opportunity for praising kids is in the first ten seconds.
How should you praise?	Compliment the action, effort, or intent of the child as opposed to the results. Find a phrase from the list of Top One Hundred Phrases of Praise. Have fun, and add a few of your own.

10. *Have an attitude of gratitude. Please* and *thank you* are often called the *magic words*. They can create an atmosphere of respect, appreciation, and gratitude between you and your child. Saying please before simple requests can inspire cooperation. In essence, you are asking for help instead of issuing a demand of obedience. When you say thank you to your child, you are acknowledging good thoughts, deeds, and actions.

According to Deborah Norville, Emmy Award–winning television journalist and best-selling author of *Thank You Power*, the benefits of saying thank you can help you and your child become happier and healthier as well as more joyful, creative, enthusiastic, determined, productive, and successful. People who practice saying thank you can inspire those around them to do well and enjoy all of life's blessings. Norville says thank you power can work miracles.[1]

POSITIVE COMMUNICATION

The Top Ten Rules of Praise	Key Points
1. Praise is the perfect communication.	Positive communication can create self-confidence, self-esteem, trust, and loving relationships with your child.
2. Praise your child's efforts.	Compliment your child's effort and personal characteristics rather than results.
3. Capture your child's attention.	When talking to your child, eliminate distractions and get face to face for best results.
4. Be specific with praise.	Identify and state the behavior in the compliment. "I like the way you. . . ."
5. Get eye to eye.	The best positive parent-child communication is eye to eye.
6. Use the Top One Hundred Phrases of Praise.	Use any compliment from this list to praise your child.
7. Practice the sandwich technique.	For positive redirection: identify the behavior, make the correction, and close with encouragement.
8. Be a good listener.	Listen to your child for effective communication.
9. Ask the three praise questions.	Learn the following: *what* actions you should praise, *when* you should praise them, and *how* you should praise your kids.
10. Have an attitude of gratitude.	There is power in *please* and *thank you*.

RULES OF PLAY

Babies are not born with personalized parenting manuals. It's all a guessing game for parents, based on astute observations as well as trial and error. It can be challenging to figure out just how much is enough stimulation. The key is to stop game play before your infant has mentally closed the window of learning. Also, try to emphasize activities that include "tummy time" for your baby to strengthen the upper body, head, neck and shoulders. Here are the ten rules of play.

THE TOP TEN TIPS FOR PLAYING WITH KIDS
FROM BIRTH TO AGE TWO

1. *Timing is everything.* A happy and healthy, well-rested, recently fed, and dry-diapered baby is most receptive to play. Schedule your game play about thirty to sixty minutes after meal and nap times for best results.

2. *Create a comfortable environment.* Warm air, a soft surface, gentle classical music in the background, and visual stimulation create a great play atmosphere. Be sure all of the elements of physical comfort are in place before you play games with your baby.

3. *Use a soothing voice.* Babies respond to simple words and soft animated voices spoken in a mid- to higher-pitched tone. If you have a deep, husky, or loud voice, think about taking it down to a softer level. Here's a hint to dads: it may feel silly to talk to your baby in a different voice, but it could bring a more positive response. It might be worth a try.

4. *Reduce distractions.* Look at your play area and see if there are objects, toys, or loud sounds that might compete for your child's attention when you're playing Proud Parents' games. Also, lower the lights and turn off the television because they are definitely eye-catchers. You want to be

the center of your baby's world for those brief few minutes of game play.

5. *Maintain the magic touch.* Stay in physical contact with your child as a form of love and reassurance as much as possible. Kids are more likely to try new games or physical skills if they feel a connection to a loved one. A parent's touch can give baby the confidence to explore a new environment.

6. *The eyes have it.* Maintain eye-to-eye contact when playing games with your child. The visual connection can make all the difference in the world. There are several options. You can get on the floor with your baby or use an infant seat to prop up your little one on a large, flat surface like a table. If you are using an infant seat, *always* attach the security straps, and *never* leave your baby unattended.

7. *Variety is the spice of life in child's play.* Select different types of games and activities that use an assortment of toys. Consider small, medium, and large objects as well as colorful eye teasers and black-and-white items that provide contrast. Engage the sense of touch with soft, fuzzy, or silky fabrics. Use toys that shake, rattle, and roll as well as those that play music.

8. *Keep it short and sweet.* Babies have a natural sense of curiosity and love to play with caring family members and adults. There is a very brief time span, however, in which they are eager and receptive. It could last a few seconds to a few minutes. Learn to read your child's cues so you might avoid sensory overload. If your baby is happy and smiling, that's a good sign. However, if your infant stops looking at you, turns his head away, rubs his eyes, or cries, then it's time to stop. Playing the game too long creates frustration from overstimulation.

9. *Get into a routine.* Try to consistently play games with your child each day. This way your baby will look forward to the activity with anticipation. For example, if you select one game to play every afternoon after

lunch or nap time, your baby will more likely be receptive and gain confidence in trying new challenges. Routines are critical to a baby's growth and development.

10. *Be aware of special circumstances.* Assuming you have followed these guidelines and you are playing with a well-rested and recently fed and diapered baby, there are a few additional factors to keep in mind. At different times throughout the first twelve months to two years, your child will be in various stages of teething. Emerging teeth can cause discomfort, small fevers, and gum pain or sensitivity. If you notice an unexplained irritable mood in your child, it might be best to hold game play for another day. Let common sense be your guide.

TOP TEN TIPS FOR PLAYING WITH TODDLERS AND PRESCHOOLERS

1. *Make it fun.* Kids will play games if they are having fun. The more they enjoy an activity, the longer they will stay focused on it. Also, it can become a happy memory and children will look forward to playing again another day. Child's play promotes learning on many levels, and it can increase the chance of your child becoming well-rounded and coordinated early in life. So whatever games you play with your child, make them fun.

2. *Know your child.* Through time, you will begin to discover your child's preferences, temperament, moods, and favorite toys and activities. You may begin to notice the best time of day to play with your toddler or preschooler. Is it morning, afternoon, or evening? Certain colors as well as different types of music may seem to draw a greater response from your child. In the first few months, you may begin to observe clues that indicate whether your baby is primarily a visual, auditory, or kinesthetic

learner. By about twelve months, you might possibly be able to determine your child's learning style order. (For more information, read chapter 3 on learning styles.) Understanding your child's strengths and weaknesses will help you formulate a method of good communication and provide information to use as a source of motivation.

3. *Keep it short.* Kids of all ages generally have short attention spans. So if you want to make playtime pleasurable, it is recommended to keep the total game time to ten minutes. Learn to recognize your child's verbal and nonverbal cues that indicate interest, enjoyment, fatigue, or boredom. Are you seeing smiles of joy or frowns of frustration? Is your child looking at you during the activity, or is he looking everywhere but you? Here is a tip about time: babies might play for two to four minutes, toddlers four to six, and preschoolers up to ten. If you are the kind of parent who loses track of time, consider setting an alarm to let you know when to wrap it up. A good rule is the younger the child, the shorter the game.

4. *Age-appropriate activities are best.* Before selecting games, check out your child's age group and investigate the normal range of skill development for that age group. Find out where your child fits regarding developmental abilities. There are a variety of areas where your child might be advanced, right on track, or a little lagging. Remember that kids develop at different times and rates. Most children eventually catch up by the time they enter elementary school. Be sure to choose games that reinforce your child's strengths as well as those that improve weaknesses. In all game play, however, it is critical to praise effort and maintain realistic expectations. The long-term goal, which will take years to achieve, is to raise an active, balanced, and coordinated kid.

5. *Positive communication is essential.* Positive words of encouragement can work wonders for a child's self-esteem. Be sure to get eye to eye with your child and select upbeat and cheerful phrases that praise his

or her efforts during game play. General guidelines are to use concise language of ten words or less. Choose words that are happy in nature. Consider giving directions in an animated voice with words that evoke visual images, such as, "Throw the ball up in the air like it is flying over a rainbow." Include nonverbal communication like clapping, high fives, smiles, thumbs-up, and facial expressions of approval.

6. *Build confidence as you increase the challenge.* All games should result in a successful conclusion for your child. Repeat them many times, and gradually increase the challenge. When your child gets it right, remember to cheer with positive words to communicate that game play can be great fun. Keep up this pattern and your youngster will likely develop a love of learning.

7. *Be persistent and consistent in playing Proud Parents' games.* Commit to a weekly schedule of playing parent-and-child games. An ideal plan includes engaging in activities an average of three to four times each week and for maximum benefits every day. Repetition creates a successful learning environment. The more you expose your baby to positive learning experiences, the faster your child's brain will develop in the first six years. So be committed to thirty to forty minutes of planned purposeful game play each week.

8. *Develop the total child by working on a variety of skills.* When you are creating a personalized Proud Parents' game plan, consider including activities that address fine and gross motor skills, coordination, balance, strength, flexibility, sensory, visual, cognitive, hearing, auditory, tactile, psychological, social, and emotional needs. Develop the total child in the first six years to build a strong foundation.

9. *Be organized and well-prepared for game play.* Take a few minutes before you begin playtime with your child to figure out what you will need for the activity. Collect the supplies, prepare an area, and review the rules and

objectives. Start with a game plan, but be flexible if your child suggests a variation. It could be more fun than the original idea. Also, by following your child's suggestions, you are encouraging leadership skills and showing that you respect his or her opinion. This interaction can result in developing self-confidence and a strong self-image.

10. *Leave your child asking for more.* This last rule is probably one of the most important. Be careful to observe your child's interest in the game and try to reach a successful conclusion while you are both still having fun. Promise a return to the activity another day, and follow through on your word. By keeping your promise, you will help your child develop the ability to trust, which is critical to future interpersonal relationships.

PART TWO

Games to Play with Your Child

Ready, Set, Play

Welcome to the parent and child interactive games section of this book. If you have read part 1 on how your child develops coordination, then you probably have an understanding of what is most likely taking place inside your child's brain and body as you use the Proud Parents' plan. That knowledge can be very helpful because it will enable you to focus on the many aspects of movement, coordination, brain growth, sensory development, and fine and gross motor skills.

If you jumped right to this page without reading the background information in part 1, that's okay, too, because the goal of this book is to get started playing games with your child. As always, adapt skill levels and game choices to accomodate special needs kids. At some point, however, it is still a good idea to read part 1 for a general overview of coordination and the physical, neurological, emotional, and intellectual benefits this program can provide.

The games are divided into four age groups that will help you locate a starting point: "Crib Capers in the First Twelve Months;" "Athletic Activities for One, Two, and You;" "Building Blocks for Three-Year-Olds;" and "The Golden Years: Four- to Six-Year-Olds." For your convenience, activities are alphabetically listed. Also, there are user-friendly charts at the end of each chapter to help you select games that teach seventeen different aspects of coordination as well as the supplies required for each.

Here is a brief explanation of benefits:

- *Fine Motor Skills:* Small muscle movement is the foundation of fine motor skills to control the hands and fingers, which are needed to reach, grasp, write, draw, self-dress, play a musical instrument, and use a computer. Other important uses for the hands and fingers include developing ball skills in sports and manipulating toys and tools. See chapter 5 for more information on fine motor development.

- *Gross Motor Skills:* The control of the large muscles of the body will help your child learn to roll, sit, stand, walk, run, skip, hop, gallop, and jump. It has an impact on torso strength, arm and leg use, balance, movement, strength, endurance, quickness, speed, sports fundamentals, musical development, artistic pursuits, and overall health and fitness. See chapter 7 for more information on gross motor development.

- *Eye-Hand Coordination:* The *eyes* are the starting point for eye-hand coordination because your child needs to see accurately before the hands can respond. Begin playing eye-tracking games from birth with colorful toys, balls, and moving lights. Advance to catching, throwing and hitting balloons, bubbles, and balls of all kinds. Early eye-hand stimulation will result in hard-wiring your child's brain for later coordination in sports, music, art, and academics.

- *Eye-Foot Coordination:* Similar to eye-hand coordination, the brain must see an object before the feet can respond to it. This applies to total body movement, such as walking, running, hopping, skipping, and stair climbing as well as kicking balls and riding bikes. Once again, early exposure is the key because eye-foot coordination begins at birth, but it is never too late to improve at any age.

- *Arms and Shoulders:* The development of the upper body involves arm strength and shoulder range of motion. This area also includes upper torso control, which has a direct impact on fine motor skills and eye-hand coordination.

- *Hands and Fingers:* Fine motor skills require the ability to use the three small individual finger joints for self-care, eating, cutting with scissors, picking up objects, and manipulating balls, clubs, rackets, and bats.

- *Legs and Feet:* Children who learn to use their lower limbs quickly and effectively often have more successful life experiences in school, sports, and life. This involves overall balance, graceful movement, and the ability to navigate through environments with body control.

- *Core Strength:* Body movement begins with core or abdominal strength and ends with the successful use of the arms, hands, legs, and feet. Kids with strong core muscles in stomach and lower back also have good posture and head and neck control.

- *Balance:* This is an intangible element of coordination that involves the brain and inner ear as well as the legs and feet. Kids who move with balance and body control often rise to the top of most social situations as well as sporting activities, academics, music, and art.

- *Cognitive and Brain:* Everything begins with the brain. The great miracle of brain growth begins at birth and continues throughout life. Kids who are exposed to stimulating sights, sounds, scents, textures, movement, and intellectual challenges often have a larger and more efficient neural network. The human brain also works on the use-it-or-lose-it theory of development. As a result, it is important to give your child as much input as possible throughout his life for an excellent head start. See chapter 4 for more information on building better brains.

- *Flexibility:* The muscles, ligaments, and tendons in your child's body readily respond to activities that promote flexibility. This element is critical to maintaining health, strength, and the prevention of injuries in later life.

- *Quickness:* This physical characteristic relies on two factors: quickness training and your child's genetic predisposition for having quick hands or feet. That means some children are naturally wired for speed, but most kids can improve in this area with practice.

- *Visual Acuity:* Your child's brain develops vision in stages from birth through about age ten. Parental feedback in these early years make all the difference to help children build layers of knowledge that serve as a foundation for academics, athletics, art, music, sports, and overall intelligence.

- *Spatial Awareness:* This is another intangible element of coordination that helps your child become aware of elements in his environment. Spatial awareness relies on a combination of accurate visual information and overall body control. It also helps kids gauge distances, walk on uneven surfaces, and become adept at sports.

- *Depth Perception:* The eyes and brain must work together to help kids discover how to safely move through everyday environments in classrooms, playgrounds, and on sports fields. Depth perception works hand-in-hand with spatial awareness.

- *Midline Crossing:* This skill enables your child to use one side of the body to reach across and work with the other. For example, a coordinated kid can move the right hand to pick up a toy on the left side of his or her body. Midline crossing is also evident in sports that require hitting balls on both sides of the body such as backhands and forehands in tennis.

- *Bilateral Limb Use:* The ability to use both arms and feet to perform different tasks at the same time is the essence of bilateral limb use. This aspect of coordination relies on sound neurological wiring, which helps to integrate the two hemispheres of your child's brain. Examples of bilateral arm and hand use include playing the piano, manipulating clay, dressing with buttons, throwing and catching a ball, and cutting paper with scissors. Bilateral leg use is found in gross motor movements such as walking, skipping, playing sports, and driving a car.

- *Level of Difficulty:* Each game is rated *easy, moderate,* or *difficult* according to the challenge it might provide the average child. There are also tips on how to adapt skill levels to make games easier or more challenging for children. This is ideal for special-needs kids, who can play the same games with a few minor adaptations. Also kids develop at different ages and stages. Many games in the younger or older age groups might be appropriate for your child. Experiment, be flexible, and have fun.

- *Special Note:* You may notice small drawings of lying, sitting, standing, and walking babies in the "Crib Capers in the First Twelve Months" chapter. This is a quick tip to guide you in selecting appropriate activities for your child. For example, a game that requires your baby's ability to sit without help would not work for a newborn infant. However, a walking baby can play games designed for a lying baby. This method of identifying games to play is based on your child's unique physical development rather than age.

DESIGN YOUR OWN PROUD PARENTS' PROGRAM

For your convenience, the games charts are further broken into two important categories: fine and gross motor skills. Try to play at least one game from each category for your child's well-rounded development. It is also important to include games that involve both fine and gross motor skills and total body stimulation. You will also find a blank record-keeping chart in the appendix that can be photocopied and used to track your child's progress.

Here are a few tips before you begin:

- Limit games to ten minutes or less, and repeat them often for optimal learning.
- Be sure your child is recently fed, rested, and healthy because hunger, fatigue, and illness make it difficult for your baby to focus on having fun.
- Be sensitive to your child's level of interest in the game. Smiles, happy faces, and eye contact are indications that something good is happening. If your child is crying, squirming, or disinterested, it would be best to change, adjust, or halt the activity.
- Create a calm, peaceful atmosphere with a safe and clutter-free play area. Reduce distractions such as loud sounds, bright lights, or objects that could compete for your child's attention. Play soothing, classical background music or your child's favorite tunes for auditory stimulation.
- Store game supplies in a safe place when finished, and always supervise your child when playing Proud Parents' activities.
- Use positive verbal feedback to promote parent and child bonding as well as emotional security and self-confidence.
- Talk to your child during game time for speech and language development. Verbally describe the action, name body parts, identify left and right positions, and praise your baby's efforts for positive feedback.

Now that you know the basic rules of play and understand the elements of coordination, it is time to select an activity. It's that easy. Have fun, and make memories while you help your child become an athletic, balanced, and coordinated kid.

11

Crib Capers in the
First Twelve Months

Airplane Arms

Baby Burrito

Black Dot

Bottle Tambourines

Buckets of Fun

Chasing Reflections

Clapping Feet

Eye Catchers: Beads and Baubles

Face-to-Face

Floortime Face-to-Face

Flyaway Baby

Follow That Word

Hand Ball

Happy Hands and Toes

Here I Am!

Hip-Hip Hooray

Humpty Dumpty

In the Spotlight

Leg Stretch

Little Drummer Boy or Girl

London Bridge

Magic Cups

Midline Jingle Jangles

Mirror, Mirror

Monkey Business

Off to the Zoo

Open, Shut Them
Palmar Grasp
Pat-a-Cake
Pillow Crawl
Pull-Up Proud
Row Your Boat
Shake, Rattle, and Roll
Sideways Rolls
Sit and Toss Across
Slapping Bath Bubbles
Snuggly Hugs
Squeeze It

Stand up Strong
Straw Pull
Swat the Mobile
Table Tapping
Tear It Up
Teeter-Totter Stool
Towel Tug
Tummy Swimming
Walk with Me
Where's the Toy?
Wiggly Piggly

GAME: Airplane Arms

OBJECT: To improve fine motor skills, eye-hand coordination, hand grasping, midline crossing, language skills, depth perception, spatial awareness, auditory processing, language acquisition, shoulder range of motion, and brain stimulation.

SUPPLIES: None needed.

RULES OF PLAY: Use your baby's arms as wings to fly an airplane. Begin by placing your alert baby on the floor faceup. Encourage him or her to grasp your fingers as you sit or kneel in front of him or her. Gently extend your child's arms out to the sides and hold the stretch for ten seconds. Next, move the arms up and down along the floor in the same and opposite directions. Vocalize engine noises for auditory stimulation and language development as you describe imaginative views from the air. For skill adaptation, grasp your child's hands or wrists and manipulate his or her arm movement.

LEVEL OF DIFFICULTY: Easy.

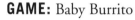

GAME: Baby Burrito

OBJECT: To improve fine and gross motor skills, eye-hand coordination, arm and leg strength, balance, flexibility, language acquisition, emotional security, spatial awareness, and visual and brain stimulation.

SUPPLIES: A large blanket or towel.

RULES OF PLAY: Spread the blanket on the floor, and place your baby faceup in the middle of it. For muscle relaxation, massage your body from head to toe. Pretend each body part is an ingredient. The head and neck could be the ground beef and the shoulders refried beans. The arms are avocado, the hands lettuce, the stomach cheese, the legs sour cream, and the feet salsa. Then lightly wrap up your child in the tortilla blanket and allow him or her to escape. For skill adaptation, manipulate your child's arms and legs to help him or her escape from the tortilla blanket.

LEVEL OF DIFFICULTY: Easy.

GAME: Black Dot

OBJECT: To improve fine motor skills, eye-hand coordination, eye-tracking movements, visual development, depth perception, spatial awareness, auditory stimulation, language development, and brain development.

SUPPLIES: A copy of the dot found in the appendix.

RULES OF PLAY: Engage your child with this visual game of tracking a black-and-white object with the eyes. Place your baby in a safe seat and hold the black dot about twelve inches away. Slowly move it side to side, up and down, in circles, or any direction. Sing songs or talk while you play. As your baby's visual skills improve, encourage him or her to reach out and touch the dot. For midline crossing, place the dot on one side of your child's body and guide the opposite hand to touch it. For skill adaptation, increase or decrease the distance between the dot and your child's eyes.

LEVEL OF DIFFICULTY: Easy.

GAME: Bottle Tambourines

OBJECT: To improve fine motor skills, eye-hand coordination, auditory processing, visual development, depth perception, hand grasping, arm and shoulder strength, and brain stimulation.

SUPPLIES: Two empty clear plastic baby bottles or small disposable water bottles, nontoxic glue, and lively music. Visual eye-catchers can be colorful beads, confetti, coins, or dried beans.

RULES OF PLAY: Make small colorful bottle shakers to develop your child's hand-grasping skills. Pour the eye-catchers into the bottles about three-quarters full. Glue the lids on securely and let them dry. Place one shaker in each of your child's hands. For skill adaptation, help your child grasp the bottle and slowly turn it upside down to watch the eye-catchers shift. Advanced levels include shaking the bottles to the beat of the music.

LEVEL OF DIFFICULTY: Easy.

GAME: Buckets of Fun

OBJECT: To improve fine motor skills, eye-hand coordination, hand grasping, midline crossing, spatial awareness, depth perception, voluntary release of the hands, and brain stimulation.

SUPPLIES: A plastic bucket and a handful of child-safe toys such as blocks.

RULES OF PLAY: Place the bucket in your child's lap with the toys positioned all around, on the right, left, and center. Encourage your child to grasp the toy and voluntarily release it into the bucket. Empty and refill. Also use the nondominant hand, as well as midline crossing, which includes reaching across the body to manipulate objects. Talk to your child about the position and color of the objects. Be sure to provide solid back support if your baby is in the early stages of sitting. For skill adaptation, guide your child's hand to grasp the toy and help him or her drop it into the bucket. Advanced levels can make it a game—count the number of toys picked up or play for speed.

LEVEL OF DIFFICULTY: Moderate.

GAME: Chasing Reflections

OBJECT: To improve gross motor skills, eye-hand and eye-foot coordination, crawling movements, midline crossing, bilateral limb use, shoulder strength, visual stimulation, cognitive development, facial recognition, and tummy play time.

SUPPLIES: A large, child-safe mirror.

RULES OF PLAY: Place your baby on the floor in a crawling position and hold a mirror at floor level about twelve inches in front of your child's line of vision. Move the mirror forward inch by inch and encourage your baby to crawl toward it. After a few strides, allow your child to reach the mirror, and then start again. For skill adaptation, increase or decrease the length of the crawling distance to the mirror.

LEVEL OF DIFFICULTY: Easy.

GAME: Clapping Feet

OBJECT: To improve gross motor skills, eye-foot coordination, midline crossing, bilateral limb use, eye tracking, leg and hip range of motion, spatial awareness, depth perception, core strength, flexibility, balance, auditory processing, language acquisition, and visual and brain stimulation.

SUPPLIES: Lively music.

RULES OF PLAY: Place your baby on his or her back on a soft surface. Your child's arms and legs should move freely. Sit in front of your child and gently grasp his or her ankles, one in each hand. The action is to bring your baby's feet up to his or her stomach and softly clap the soles of his or her feet to the beat of lively music. Recite rhymes or talk about the parts of the body in motion. For skill adaptation, encourage your child to bring his or her feet together without help.

LEVEL OF DIFFICULTY: Easy.

GAME: Eye Catchers: Beads and Baubles

OBJECT: To improve fine motor skills, eye-hand coordination, eye tracking, hand grasping, midline crossing, attention span, auditory processing, language acquisition, spatial awareness, depth perception, and brain stimulation.

SUPPLIES: Dangling colorful beads, a shiny necklace, or a ribbon.

RULES OF PLAY: Your baby is sitting or lying faceup. Hold the object at your child's eye level and move it sideways, high and low, and in a circular motion. Allow your baby time to follow the object with his or her eyes, and occasionally lower it into grasping range. For midline crossing, encourage your baby to reach across the body and grasp the toy with the opposite hand. For skill adaptation, guide your child's hand across the body to reach for and grasp the necklace. Advanced skills include playing a brief mini tug-of-war with your child as he or she is holding on to the necklace.

LEVEL OF DIFFICULTY: Easy.

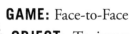

GAME: Face-to-Face

OBJECT: To improve gross motor skills; eye-hand coordination; core, shoulder, hand, head, and neck strength; visual and cognitive functioning, language acquisition, facial recognition, eye-tracking stimulation, and tummy play time.

SUPPLIES: None needed.

RULES OF PLAY: Hold your baby securely at the torso and look directly into your baby's eyes. Speak in animated tones, with smiles and exaggerated facial gestures. Move your baby away, close, up and down, and to the right and left. Describe your child's position and location. For skill adaptation, increase or decrease the distance between your face and your child's face.

LEVEL OF DIFFICULTY: Easy.

GAME: Floortime Face-to-Face

OBJECT: To improve gross motor skills; eye-hand coordination; core, shoulder, hand, head, and neck strength; visual and cognitive functioning, language acquisition, facial recognition, and precrawling skills.

SUPPLIES: A large blanket or towel.

RULES OF PLAY: Place your baby stomach side down on the floor on a soft blanket. You are face-to-face with your child, a few inches apart. Play a facial feature recognition game. For example, point to your nose and say, "This is my nose. Where is (baby's name)'s nose?" Point to your baby's nose and exclaim, "There it is!" Identify eyes, ears, teeth, tongue, hair, eyebrows, eyelashes, chin, cheeks, and the neck. For skill adaptation, ask your baby to point to his or her nose with little or no guidance.

LEVEL OF DIFFICULTY: Easy.

GAME: Flyaway Baby

OBJECT: To improve fine and gross motor movements; eye-hand coordination; core, head, and neck strength; balance and vestibular (position of head on shoulders) functioning; and cognitive, language, tummy play time, and spatial skills.

SUPPLIES: Colorful necklace.

RULES OF PLAY: Place your infant across your lap or thighs stomach-side down while you are sitting on a chair. Your child's head, neck, arms, hands, legs, and feet should extend beyond your lap. The support is under your child's abdominals. Encourage your baby to lift his or her head and look up at the dangling beads, which you are holding in front of the eyes. The game is for your baby to reach out and grasp the beads with one or both hands. For skill adaptation, increase or decrease the distance between your child's hands and the dangling beads. Advanced levels include gently moving the beads for challenging grasping.

LEVEL OF DIFFICULTY: Easy.

GAME: Follow That Word

OBJECT: To improve gross motor skills, core strength, spatial aware-ness, head and neck support, balance, brain stimulation, and visual development.

SUPPLIES: None needed.

RULES OF PLAY: Hold your baby securely at the torso and under the arms. Begin in a face-to-face position. Lift your child above your head and say, "You are *high* above (Mommy's or Daddy's) head." Gently lower your baby to the ground and say, "Now, you are *low* to the ground." Repeat with positions of left, right, center, under your arms or, legs, toes-to-toes, and nose-to-nose. For skill adaptation, increase or decrease the distance between you and your child as you lift him or her through the game.

LEVEL OF DIFFICULTY: Easy.

GAME: Hand Ball

OBJECT: To develop fine motor skills, eye-hand coordination, eye track-ing, finger dexterity, core strength, overall balance, arm and shoulder range of motion, depth perception, spatial awareness, and an introduction to ball play.

SUPPLIES: A small child-safe ball.

RULES OF PLAY: Sit on the floor directly facing your baby, who is also sitting comfortably with-out help. Hold the ball in your hands and gently roll or place it in your child's hands. Encourage your baby to grasp the ball and hand it back to you. Repeat. As skills improve, increase the distance.

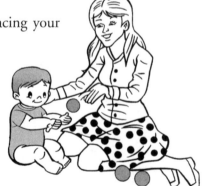

Describe the action: "Now I am rolling the ball to you. Good catch. Try to send it back to me." For skill adaptation, increase or decrease the distance between your hands and your child's hands.

LEVEL OF DIFFICULTY: Moderate.

GAME: Happy Hands and Toes

OBJECT: To improve fine and gross motor skills, eye-hand and eye-foot coordination, midline crossing, cross-crawl movements, core strength, flexibility, eye tracking, auditory processing, language development, spatial awareness, depth perception, and cognitive stimulation.

SUPPLIES: None needed.

RULES OF PLAY: Sit on the floor or a bed next to your child, who is lying on his or her back. Hold your baby's right hand and left foot and join them at the center of the child's body. As you do so, name the moving body parts. Encourage your child to grab his or her toes placing his or her tiny hands around his or her feet. Repeat and reverse hands and feet. This game has powerful long-term effects because it increases neurological connections between the right and left hemispheres of the brain. For skill adaptation, massage your child's arms and legs prior to playing the game for muscle relaxation.

LEVEL OF DIFFICULTY: Easy.

GAME: Here I Am!

OBJECT: To improve fine motor skills, eye-hand coordination, eye tracking, spatial awareness, depth perception, hand grasping, memory, emotional security, auditory processing, and brain stimulation.

SUPPLIES: A baby blanket.

RULES OF PLAY: Place your child in a high chair and get eye-to-eye with your baby. Put a blanket over your head and say, "It is (Mommy or Daddy). Where am I?" When your child pulls the blanket off your head exclaim, "Here I am!" Repeat the action from the right, left, behind, and below the chair. Always allow your baby to find you. This develops visual tracking and emotional security that comes with knowledge that you are nearby even if your child cannot see you. For skill adaptation, guide your child's hands onto the blanket and help him or her lift it off your head.

LEVEL OF DIFFICULTY: Easy.

GAME: Hip-Hip Hooray

OBJECT: To improve gross motor skills, eye-foot coordination, midline crossing, bilateral limb use, eye-tracking, leg and hip range of motion, spatial awareness, strength, flexibility, and visual and brain stimulation.

SUPPLIES: None needed.

RULES OF PLAY: Place your baby on his or her back on a soft and safe surface. Sit in front of your child and hold his or her upper thighs just below the hips. Pull the knees up to the chest and hold for five seconds. Now rotate them to the right and left. The movement should come from the hips and not the entire torso. Finally, release your child's thighs and gently extend the legs to stretch them out. For skill adaptation, massage the hips, legs, and thighs before the game for muscle relaxation.

LEVEL OF DIFFICULTY: Easy.

GAME: Humpty Dumpty

OBJECT: To improve fine and gross motor skills, eye-hand coordination, overall balance, core strength, flexibility, arm range of motion, auditory processing, language acquisition, spatial awareness, depth perception, and brain stimulation.

SUPPLIES: None needed.

RULES OF PLAY: Your child should sit independently on the floor with you by his side. Place one hand on your child's chest and one on the back. Gently rock your baby back and forth about an inch as you recite "Humpty Dumpty." When you get to the second line, softly push your child backward while maintaining back support. Encourage your child to extend the arms and hands in the direction of the push as a means of protection. Return your child to a sitting position and repeat. For skill adaptation, extend your child's arms backward before tipping to prepare for the Humpty Dumpty fall. Advanced levels can include pushing in several directions such as right and left, each time extending the arms in the direction of the fall.

LEVEL OF DIFFICULTY: Moderate.

RHYME: *Humpty Dumpty*

> Humpty Dumpty sat on a wall.
>
> Humpty Dumpty had a great fall. (*Gently nudge baby.*)
>
> All the King's horses and all the king's men
>
> Were able to put Humpty together again.
>
> (*Help baby sit up again. Clap hands and cheer.*)

GAME: In the Spotlight

OBJECT: To improve visual acuity, eye-tracking skills, eye-muscle strength, spatial awareness, depth perception, language development, and brain stimulation.

SUPPLIES: A flashlight.

RULES OF PLAY: Hold your child in your arms and go into a darkened bathroom. Turn the flashlight on and create a moving visual light display on a wall for eye-tracking skills. For skill adaptation, increase or decrease the distance to the moving light on the wall.

LEVEL OF DIFFICULTY: Easy.

GAME: Leg Stretch

OBJECT: To improve gross motor skills, eye-foot coordination, leg and core strength, flexibility, bilateral limb use, auditory processing, language development, and brain stimulation.

SUPPLIES: A blanket.

RULES OF PLAY: Place your alert baby on a large, safe surface stomach-side up. Kneel in front of your child. Stretch one leg at a time. First relax your baby's leg by supporting it under the knee joint with one hand. Slowly and carefully try to extend your child's leg into a straightened position. Hold the stretch for ten seconds and gently release. Repeat two to four times. Switch legs. For skill adaptation, gently massage the leg muscles prior to the stretch to release tension.

LEVEL OF DIFFICULTY: Easy.

GAME: Little Drummer Boy or Girl

OBJECT: To improve fine and gross motor skills, eye-hand coordination, hand grasping, bilateral hand use, sitting skills, depth perception, auditory processing, eye-tracking skills, and brain stimulation.

SUPPLIES: Two wooden cooking spoons and a plastic or metal mixing bowl.

RULES OF PLAY: Place your baby in a chair, or a strong sitter can play on the floor. Give your child two wooden spoons, one for each hand, and an upside-down mixing bowl. Show your child how to strike the bowl to make noise. For skill adaptation, hold your child's hands while he or she is grasping the spoons and manipulate the hands into a drumming motion. Advanced levels can drum to the beat of lively music.

LEVEL OF DIFFICULTY: Easy.

GAME: London Bridge

OBJECT: To improve gross motor skills, spatial awareness, depth perception, eye-hand coordination, balance, flexibility, core strength, brain stimulation, tummy play time, midline crossing, and the protective reaction of using the arms and hands to break a forward fall.

SUPPLIES: None needed.

RULES OF PLAY: Place your baby on the floor stomach-side down. While securely holding your baby at midtorso, lift him or her a few inches off the floor. Your child's body should be parallel to the floor. The action is to gently tip your baby's upper body and arms forward to encourage your child's hands to touch the floor. Repeat the tipping action each time you slowly sing the phrase, "London Bridge is falling down." For skill adaptation, increase or decrease the tipping angle.

LEVEL OF DIFFICULTY: Moderate.

LYRICS: *London Bridge*

> London Bridge is falling down
> Falling down, falling down.
> London Bridge is falling down,
> My fair lady.

GAME: Magic Cups

OBJECT: To develop fine motor skills, eye-hand coordination, hand-grasping; visual tracking, depth perception, spatial awareness, language development, and brain stimulation.

SUPPLIES: A small toy and two colored plastic cups.

RULES OF PLAY: Your child should sit in a high chair or at a table. Display a small child-safe toy and place it on the flat surface in front of your child.

Then cover the toy with an upside-down cup. Ask your child to find the toy. When your child lifts the cup to find the object, praise his or her efforts. Repeat. For skill adaptation, guide your child's hand to lift the cup and find the toy. Advanced levels include adding a second cup to the mix. Use one toy and move the cups around before allowing your child to find the hidden object.

LEVEL OF DIFFICULTY: Moderate.

GAME: Midline Jingle Jangles

OBJECT: To develop fine motor skills, eye-hand coordination, midline crossing, hand grasping, eye tracking, auditory processing, depth perception, spatial awareness, and brain stimulation.

SUPPLIES: A child-safe sparkling necklace and a baby blanket.

RULES OF PLAY: Your alert baby is in a sitting position. You are kneeling in front of your child. Dangle the necklace along the center of his or her body. Move it to the right, and as that side's hand reaches for the necklace, slowly draw it toward the left. Finally, the right hand should grasp the necklace when it is firmly over the left shoulder. If your child drops the right hand and starts to use the left, go back and reengage the right hand. Repeat the action for the opposite side. For skill adaptation, guide your child's hand toward the dangling necklace and help him grasp it. Advanced levels include using two necklaces, each hand grasping a necklace, one at a time. Hold for a few seconds and release.

LEVEL OF DIFFICULTY: Easy.

GAME: Mirror, Mirror

OBJECT: To develop visual acuity, eye tracking, facial recognition, auditory processing, language acquisition, and brain stimulation.

SUPPLIES: A small unbreakable mirror.

RULES OF PLAY: Place your child on your lap with his or her back against your chest. Securely hold your child with one hand, and hold a mirror in the other. You are both looking at the mirror, which is about twelve inches in front of your child's eyes. Slowly move the mirror a few inches side to side, up and down, and in circular motions. Make sure your baby's eyes are following the mirror as you talk about the position of the mirror in relation to your child. Is it high, low, right, or left? For skill adaptation, place the mirror closer to your child's eyes. Advanced levels include moving the mirror faster to promote vision and eye-tracking abilities.

LEVEL OF DIFFICULTY: Easy.

GAME: Monkey Business

OBJECT: To develop fine and gross motor skills, eye-hand coordination, shoulder and arm range of motion, finger dexterity, eye tracking, spatial awareness, depth perception, midline crossing, tummy play time, and auditory and brain stimulation.

SUPPLIES: A small stuffed monkey or other plush toy and a two-foot length of string.

RULES OF PLAY: Attach the string to the monkey's tail. Your child can be sitting in a safety seat, lying on his or her back, or try tummy time on the floor. Dangle the monkey within your child's hand-striking distance. Encourage him or her to swat, swipe, or grab the monkey with one or both hands. Provide stimulation for the right and left hands. For skill adaptation, place your child's hand directly onto the stationary dangling monkey and push it into action. Advanced levels can try to hit the monkey while in motion.

LEVEL OF DIFFICULTY: Moderate.

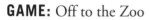

GAME: Off to the Zoo

OBJECT: To develop fine and gross motor skills; shoulder, arm, hand, and core strength; cross-limb movements; leg and hip flexibility; spatial awareness; depth perception; balance; midline crossing, quickness; tummy play time; and cognitive, visual, and auditory stimulation.

SUPPLIES: None needed.

RULES OF PLAY: Get down on the floor on your hands and knees with your child. Pretend you are a variety of zoo animals, such as a tiger, lion, bear, elephant, rhinoceros, or giraffe. Make animal noises as you crawl at various speeds and patterns. Try playing a crawling version of zoo follow-the-leader or a fun game of zoo chase with your baby. For skill adaptation, increase or decrease the intensity and pace of animal crawling.

LEVEL OF DIFFICULTY: Easy.

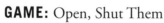

GAME: Open, Shut Them

OBJECT: To develop fine motor and eye-hand coordination, finger dexterity, auditory processing, clapping skills, depth perception, and visual and brain stimulation.

SUPPLIES: Safety seat.

RULES OF PLAY: Place your child in a safety seat. Follow the directions of the rhyme for finger and hand manipulation. Chant the rhyme as you play and encourage your child to copy your actions. Repeat several times. For skill adaptation, manipulate your child's hand to follow the directions of the rhyme. Advanced levels can play at a faster pace.

LEVEL OF DIFFICULTY: Moderate.

Rhyme	Action
Open, shut them.	*Open and close the fingers of your hand.*
Open, shut them.	*Repeat action.*
Give a little clap.	*Clap your hands.*
Open, shut them.	*Open and close your hand.*
Open, shut them.	*Repeat action.*
Clap them on your lap.	*Clap hands gently on the top of your thighs.*

GAME: Palmar Grasp

OBJECT: To improve fine motor skills, midline crossing, eye-tracking movements, arm strength, shoulder range of motion, hand-grasping skills, depth perception, and visual, auditory, and brain stimulation.

SUPPLIES: A child-safe rattle.

RULES OF PLAY: Your infant should be faceup on a soft and safe surface. Select a favorite rattle and shake it to engage your child's attention. Move it side to side about twelve inches in front of your child's face. When your baby lifts a hand toward the object, bring it within grasping range and allow your child to hold it. For skill adaptation, continue to securely hold your child's hand with the rattle inside it. Shake it together. Advanced levels include midline crossing, which is grasping the rattle on the opposite side of the body. For example, the right hand reaches across to the left side.

LEVEL OF DIFFICULTY: Easy.

GAME: Pat-a-Cake

OBJECT: To improve fine motor skills, eye-hand coordination, finger dexterity, arm strength, hand-clapping skills, depth perception, and auditory, visual, and cognitive development.

SUPPLIES: None needed.

RULES OF PLAY: Place your infant in a safety seat. Face your baby and demonstrate how to clap your hands as you recite the rhyme. For skill adaptation, place your child's hands in your own and do it together. Advanced levels include allowing him or her to independently clap to the rhyme.

LEVEL OF DIFFICULTY: Easy.

RHYME: *Pat-a-Cake (Mother Goose)*

> Pat-a-cake, pat-a-cake,
> Baker's man!
> So I do, master,
> As fast as I can.
>
> Pat it, and prick it,
> And mark it with B,
> Put it in the oven
> For (baby's name) and me.

GAME: Pillow Crawl

OBJECT: To improve gross motor skills, eye-hand and eye-foot coordination, cross crawling, balance, core strength, arm and leg flexibility, quickness, spatial awareness, depth perception, tummy play time, and visual and brain development.

SUPPLIES: Sofa cushions, pillows of all shapes and sizes, and rolled-up towels.

RULES OF PLAY: Place your baby on the floor in a crawling position. Place a small pillow or cylindrical-shaped towel roll under his or her tummy to develop upper body strength and coordination. Encourage your baby to crawl over the cushion leading with the hands. The knees and feet will follow.

For skill adaptation, make a smaller towel roll and then guide your child's hands over the roll followed by the feet. For advanced levels, increase the size of the towel roll and add more cushions and pillows of various sizes. Create a pillow obstacle course.

LEVEL OF DIFFICULTY: Difficult.

GAME: Pull-Up Proud

OBJECT: To encourage fine and gross motor skills; shoulder, core, arm, and leg strength; balance; flexibility; standing development; spatial awareness; depth perception; and auditory and brain stimulation.

SUPPLIES: None needed.

RULES OF PLAY: Place your child in a sitting position on the floor. Offer support from your hands and encourage your baby to pull up into a standing position. Hold the stand for about ten seconds and help your baby to sit down again. Repeat the action several times. For skill adaptation, offer more support when moving into a pull-up position.

LEVEL OF DIFFICULTY: Moderate.

GAME: Row Your Boat

OBJECT: To develop gross motor skills, balance, a protective reflex action, abdominal strength, spatial awareness, arm and shoulder stability, and visual and brain stimulation.

SUPPLIES: None needed.

RULES OF PLAY: Place your baby in a sitting position on the floor. You should be facing your child, directly in front. Place your one hand on his right side and one on the left at the waist or mid-torso. Sing the song "Row Your Boat," and sway your baby a few inches from side to side. When you reach the end of the song, tip your baby sideways so he will learn to reach the arms toward the floor to protect against the fall. For skill adaptation, guide your child's arms out to the side before tipping him into the final sideways fall. Advanced levels can handle a greater sideways swaying motion.

LEVEL OF DIFFICULTY: Difficult.

LYRICS: *Row Your Boat*

> Row, row, row your boat
> Gently down the stream
> Merrily, merrily, merrily, merrily
> Life is but a dream!
>
> Row, row, row your boat,
> Gently as can be
> Place your arms side to side,
> You'll stay out of the sea!
>
> Row, row, row your boat
> Gently to and fro
> Stretch your hands out to the side
> Or in the lake you go!

GAME: Shake, Rattle, and Roll

OBJECT: To develop fine and gross motor coordination, eye-hand and hand-grasping skills, arm and shoulder range of motion, bilateral limb use, midline crossing, auditory processing, visual acuity, and brain stimulation.

SUPPLIES: Two toy rattles and lively music.

RULES OF PLAY: Your baby is in an independent sitting position or a safety seat. Give your child a rattle for each hand. For skill adaptation, place the rattle in your child's hand and move it up and down to initiate action and sound. Advanced levels include playing your child's favorite music and shaking the rattles to the beat of the song.

LEVEL OF DIFFICULTY: Easy.

GAME: Sideways Rolls

OBJECT: To develop gross motor skills; torso, back, and shoulder strength; eye-hand and eye-foot coordination, tummy play time; and side-to-side muscle control that leads to rolling from front to back or back to front.

SUPPLIES: None needed.

RULES OF PLAY: Place your alert infant on his or her back on a flat safe surface. Kneel in front of your child. Gently hold your baby at his or her sides using your arms, forearms, and hands. Now gently roll your child to his or her tummy. Try to prop your baby on his or her forearms and hands. Allow your child to remain in this position for about a minute and repeat the action back-to-front, and front-to-back several times. For skill adaptation, help your baby remain propped up on the forearms by supporting or lifting the chest and shoulders off the surface. This builds shoulder, head, and torso strength.

LEVEL OF DIFFICULTY: Easy.

GAME: Sit and Toss Across

OBJECT: To improve fine and gross motor skills, eye-hand coordination, manual dexterity, visual stimulation, early throwing skills, spatial awareness, depth perception, arm control, and brain stimulation.

SUPPLIES: A moderate-sized ball about six to eight inches in diameter and an empty laundry basket.

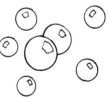

RULES OF PLAY: Put laundry basket on its side and place your child in a sitting position about two to three feet away from the opening. The basket should resemble a soccer goal. Give your child a ball and encourage him or her to toss the ball into the goal and, if possible, retrieve it from the basket and toss it again. For skill adaptation, increase or decrease the throwing distance.

LEVEL OF DIFFICULTY: Moderate.

GAME: Slapping Bath Bubbles

OBJECT: To develop fine motor skills, eye-hand coordination, finger dexterity, spatial skills, depth perception, and visual and brain stimulation.

SUPPLIES: Bubble bath solution.

RULES OF PLAY: Fill a bathtub with lukewarm water and bubble bath solution. Encourage your child to take a bath and slap or pop the bubbles with one or both hands until the bubbles disappear. For skill adaptation, hold your child's hands and manipulate the action of slapping the bubbles. Advanced levels include using the tip of the index fingers of both hands to pop bubbles.

LEVEL OF DIFFICULTY: Easy.

RHYME: *The Bubble Song*

> There was a little froggy with four tiny limbs
> I put it in my bathtub to see if he could swim.
> He hopped atop the bubbles like lily pads of soap
> And now he's in my bathtub with a bubble in his throat.
> Bubble, bubble, bubble—pop, pop, pop!![1]

GAME: Snuggly Hugs

OBJECT: To develop gross motor skills, hand, arm, and upper-body strength, midline crossing, spatial awareness, flexibility, and shoulder range of motion.

SUPPLIES: None needed.

RULES OF PLAY: Place your alert baby on his or her back on a safe surface. Kneel in front of your child. Put your thumbs inside your baby's palms and wrap your fingers around the backs of the hands. Stretch your child's arms out wide at shoulder height and then immediately bring them back across the chest in a crisscross fashion that feels like a loving, snuggly hug. Repeat several times. For skill adaptation, hold your child's hands or wrists to manipulate the arms.

LEVEL OF DIFFICULTY: Easy.

GAME: Squeeze It

OBJECT: To develop fine motor skills, hand strength, grasping skills, depth perception, auditory processing, tummy play time, and brain and visual stimulation.

SUPPLIES: Two small, squeezable baby toys that make noise.

RULES OF PLAY: Give your child two squeezable noise-making toys, one for each hand, and encourage him or her to open up the fingers of the hand and squeeze the toys to make noise. Variations include squeezing one hand at a time or both hands at once. To engage midline crossing, encourage your baby to reach across the body to grasp the toy. Try placing your baby on his or her back for tummy play time during this activity. For skill adaptation, place your hands around your child's and demonstrate how to squeeze the toy. Advanced levels can try to squeeze the toys to the beat of a favorite song.

LEVEL OF DIFFICULTY: Easy.

GAME: Stand Up Strong

OBJECT: To improve gross motor skills, leg and hip strength, balance, flexibility, spatial awareness, depth perception, brain stimulation, and eye-foot control needed for standing and prewalking skills.

SUPPLIES: None needed.

RULES OF PLAY: Your child is in a balanced sitting position on the floor. Allow your child to grasp your hand or fingers and provide support to help him or her stand up. Continue until he or she develops balance in the feet, legs, and hips. For skill adaptation, grasp your child's hands or wrists and pull him or her into a standing position. Advanced levels include gradually letting go of one hand. When balance improves, release both hands.

LEVEL OF DIFFICULTY: Moderate.

GAME: Straw Pull

OBJECT: To improve fine motor skills, eye-hand coordination, finger dexterity, the pincer grasp, spatial awareness, depth perception, and visual and brain development.

SUPPLIES: Child-safe modeling dough and four tall drinking straws cut to four-inch lengths.

RULES OF PLAY: Place your baby in a safety seat or on your lap. Shape modeling dough into a small ball about two inches in diameter and hold it in front of your child. Demonstrate how to push a straw into the ball using the pincer grasp with the thumb and index finger. Now your child should push the straw completely through the ball using the index finger. When the straw exits the other side, pull it out with the pincer grasp. Repeat using different entry spots on the ball. For skill adaptation, allow your child to grasp the straw with the fist and guide the hand to insert the straw into the dough. Advanced levels can use both hands to manipulate the straw and dough.

LEVEL OF DIFFICULTY: Moderate.

GAME: Swat the Mobile

OBJECT: To improve fine motor skills, eye-hand and eye-foot coordination, manual dexterity, spatial awareness, depth perception, eye tracking, tummy play time, and brain stimulation.

SUPPLIES: A colorful crib mobile.

RULES OF PLAY: Your baby is on his or her back. Unhook the crib mobile and lower it within your baby's hand reach. Encourage your child to grasp the dangling objects with one or both hands or kick with the feet. Describe the action of the game for language development. Try placing your baby on his or her tummy during this activity for tummy play time. For skill adaptation, bring the mobile down to your child's hands and guide them to touch or swat the mobile. Advanced levels can try to swat it with the feet. Safety alert includes making sure your child's hands or feet do not get tangled in the hanging string.

LEVEL OF DIFFICULTY: Moderate.

GAME: Table Tapping

OBJECT: To develop fine motor skills, eye-hand coordination, hand grasping, finger dexterity, depth perception, spatial awareness, eye tracking, auditory processing, and brain development.

SUPPLIES: Two toy blocks and lively music.

RULES OF PLAY: Place your child in a high chair or on your lap at a kitchen table. Place one block in the front and center of your child. Observe his or her hand selection for possible clues on handedness. Put the second block in your child's free hand. Play lively music and show your child how to tap the blocks on the surface to the beat of the song. Variations include tapping the blocks together similar to hand clapping. For skill adaptation, manipulate your child's hands through the action. For advanced levels, tape a few pieces of paper on the table for tapping targets.

LEVEL OF DIFFICULTY: Easy.

GAME: Tear It Up

OBJECT: To improve fine motor skills, eye-hand coordination, hand grasping, finger dexterity, depth perception, balance, visual stimulation, and brain development.

SUPPLIES: Paper of any size and color.

RULES OF PLAY: Place your child in a safety seat, on your lap, or on the floor. Give him or her a piece of paper approximately the size of a four-inch square. Demonstrate the skill of grasping the paper with both hands and tearing it in half. Then help your child do the same. For skill adaptation, offer your child a smaller piece of paper to tear for easier hand grasping. Advanced levels can try to tear the paper into tiny pieces.

LEVEL OF DIFFICULTY: Easy.

GAME: Teeter-Totter Stool

OBJECT: To develop fine and gross motor skills, eye-hand and eye-foot coordination, core strength, lower-back flexibility, balance, spatial awareness, depth perception, visual acuity, and brain stimulation.

SUPPLIES: A small stool and three to six small toys or stuffed animals.

RULES OF PLAY: Place your child on a stool with his feet flat on the floor. Place the toys on the floor in front, right, and left of your child. Sit directly behind your child for support. Name the toy on your child's right and ask him or her to pick it up. As your baby reaches to his or her right, hold the left thigh down with your hand. When reaching for the toy on the left side, hold your child's or her right thigh. For the toy in the center, offer support where it is needed, but allow your child to find his center of balance through trial and error. For skill adaptation, offer more torso support through the action and guide your child's hand toward the toy. Advanced levels need less torso support and can reach the toy from longer distances.

LEVEL OF DIFFICULTY: Difficult.

GAME: Towel Tug

OBJECT: To improve fine and gross motor skills, eye-hand coordination, core strength, back control, balance, hand grasping, arm range of motion, eye tracking, and brain development.

SUPPLIES: A small bath towel.

RULES OF PLAY: Sit on the floor facing your child with your legs in front of your body either in a cross-legged or open *V* shape. Both you and your baby each hold one end of the towel to start the towel tug-of-war. Your arms are straight, and the towel should be taut. Now gently pull the towel back and forth a few inches. For skill adaptation, gently tug the towel a few inches. Advanced levels can handle longer pulls and shifting to the right and left. Your baby will learn to balance by using the hips, lower back, and abdominal muscles.

LEVEL OF DIFFICULTY: Moderate.

GAME: Tummy Swimming

OBJECT: To improve gross motor skills, eye-hand and eye-foot coordination, bilateral limb use, torso strength, balance, flexibility, shoulder range of motion, spatial awareness, tummy play time, and brain development.

SUPPLIES: None needed.

RULES OF PLAY: Place your alert baby on a large, safe area like a bed or the floor. Your child should be stomach-side down. You are kneeling in front of your child. Gently hold your baby's arms out to the sides to simulate the arm movements of the breaststroke. Also show your child how to move his or her legs in the flutter kick motion used in swimming. This is a great activity that follows the "back to sleep, tummy to play" philosophy currently suggested by many pediatricians. For skill adaptation, manipulate your child's limbs through the game. Advanced levels can try to swim for speed with fast arm motion and leg kicks.

LEVEL OF DIFFICULTY: Easy.

GAME: Walk with Me

OBJECT: To improve gross motor skills, eye-foot coordination, balance, core strength, hip and leg flexibility, visual awareness, depth perception, and brain development.

SUPPLIES: None needed.

RULES OF PLAY: Hold your child in an upright position with his or her feet on the floor. You are offering support by holding your baby's torso under the arms. Your baby's hands, arms, and legs should be free to develop balance and prewalking skills. For skill adaptation, offer more support so your child has limited weight bearing on his or her feet. As balance increases, gradually reduce the level of support.

LEVEL OF DIFFICULTY: Easy.

GAME: Where's the Toy?

OBJECT: To improve fine motor skills, eye-hand coordination, bilateral limb use, hand grasping, spatial awareness, depth perception, visual tracking, core strength, and brain development.

SUPPLIES: A small toy and an empty shoe or gift box with a lid. The box should be big enough to hide the toy.

RULES OF PLAY: Place your child in a safety seat or on the floor. Show your child the toy, name it, and place it inside the box.

Close the lid, shake the box, place it back on the floor, and ask your child, "Where is the (name the toy)?" Let your baby respond by looking for it inside the box. For skill adaptation, use a box without a lid and cover it with a towel or blanket. Advanced levels can place additional objects over the box.
LEVEL OF DIFFICULTY: Easy.

GAME: Wiggly Piggly

OBJECT: To develop fine motor skills, eye-hand and eye-foot coordination, wrist flexibility, manual dexterity, and depth perception, visual and brain stimulation.

SUPPLIES: None needed.

RULES OF PLAY: Place your alert baby on his back on a safe surface. Kneel in front of your child. Gently hold your child's fingers in your hand and close them into a fist. Then open the thumb and fingers one at a time until they are completely extended. The stretch should be slow and steady. Play with the left and right hands. As you stretch each finger recite the rhyme "This Little Piggy Went to Market." Variations include the same game with your child's feet. For skill adaptation, straighten the finger as much as it will go but do not force it beyond a normal range of motion. For advanced levels, play at a faster pace.

LEVEL OF DIFFICULTY: Easy.

RHYME: *This Little Piggy Went to Market*
> This little piggy went to market,
> This little piggy stayed at home,
> This little piggy had roast beef,
> This little piggy had none.
> And this little piggy went,
> "Wee, wee, wee," all the way home.

Game: The First Twelve Months	Fine Motor	Gross Motor	Arms & Shoulders	Hands & Fingers	Legs & Feet	Core Strength	Balance	Cognitive & Brain	Flexibility	Quickness	Visual	Spatial Awareness	Depth Perception	Eye-Hand	Eye-Foot	Midline Crossing	Bilateral Limb	Supplies
Airplane Arms	•	•	•	•		•		•	•		•	•		•		•	•	None
Baby Burrito	•	•	•	•	•	•		•	•		•	•	•	•	•		•	Blanket
Black Dot	•			•		•					•		•	•			•	See appendix
Bottle Tambourines	•		•	•				•	•	•	•		•	•	•		•	•	Bottles, glue, beads, music
Buckets of Fun	•		•	•		•		•			•	•	•	•		•	•	Bucket, blocks
Chasing Reflections		•	•	•	•	•	•	•			•	•		•			•	Child-safe mirror
Clapping Feet		•			•	•	•	•			•	•	•		•	•		•	Music
Eye Catchers: Beads and Baubles	•		•	•				•	•		•	•		•		•	•	Shiny necklace or ribbon
Face-to-face		•	•	•		•	•		•			•	•	•	•		•	None
Floortime Face-to-Face	•		•	•	•	•	•	•	•	•	•	•	•	•			•	•	Shiny necklace
Flyaway Baby	•	•	•	•	•	•	•	•	•		•	•	•	•			•	Shiny necklace
Follow That Word		•	•	•	•	•		•			•	•	•					None
Hand Ball	•	•	•	•		•	•		•		•	•	•	•	•		•	•	Small child-safe ball
Happy Hands and Toes	•	•	•	•	•	•	•	•	•	•	•	•	•	•	•	•	•	None
Here I Am!	•		•			•	•	•			•	•	•	•			•	Blanket
Hip-Hip Hooray		•		•	•	•	•	•			•	•	•			•	•	None
Humpty Dumpty	•	•	•	•	•	•	•				•	•		•	•	•	•	None
In the Spotlight		•	•	•		•	•		•		•	•	•	•			•	Flashlight
Leg Stretch		•			•	•	•				•	•			•	•	•	None
Little Drummer Boy or Girl	•	•	•	•		•	•		•	•		•		•	•		•	•	Wooden spoons, mixing bowl

Game: The First Twelve Months	Fine Motor	Gross Motor	Arms & Shoulders	Hands & Fingers	Legs & Feet	Core Strength	Balance	Cognitive & Brain	Flexibility	Quickness	Visual	Spatial Awareness	Depth Perception	Eye-Hand	Eye-Foot	Midline Crossing	Bilateral Limb	Supplies
London Bridge		•	•	•		•	•	•		•	•	•	•	•	•	•	•	None
Magic Cups	•		•	•		•	•		•	•	•	•	•	•			•	Plastic cups, small toy
Midline Jingle Jangles	•		•	•		•	•	•			•	•	•	•		•	•	Colorful necklace, blanket
Mirror, Mirror						•	•	•			•	•	•			•	•	Child-safe mirror
Monkey Business	•	•	•	•		•	•	•		•	•	•	•	•			•	Stuffed animal, string
Off to the Zoo	•	•	•	•	•	•	•	•	•	•	•	•	•	•	•		•	None
Open, Shut Them	•		•	•		•	•	•		•	•	•	•	•		•	•	None
Palmar Grasp	•		•	•			•			•	•	•	•	•		•	•	Rattle
Pat-a-Cake	•		•	•		•	•	•		•	•	•		•			•	None
Pillow Crawl	•	•	•	•	•	•	•	•	•	•	•	•	•	•	•	•	•	Pillows, sofa cushions, towels
Pull-Up Proud	•	•	•	•	•	•	•	•	•	•	•	•	•	•	•	•	•	None
Row Your Boat	•	•	•	•	•	•	•	•	•	•	•	•	•	•	•	•	•	None
Shake, Rattle, and Roll	•	•	•	•		•	•	•	•	•	•	•	•	•		•	•	Two rattles, lively music
Sideways Rolls		•	•	•	•	•	•	•			•	•	•	•	•			None
Sit and Toss Across	•	•	•	•	•	•	•	•	•		•	•	•	•		•	•	Laundry basket, medium-sized ball
Slapping Bath Bubbles	•		•	•		•	•	•	•	•	•	•	•	•		•	•	Bubble bath solution
Snuggly Hugs	•	•	•	•		•		•	•		•	•	•	•		•	•	None
Squeeze It	•		•	•		•	•	•			•	•	•	•		•	•	Two squeeze toys
Stand Up Strong	•	•	•	•	•	•	•	•	•	•	•	•	•	•	•		•	None

Game: The First Twelve Months	Fine Motor	Gross Motor	Arms & Shoulders	Hands & Fingers	Legs & Feet	Core Strength	Balance	Cognitive & Brain	Flexibility	Quickness	Visual	Spatial Awareness	Depth Perception	Eye-Hand	Eye-Foot	Midline Crossing	Bilateral Limb	Supplies
Straw Pull	•	•	•		•	•	•	•			•	•	•	•			•	Modeling dough, drinking straws
Swat the Mobile	•		•		•			•		•	•	•	•	•	•	•	•	Crib mobile
Table Tapping	•	•	•	•		•	•	•	•	•	•	•	•	•		•	•	Two toy blocks, music
Tear It Up	•		•	•		•	•	•	•		•	•	•	•			•	Paper
Teeter-Totter Stool	•	•	•	•	•	•	•	•	•	•	•	•	•	•	•	•	•	Child's stool, six small toys
Towel Tug	•	•	•	•	•	•	•	•	•	•	•	•	•	•		•	•	Towel
Tummy Swimming		•	•	•	•	•	•	•	•		•	•	•	•	•		•	None
Walk with Me	•	•	•		•	•	•	•	•	•	•	•	•	•	•	•	•	None
Where's the Toy?	•	•	•	•		•	•	•	•		•	•	•	•		•	•	Small toy, shoe box
Wiggly Piggly	•			•			•	•	•	•	•	•	•	•		•	•	None

12

Athletic Activities
for One, Two, and You

Air Ball

Beanbag Basketball

Beginning Bubbles

Bitty Boxing

Block Towers

Bubble Hunting

Bunny Hopscotch

Cereal Drops

Chalk It Up

Clothespin Drops

Colorful Yarn Balls

Copy Me Clapping Hands

Dog Walk

Dough Balls

Dress Up

Fancy Finger Follies

Finger Painting

Finger Snaps

Floating Feathers

Giant Stomping

Googly Golf

Hallway Soccer

Heel-Toe Walking

Inchworm Races

Magazine Tear Art

Musical Hands

Nose Circles

Perky Penguin

Ping-Pong Bubble Bath

Pop Goes the Pillowcase Pal

Power Pull Toys

Quick Toy Grab

Rainbow Arms

Ready, Aim, Roll

Ring-Around-the-Rosy:
    Sitting Cross-Legged

Roller Ball

Silky Swirling Kites

Squishy Snips

Stringing Beads

Super Snow Angels

Tasty Tongue Twisters

Ten Little Jumping Beans

Three-Legged Dog

Tissue Crunch n' Toss

Up and Down

Wacky Waving

GAME: Air Ball

OBJECT: To improve fine and gross motor skills; eye-hand coordination; visual, spatial, and cognitive development; balance; quickness; fitness; leg strength; and brain stimulation.

SUPPLIES: An inflated balloon.

RULES OF PLAY: Use your hands to tap the balloon back and forth to your child. Options are counting the number of taps, singing a song while you play, or playing to your child's favorite music. If the balloon lands on the floor, pick it up and start over. For skill adaptation, increase or decrease the size of the inflated balloon.

LEVEL OF DIFFICULTY: Easy.

GAME: Beanbag Basketball

OBJECT: To improve fine and gross motor skills, eye-hand coordination, man-

ual dexterity, arm and shoulder range of motion, hand grasping, and visual, spatial, and brain development.

SUPPLIES: Six beanbags and a laundry basket.

RULES OF PLAY: Begin in a balanced standing position. Place a laundry basket about three feet from your child. The goal is to try to shoot or throw the beanbag into the basket. For skill adaptation, increase or decrease the shooting distance.

LEVEL OF DIFFICULTY: Easy.

GAME: Beginning Bubbles

OBJECT: To develop fine motor skills, eye-hand coordination, core strength, control of breath, balance, auditory processing, language acquisition, spatial awareness, depth perception, and visual and brain stimulation.

SUPPLIES: Bubble solution and a wand.

RULES OF PLAY: Sit on the floor, facing your child. Dip the wand into the bottle of bubble solution, then demonstrate how to take a deep breath from your lungs and blow a bubble. Repeat the preparation, then hold the wand in front of your child's mouth. Encourage him or her to blow air through the wand. For skill adaptation, practice blowing air out of the mouth against objects such as a facial tissue. Then transfer the skill to a bubble wand. Advanced levels can independently hold the wand.

LEVEL OF DIFFICULTY: Easy to moderate.

GAME: Bitty Boxing

OBJECT: To improve fine and gross motor skills, eye-hand coordination, fitness, depth perception, spatial awareness, bilateral hand use, and visual and cognitive development.

SUPPLIES: A beach ball, a large pillowcase, and a six-foot length of rope.

RULES OF PLAY: Place the ball inside the pillowcase and tie the rope around the open end. Tie the other end to a tree limb or any high horizontal object, such as a patio cover. The ball should be low enough for your child to easily reach. Show your child how to punch, tap, and hit the dangling ball with the left and right hands. For skill adaptation, place your child's hand on the stationary ball and push it into action. Advanced levels can try to hit the ball while the body is in motion.

LEVEL OF DIFFICULTY: Moderate to difficult.

GAME: Block Towers

OBJECT: To improve fine motor skills, eye-hand coordination, hand-grasping, spatial awareness, depth perception, visual development, and cognitive and spatial skills.

SUPPLIES: Six plastic *ABC* blocks.

RULES OF PLAY: Place your child in a safety seat or at a table. Play on a level surface, such as a table, tray, or hard floor. Encourage your child to create a two- to three-block tower, and then knock it down. For skill adaptation, increase or decrease the number of blocks in the tower.

LEVEL OF DIFFICULTY: Easy.

GAME: Bubble Hunting

OBJECT: To improve fine and gross motor skills, eye-hand and eye-foot coordination, visual and eye-tracking stimulation, midline crossing, footwork, quickness, jumping skills, and fitness.

SUPPLIES: Bubble solution and wand.

RULES OF PLAY: An adult can blow streams of bubbles into the air while the child chases them down and pops them. Two methods of bubble popping are recommended: clapping hands around the bubbles, which promotes eye-hand coordination and spatial development, and finger poking, which helps develop the small muscles of the fingers and hands. Variations include stepping on bubbles that have reached the ground. For skill adaptation, try swatting bubbles with one hand or stomping on them as they land on the ground. Advanced levels can include kicking bubbles in the air before they hit the ground.

LEVEL OF DIFFICULTY: Easy.

GAME: Bunny Hopscotch

OBJECT: To improve gross motor skills, eye-foot coordination; balance, jumping, quickness, leg strength, ankle flexibility; spatial awareness, depth perception, and visual and brain development.

SUPPLIES: Sidewalk chalk.

RULES OF PLAY: Use sidewalk chalk to create a hopscotch grid of eight squares. The squares should be at least twice as large as your child's feet. Number them from one to eight. First demonstrate the game using two-footed landings in each square. The goal is to learn to press the knees and feet together for takeoffs and landings. For skill adaptation, help your child walk through the squares, then try hopping with two feet using a staggered landing. Other options include holding your child's hands while he or she hops across the squares. Also, draw larger hopscotch squares.

LEVEL OF DIFFICULTY: Moderate.

GAME: Cereal Drops

OBJECT: To improve fine motor skills, eye-hand coordination, manual dexterity, hand-grasping and pincer grip movements, and visual and cognitive development.

SUPPLIES: Round or oval-shaped pieces of cereal, an empty bowl, and a clean empty egg carton.

RULES OF PLAY: Your child should be seated at a table. Pour cereal into a small bowl and give your child an empty egg carton. Encourage your child to pick up one piece of cereal at a time, using the pincer grip with the thumb and index finger, then drop it into the individual egg holes. Make it an educational game and introduce counting skills with each drop of cereal. After your child has placed one or two pieces of cereal into each egg hole, he or she can eat the same number of cereal pieces for a snack. For skill adaptation, use cereals that come in larger shapes for easier grasping and use muffin tins or larger bowls in place of egg cartons.

LEVEL OF DIFFICULTY: Easy.

GAME: Chalk It Up

OBJECT: To improve fine motor skills, eye-hand coordination, hand grasping, pre-writing skills, depth perception, visual development, spatial awareness, eye tracking, and brain stimulation.

SUPPLIES: Chalk, a chalkboard of any size, and an eraser or a wet paper towel.

RULES OF PLAY: Give your child a stick of chalk and demonstrate how to make lines on a chalkboard as well as how to make basic lines, dots, shapes, such as circles, triangles, squares, letters, numbers, happy faces, and people. Also show your child how to draw the infinity sign (∞) to improve brain activity and coordination. Helpful hints include actually guiding your child's hand when needed during the process. For skill adaptation, create dots for your child to connect to make shapes. Advanced levels should use the nondominant hand to draw.

LEVEL OF DIFFICULTY: Easy.

GAME: Clothespin Drops

OBJECT: To develop fine motor skills, eye-hand coordination, visual and spatial awareness, depth perception, pincer grasps, finger dexterity, and brain development.

SUPPLIES: A wide-mouthed bottle or bowl and clothespins or small craft sticks.

RULES OF PLAY: Your child should stand directly over a wide-mouth bottle and try to drop the objects into it. Hold the clothespin using the tripod grasp of the thumb and the first two fingers over the opening of the bottle. For skill adaptation, use a very wide bowl. To increase the level of difficulty, close one eye and make the drops. Then close the other eye and repeat the action.

LEVEL OF DIFFICULTY: Easy.

GAME: Colorful Yarn Balls

OBJECT: To develop fine motor skills, eye-hand coordination, the tripod grasp, eye tracking, depth perception, arm and shoulder range of motion, bilateral limb use, and brain development.

SUPPLIES: A small and colorful ball of yarn about two inches in diameter.

RULES OF PLAY: Your child should be in a sitting position on the floor. Place the ball of yarn about three feet in front of your child and place the end of the yarn in your baby's hand. Demonstrate how to use the thumb and fingers of the hand to grasp at the string. Try to use alternating hands to pull the string toward the body in a controlled manner. For skill adaptation, easier grasping includes holding the string with the fingers and palm. For a greater challenge, pull the string faster with a hand-over-hand action.

LEVEL OF DIFFICULTY: Difficult.

GAME: Copy Me Clapping Hands

OBJECT: To develop fine motor skills, eye-hand and eye-foot coordination, auditory skills, hand-clapping rhythm, and visual, auditory, memory, and brain stimulation.

SUPPLIES: None needed.

RULES OF PLAY: Create a fun eye-hand and auditory game of clapping patterns that are easy for your child to imitate. Examples of clapping patterns are: Easy: Clap, clap, pause, clap. Medium: Clap, clap, pause, clap, clap. Hard: Clap, clap, clap, pause, clap, clap, clap. Your child should be able to copy at least three to four claps in one pattern. As auditory memory improves, so will your child's ability to copy sounds. Variations include tapping hands to feet along with basic hand clapping patterns. For example, clap, clap, tap foot and clap. To adapt skills, reduce or increase the number of elements in a set.

LEVEL OF DIFFICULTY: Easy to moderate.

GAME: Dog Walk

OBJECT: To improve gross motor skills, eye-hand and eye-foot coordination, cross-crawl movement, shoulder range of motion, core strength; spatial awareness, visual acuity, and brain stimulation.

SUPPLIES: Lively music.

RULES OF PLAY: Get on all fours with your hands and feet (no knees) as you try to walk on the floor. Play follow-the-leader while you move around the room. For skill adaptation, allow your child to dog walk on the knees then gradually raise the legs to use hands and feet. Advanced levels can dog walk in circles, squares, *S* curves, or any random movement. Dog walk for speed and race to a finish line.

LEVEL OF DIFFICULTY: Easy.

GAME: Dough Balls

OBJECT: To improve fine motor development, eye-hand coordination, finger dexterity, arm range of motion, hand strength, and visual and brain stimulation.

SUPPLIES: Child's modeling dough, which can be purchased or homemade. (See appendix for recipe).

RULES OF PLAY: Place a tablespoon-size wad of modeling dough into the palm of your child's hand. Demonstrate how to rub the palms together in a circular motion to form the dough into a ball. Then let your child do it. For skill adaptation, prestart a dough ball and guide your child's hands through the motion of forming it into a round shape. Advanced levels can make several dough balls and press them together to create shapes such as snowmen, animals, or segmented insects like caterpillars. Also use the index finger to poke holes in the dough to create facial features.

LEVEL OF DIFFICULTY: Easy.

GAME: Dress Up

OBJECT: To improve fine motor skills, eye-hand and eye-foot coordination, manual dexterity, spatial abilities, depth perception, creativity, bilateral hand use, pincer grasp, and brain stimulation.

SUPPLIES: An assortment of play dress-up clothing for children, which can include costumes or discarded adult clothing and accessories such as dresses, hats, shoes, jewelry, jackets, and ties. Halloween costumes are also fun.

RULES OF PLAY: Collect various types of clothing for your child to wear in dramatic play. Invite your child to put on a performance pretending to be various characters in costume. For skill adaptation, use clothing that is easy to slip over the head and arms. Advanced play includes clothing with buttons, zippers, snaps, and tying bows.

LEVEL OF DIFFICULTY: Easy.

GAME: Fancy Finger Follies

OBJECT: To improve fine motor skills, eye-hand coordination, finger dexterity, flexibility, hand strength, spatial awareness, and brain development.

SUPPLIES: None needed.

RULES OF PLAY: Place your palms so they are facing each other. Match your fingers so the thumbs, index fingers, middle fingers, ring fingers, and pinkies of both hands touch one another. Push your fingertips against each other. Try to make shapes such as circles, ovals, triangles, and hearts. For skill adaptation, press the fingertips and heels of the hands or wrists together. Thumbs are not touching. Try to create a small opening between the hands, and then press the palms together to close the opening. Alternate between the two movements. Advanced skills include bending at the individual finger joints as the fingertips are pressed together.

LEVEL OF DIFFICULTY: Difficult.

GAME: Finger Painting

OBJECT: To improve fine motor skills, eye-hand coordination, finger strength and flexibility, creativity, and visual and brain stimulation.

SUPPLIES: Child-safe finger paint, disposable plastic plate, newspaper, and craft paper of any size.

RULES OF PLAY: Your child is in a seated position at a table or flat surface. Place newspaper on the painting area for protection. Also, your child should wear clothes that can get dirty or an adult-sized t-shirt as a painting smock. Pour a tablespoon of paint onto a plastic plate and place it in front of your child along with the paper. Have your child dip his or her index finger into the paint and smear it on the paper. Include a variety of colors for interesting designs. For skill adaptation, pour one color at a time on the plate.

LEVEL OF DIFFICULTY: Easy.

GAME: Finger Snaps (Isometric Finger Movements)

OBJECT: To improve fine motor skills, eye-hand coordination, finger dexterity, flexibility, hand strength, spatial awareness, and brain development.

SUPPLIES: None needed.

RULES OF PLAY: Teach your child how to snap fingers by placing your thumb and middle finger together so the pads of the fingertips are touching. Thrust your middle finger down. Your thumb ends up pointing upward while your middle finger taps the palm of your hand. For skill adaptation, guide your child's fingers through the snapping motion. For advanced skills try snapping fingers to music.

LEVEL OF DIFFICULTY: Difficult.

GAME: Floating Feathers

OBJECT: To develop fine motor skills, eye-hand and eye-foot coordination, eye-tracking spatial awareness, depth perception, fitness, agility, manual dexterity, and brain development.

SUPPLIES: Feathers of different sizes.

RULES OF PLAY: Toss a handful of feathers into the air and encourage your child to catch them before they reach the ground. You can blow on them in the air to create more movement and various falling patterns. For skill adaptation, use larger feathers and catch with two hands. For a greater challenge, use smaller feathers and catch with one hand.

LEVEL OF DIFFICULTY: Easy.

GAME: Giant Stomping

OBJECT: To improve gross motor skills, eye-foot coordination, balance, leg and core strength, spatial awareness, depth perception, eye tracking, and brain stimulation.

SUPPLIES: Lively music.

RULES OF PLAY: Slowly walk with long, large steps or lunges. Hold each step for two seconds. Have your child imitate your motions. The lunging action will strengthen the quadriceps muscles of the legs. Walk to the beat of the music. For skill adaptation, take smaller steps. For a greater challenge, take longer steps and hold for three to five seconds.

LEVEL OF DIFFICULTY: Easy.

GAME: Googly Golf

OBJECT: To improve fine and gross motor skills, eye-hand coordination, balance, finger dexterity, eye tracking, aiming toward targets, spatial awareness, depth perception, and cognitive thinking.

SUPPLIES: A child's small plastic golf club, tennis balls, and an empty wastebasket.

RULES OF PLAY: Place the wastebasket on its side a few feet from your child. Draw silly faces on the tennis balls with permanent markers and put them on the floor in front of your child's feet. Teach your child to hold the club with both hands on the grip. The right hand should be at the bottom of the grip for a right-hander, opposite for the left. (Avoid placing the hands directly on top of each other.) To putt, place the club head behind the ball and have your child tap it into the wastebasket. For skill adaptation, replace the wastebasket with a large cardboard box and use a larger foam ball. For a greater challenge, create a putting path with several buckets, wastebaskets, or empty tin cans.

LEVEL OF DIFFICULTY: Easy.

GAME: Hallway Soccer

OBJECT: To improve gross motor skills, eye-foot coordination, leg strength, balance, kicking abilities, eye tracking, spatial awareness, bilateral limb use, depth perception, fitness, and brain stimulation.

SUPPLIES: An inflatable beach ball and a laundry basket.

RULES OF PLAY: Place a laundry basket on its side at the end of a hallway. The opening should face your child to resemble a soccer goal. For beginners, have your child stand about four feet from the goal. Place the ball in front of your child's foot and demonstrate how the foot makes contact with the ball using the arch or instep of the foot. Direct the ball into the basket. Repeat. For skill adaptation, increase or decrease the distance between your child and the laundry basket.

LEVEL OF DIFFICULTY: Easy.

GAME: Heel-Toe Walking

OBJECT: To develop gross motor skills, eye-foot coordination, balance, flexibility, spatial awareness, depth perception, auditory processing, and brain stimulation.

SUPPLIES: None needed.

RULES OF PLAY: Try to walk in a straight line with your feet connecting on every step as closely as possible. Place your arms out at the sides like a gymnast on a balance beam. For skill adaptation, draw wide lines and mark the spots the heels could touch the ground. Other tips include holding your child's hands for guidance. For a higher level of difficulty, have your child walk in a circle, square, or *S* curve.

LEVEL OF DIFFICULTY: Easy.

GAME: Inchworm Races

OBJECT: To improve gross motor skills, core strength, leg and hip flexibility, and spatial awareness, visual development, and brain stimulation.

SUPPLIES: Lively music.

RULES OF PLAY: Sit on the floor with your legs straight out in front. Your body looks like the letter *L*, and your back is tall. Lift one leg from your hip to your toes and move it forward an inch. Then lift the other leg and move it forward an inch. This action is similar to walking on your buttocks. Have your child imitate your actions, moving forward until the music stops. For skill adaptation, instead of lifting the leg, encourage your child to push or scoot the entire leg on the floor in a forward direction. For advanced skills, try inchworm racing.

LEVEL OF DIFFICULTY: Easy.

GAME: Magazine Tear Art

OBJECT: To improve fine motor skills, eye-hand coordination, finger dexterity, hand grasping, creativity, gluing and art design, spatial skills, depth perception, language acquisition, and visual and cognitive awareness.

SUPPLIES: A collection of magazines, catalogs, newspapers, and advertisements, a glue stick, and a piece of construction paper.

RULES OF PLAY: Help your child find interesting photographs of toys, sporting activities, people, household items, and landscapes in magazines, newspapers, and advertisements. Demonstrate for your child how to tear out the pictures that are of interest to him or her using the thumb and index and middle fingers. Paper torn in any shape would be considered a success. Finally, help your child glue them onto a piece of art paper to make a collage. For skill adaptation, guide your child's hands during the tearing process.

LEVEL OF DIFFICULTY: Easy.

GAME: Musical Hands

OBJECT: To develop fine motor skills; eye-hand coordination; auditory, memory, and brain stimulation; finger dexterity; and musical abilities.

SUPPLIES: Your child's favorite music.

RULES OF PLAY: Select up to three of your child's favorite songs and clap to the beat of the music. Do it with your child to help identify and demonstrate the rhythm. For skill adaptation, select songs with simple rhythms that are easily recognized.

LEVEL OF DIFFICULTY: Easy.

GAME: Nose Circles

OBJECT: To improve head and neck strength and flexibility, spatial awareness, depth perception, midline crossing, auditory processing, language development, and brain stimulation.

SUPPLIES: One crayon per person.

RULES OF PLAY: Stand in a balanced position facing your child. Demonstrate by pretending your finger is a crayon and place it on the end of your nose. The tip of your finger extends outward to help your child visualize writing in the air. Draw dots, lines, and circles with your nose "crayon." Remember to turn your head to the right and left, and drop your chin to your chest and up again. If your child knows the letters in his or her name, try to write them. For skill adaptation, hold a piece of paper in front of your child's face with drawings of the shapes or letters to make nose circles. Make the shapes as large as possible.

LEVEL OF DIFFICULTY: Difficult.

GAME: Perky Penguin

OBJECT: To develop gross motor skills, eye-foot coordination, balance flexibility, footwork, fitness, leg and ankle strength, spatial awareness, and brain development.

SUPPLIES: Lively music.

RULES OF PLAY: Begin in a standing balanced position with your legs and heels pressed together. Your toes are turned out to the sides to form the letter *V.* Waddle like a penguin to your child's favorite music. Have your child imitate your actions. For skill adaptation, allow your child's heels to separate when walking. Strive for a loosely formed *V* shape with his or her feet.

LEVEL OF DIFFICULTY: Easy.

GAME: Ping-Pong Bubble Bath

OBJECT: To develop fine motor skills, eye-hand coordination, hand grasping, bilateral hand use, spatial awareness, depth perception, eye tracking, and visual and brain stimulation.

SUPPLIES: A new or clean fishnet used for aquariums, about six table tennis balls, and bubble bath solution.

RULES OF PLAY: Fill a bath with lukewarm water and bubble bath solution. When the tub is about one-quarter full, place your child into the water for game time. Hand your child a clean fishnet, and randomly toss about six ping-pong balls into the bath. The challenge is to scoop them out using only the fishnet. Repeat several times. For skill adaptation, use a large fishnet and draw random designs on the balls with permanent marker for better visibility.

LEVEL OF DIFFICULTY: Easy to moderate.

GAME: Pop Goes the Pillowcase Pal

OBJECT: To develop fine and gross motor skills, eye-hand coordination, manual dexterity, hand grasping, arm and shoulder range of motion, visual development, auditory processing, language development, and brain stimulation.

SUPPLIES: A twin-size pillowcase, and approximately six small stuffed animals or toys.

RULES OF PLAY: Fill a pillowcase with about a half dozen small stuffed animals or toys, tie a loose knot at the top, and place it in the middle of the floor. All players begin in a balanced standing position and walk or dance around the pillowcase. Sing the song "Pop Goes the Weasel," and dance, move, hop, or jump to the music. Be sure to move the arms, shoulders, and torso. When the song reaches the last line, your child gets to pick up the pillowcase, untie the knot, and pull out a pal. Instead of finishing with the word *weasel* to end the song, replace it with the name of the pillowcase pal. For example, "Pop goes the (monkey, teddy bear, bird, etc.)." Retie the knot and continue until the pillowcase is empty. When the game is over, teach your child one fact about each animal, such as habitat, physical description, size, or food preferences. For skill adaptation, do not tie a knot in the top of the pillowcase.

LEVEL OF DIFFICULTY: Easy.

RHYME: *Pop Goes the Weasel (Mother Goose)*

All around the cobbler's bench,

The monkey chased the weasel.

The monkey thought 'twas all in fun,

Pop goes the . . . (name the item pulled out from the pillowcase).

GAME: Power Pull Toys

OBJECT: To improve fine and gross motor skills, eye-hand and eye-foot coordination, hand grasping, spatial awareness, eye tracking, depth perception, balance, bilateral limb use, and brain stimulation.

SUPPLIES: A favorite pull toy on a string.

RULES OF PLAY: Have your child try a variety of gross motor movements such as walking, hopping, jumping or runnig while guiding a pull toy. Demonstrate for your child how to hold the end of the string with the tripod grasp, which uses the thumb and index and middle fingers. Have fun as you move in lines, circles or other fun shapes. Try playing pull-toy races or creating a path of chalk on cement for your child to follow, similar to a road or race track. Your child should alternate using the right and left hands for string pulling. For skill adaptation, grasp the string with the entire fist or loosely tie the string around your child's wrist.

LEVEL OF DIFFICULTY: Easy.

GAME: Quick Toy Grab

OBJECT: To improve fine motor skills, eye-hand coordination, depth perception, balance, eye tracking, language acquisition, hand grasping, quickness, arm and shoulder strength, and brain stimulation.

SUPPLIES: Three small toys such as stuffed animals, cars, or blocks.

RULES OF PLAY: Sit on the floor facing your child. Place the toys behind your back and offer one to your child. When he or she grabs the toy in one hand, display a second toy and extend it to your child's free hand. Finally, bring out the third toy and dangle it to create excitement. Your child will probably drop one toy to reach for the new toy. Quickly pick up the dropped toy and offer it again before your child gets attached to any particular object. For skill adaptation, decrease or increase the pace of the game.

LEVEL OF DIFFICULTY: Moderate.

GAME: Rainbow Arms

OBJECT: To improve gross motor skills, eye-hand coordination, arm strength, shoulder range of motion, fitness, flexibility, eye tracking, auditory processing, language development, and brain stimulation.

SUPPLIES: None needed.

RULES OF PLAY: Begin in a standing balanced position. Your arms are out at your sides at shoulder height. Pretend there are rainbows of colorful crayons at the tips of your fingers. Draw circles, squares, triangles, and various shapes with your "crayon" arms. Now pretend to paint the sky with lots of colors. Have your child imitate your actions. Make it a game as you draw a picture, shape, design, or a letter, and ask your child to guess its name. For skill adaptation, decrease or increase the size of the rainbow air drawing. It is also helpful if you are both facing the same direction.

LEVEL OF DIFFICULTY: Easy.

GAME: Ready, Aim, Roll

OBJECT: To improve fine motor skills, eye-hand coordination, manual dexterity, hand control, pincer grasp, spatial awareness, depth perception, eye tracking, and brain development.

SUPPLIES: A long cardboard mailing tube or an empty gift-wrap roll, a plastic bowl or bucket, and about ten small Wiffle golf balls.

RULES OF PLAY: Your child should pick up a golf ball with one hand while holding the tube with the other. Insert the ball inside the tube and aim it into the bucket. Count the number of balls that make it into the target. For skill adaptation, decrease or increase the length of the tube and the distance to the bowl or bucket.

LEVEL OF DIFFICULTY: Easy.

GAME: Ring-Around-the-Rosy: Sitting Cross-Legged

OBJECT: To develop fine and gross motor skills, overall balance, arm flexibility, core strength, hand grasping, shoulder range of motion, and brain development.

SUPPLIES: None needed.

RULES OF PLAY: Sit cross-legged on the floor facing your child. Your knees should be touching your child's knees. Hold hands and sway side to side or back and forth as you sing the nursery rhyme "Ring-Around-the-Rosy." Use gradual leaning movements of a few inches and increase the degree of the lean as your child's hip balance improves. On the last line of the song purposely fall sideways for fun. Repeat several times. For skill adaptation, shorten or lengthen the sideways lean with your child.

LEVEL OF DIFFICULTY: Easy.

LYRICS: *Ring-Around-the-Rosy*
> Ring around the rosy,
> A pocketful of posies,
> A-tishoo! A-tishoo!
> We all fall down!

GAME: Roller Ball

OBJECT: To improve fine motor skills, eye-hand coordination, finger dexterity, ball catching, eye tracking, arm control, auditory processing, visual stimulation, and brain development.

SUPPLIES: A soft playground ball at least six inches in diameter.

RULES OF PLAY: Sit on the floor facing your child with your legs opened up similar to the letter *V*. The bottom of your feet should be touching the bottom of your child's feet. Gently roll the ball on the floor toward your child. Demonstrate catching skills, which include opening the hands before the ball arrives and closing them around the ball on contact. Try to roll the ball a little to the left and right. Play for about ten to twenty catches. For skill adaptation, use a smaller or larger ball.

LEVEL OF DIFFICULTY: Easy.

GAME: Silky Swirling Kites

OBJECT: To develop fine and gross motor skills, eye-hand coordination, manual dexterity, hand grasping, arm and shoulder development, fitness, balance, and overall brain development.

SUPPLIES: Two scarves, two twelve-inch rulers, and masking, packing or duct tape.

RULES OF PLAY: To prepare the swirl sticks, use duct tape to attach a scarf to the end of a stick. You will need two swirl sticks per person. After making a swirl stick, have your child hold the end of the stick and move it in geometric shapes such as circles, ovals, and figure eights to make visual designs in the air with the swirling scarves. For skill adaptation, use a smaller scarf. Advanced skills include using two swirl sticks, one in each hand, to make dual air designs.

LEVEL OF DIFFICULTY: Easy.

GAME: Squishy Snips (Cutting Dough)

OBJECT: To improve fine motor skills, eye-hand coordination, cutting skills, finger dexterity, bilateral hand use, depth perception, spatial awareness, arm control, eye tracking, and brain stimulation.

SUPPLIES: Child's homemade playing dough (see appendix for recipe).

RULES OF PLAY: Teach your child to scoop a tablespoon of dough and roll it between the palms of the hands in an up-and-down motion to make a cylindrical snake-like shape. Show your child how to use the index and middle fingers to pretend to cut like scissors. The action is to open and close the fingers. Repeat until the snake is "finger" cut into many little pieces. For skill adaptation, make larger dough snakes and help your child with the finger movements.

LEVEL OF DIFFICULTY: Difficult.

GAME: Stringing Beads

OBJECT: To improve fine motor skills, eye-hand coordination, manual dexterity, pincer grasps, depth perception, eye tracking, spatial awareness, balance, and brain development.

SUPPLIES: Large child-safe colorful beads, an eighteen-inch length of string or yarn, and a child's blunt plastic needle. In place of a needle, wrap the end of the yarn or string with a small amount of transparent tape to create a stiff and pointy tip.

RULES OF PLAY: Pour the beads into a cereal bowl. Tie off one bead on the string about four inches from one end to prevent the beads from falling off. Then encourage your child to hold the needle or taped end using the pincer grasp. Use the other hand to hold the bead. Now place the needle through the hole in the bead to make a necklace. Design patterns of colors. Try switching hands for bilateral coordination. For skill adaptation, use larger beads with wider holes. Store supplies safely out of your child's reach, and supervise game play.

LEVEL OF DIFFICULTY: Difficult.

GAME: Super Snow Angels

OBJECT: To improve gross motor skills, eye-hand and eye-foot coordination, bilateral arm and leg movement, core strength, flexibility, spatial awareness, and brain development.

SUPPLIES: None needed.

RULES OF PLAY: Lie on your back on the floor, with your arms down by your sides and your legs pressed together. Pretend you are lying in the snow. Move your arms up to meet above your head and spread your legs wide. Then bring your arms back down to your sides and your legs back together. Have your child imitate this movement. This action develops the coordination for doing jumping jacks. For skill adaptation, stand over your child and guide his or her arms. Advanced snow angels can move quickly and independently while singing the alphabet song.

LEVEL OF DIFFICULTY: Easy.

GAME: Tasty Tongue Twisters

OBJECT: To improve head, neck, and facial muscles as well as jaw and tongue strength and flexibility necessary for articulate speaking.

SUPPLIES: Small candy-type cake decorations available at most markets.

RULES OF PLAY: Try to capture the candy using only your tongue. Place a small candy cake decoration such as a colorful dot, flower, or sprinkle above your child's upper lip. It will stick to the skin. Encourage using only the tongue to reach up and scoop the candy into the mouth. Next place sprinkles, one at a time, to the right and left sides of the mouth and below the lower lip. Wet the back of the candy with water to help it stick to the skin. For skill adaptation, use smaller or larger sprinkles, or apply a dab of peanut butter.

LEVEL OF DIFFICULTY: Easy.

GAME: Ten Little Jumping Beans

OBJECT: To improve gross motor development, eye-hand and eye-foot coordination, bilateral leg use, spatial awareness, depth perception, strength, flexibility, quickness, language development, auditory processing, and visual and brain stimulation.

SUPPLIES: None needed.

RULES OF PLAY: Start in a balanced standing position facing your child. Demonstrate how to bend your knees at the beginning of the jump using the legs, torso, body, and arms to push off the ground. Jump often as you recite the rhyme. For skill adaptation, place your hands under your child's arms at his or her torso for full guidance. Medium support involves holding your child's hands. An advanced jumping bean requires no help.

SUGGESTED RHYME: *Ten Little Jumping Beans*
(To the tune of *Ten Little Indians*)
One little, two little, three little jumping beans
Four little, five little, six little jumping beans
Seven little, eight little, nine little jumping beans
Ten little jumping beans . . . up you go! (*Double jump up.*)
(Now backwards)

Ten little, nine little, eight little jumping beans
Seven little, six little, five little jumping beans
Four little, three little, two little jumping beans,
One little jumping bean . . . way down low! (*Touch the ground.*)[1]

GAME: Three-Legged Dog

OBJECT: To improve gross motor skills; cross-crawl movement; shoulder, back, and core strength; shoulder range of motion, eye-hand and eye-foot coordination; balance; flexibility; fitness; and brain development.

SUPPLIES: Lively music.

RULES OF PLAY: Pretend to be a three-legged dog and play games while wiggling on all threes with two hands and one foot. Start on the floor on all fours with your hands and feet on the ground. Then lift one leg and hold it up in the air. Now try wiggling your body parts such as the head, shoulders, bottom, and extended leg while balancing on the hands and only one leg. Switch legs and repeat this balancing game. For skill adaptation, assist your child by supporting the torso at the back or waist during movement for better balance.

LEVEL OF DIFFICULTY: Difficult.

GAME: Tissue Crunch 'n' Toss

OBJECT: To improve fine and gross motor skills, eye-hand and eye-foot coordination, finger dexterity, hand grasping, balance, flexibility, eye tracking, depth perception, spatial awareness, catching skills, and brain development.

SUPPLIES: Tissue paper.

RULES OF PLAY: Offer your child several sheets of tissue paper and demonstrate how to crumple them into small colorful balls. Then play underhand toss and catch with them. Use both hands to toss the paper balls for total brain stimulation. Throw out the paper when you are finished with the game. For skill adaptation, make smaller or larger tissue paper balls and increase or decrease the tossing distance.

LEVEL OF DIFFICULTY: Easy.

GAME: Up and Down

OBJECT: To develop gross motor skills, balance, core strength, leg control, quickness, jumping ability, auditory processing, language development, right and left directional awareness, and brain development.

SUPPLIES: None needed.

RULES OF PLAY: Begin in balanced standing position. Demonstrate for your child how to follow the lyrics of the rhyme. Try holding your child's hands as you both jump to the right and left, up and down, and sideways with balance and control. For skill adaptation, slow down or increase the pace of the rhyme. If jumping is too difficult for your child, try walking or marching and later advance to hopping or jumping.

LEVEL OF DIFFICULTY: Easy.

Rhyme	**Action**
(Recite slowly)	
This is to the right of me	*Step or jump to the right*
This is to the left of me	*Step or jump to the left*

Rhyme	Action
This is above me	*Jump up to the sky*
And this is below.	*Squat down to the ground*
Jump right and left	*Jump right and left*
Jump right and left	*Jump high to the sky*
Up again, and down we go.	*Bend down to touch the ground[2]*

GAME: Wacky Waving

OBJECT: To develop fine motor skills, eye-hand coordination, wrist flexibility, and arm hand strength, right and left directional awareness, and brain development.

SUPPLIES: Lively music

RULES OF PLAY: Begin in sitting position next to your child. Gently hold your child's right hand in your own. Slowly, straighten the fingers and bend the wrist forward toward the inside forearm and elbow. Hold a gentle stretch for about five seconds. Now open the palm up to the sky. Hold the stretch. Move the wrist in circles. Switch and stretch the left wrist. For skill adaptation, modify the pace and range of motion of the stretch. Safety alert: never force a movement beyond your child's physical limitation.

LEVEL OF DIFFICULTY: Easy

Athletic Activities for One, Two, and You	Fine Motor	Gross Motor	Arms & Shoulders	Hands & Fingers	Legs & Feet	Core Strength	Balance	Cognitive & Brain	Flexibility	Quickness	Visual	Spatial Awareness	Depth Perception	Eye-Hand	Eye-Foot	Midline Crossing	Bilateral Limb	Supplies
Air Ball	•	•	•	•	•	•	•	•	•	•		•	•	•		•	•	Balloon
Beanbag Baseball	•	•	•	•	•		•		•	•		•	•	•	•		•	Six beanbags, laundry basket
Beginning Bubbles	•	•		•		•	•	•	•			•	•	•		•	•	Bubble solution, wand
Bitty Boxing		•	•		•		•	•	•	•	•	•	•	•		•	•	Beach ball, pillowcase, rope
Block Towers	•	•	•	•		•	•	•	•	•	•	•	•	•		•	•	Six toy blocks
Bubble Hunting	•	•	•	•	•	•	•	•	•	•	•	•	•	•	•	•	•	Bubble solution, wand
Bunny Hopscotch		•			•	•	•	•	•	•					•		•	Sidewalk chalk
Cereal Drops	•	•	•	•		•	•	•	•	•	•	•	•	•		•	•	Cereal, bowl, empty egg carton
Chalk It Up	•		•	•		•	•	•		•	•	•	•	•		•	•	Sidewalk chalk
Clothespin Drops	•	•	•	•	•	•	•	•	•	•	•	•	•	•		•	•	Clothespins or craft sticks, wide-mouth bottle
Colorful Yarn Balls	•		•	•		•	•	•	•	•	•	•	•	•		•	•	Colorful yarn balls
Copy Me Clapping Hands	•	•	•	•		•	•	•	•	•	•	•	•	•	•	•	•	None
Dog Walk	•	•	•	•	•	•	•	•	•	•	•	•	•	•		•	•	Lively music
Dough Balls	•		•	•		•	•	•	•	•	•	•	•	•		•	•	Modeling dough
Dress Up	•	•	•	•		•	•	•	•	•	•	•	•	•		•	•	Dress up clothes
Fancy Finger Follies	•		•	•		•	•	•	•	•	•	•	•	•		•	•	None

Athletic Activities for One, Two, and You	Fine Motor	Gross Motor	Arms & Shoulders	Hands & Fingers	Legs & Feet	Core Strength	Balance	Cognitive & Brain	Flexibility	Quickness	Visual	Spatial Awareness	Depth Perception	Eye-Hand	Eye-Foot	Midline Crossing	Bilateral Limb	Supplies
Finger Painting	•		•	•			•	•			•	•	•	•		•	•	Paper, child-safe paint
Finger Snaps	•		•	•			•	•	•	•	•	•	•	•		•	•	None
Floating Feathers	•	•	•	•	•	•	•	•	•	•	•	•	•	•	•	•	•	Craft feathers
Giant Stomping		•	•		•	•	•	•	•		•	•	•	•		•	•	Lively music
Googly Golf	•	•	•	•	•	•	•	•	•	•	•	•	•	•		•	•	Child's golf clubs, tennis balls, small waste basket
Hallway Soccer		•			•	•	•	•	•	•	•	•	•		•	•	•	Beach ball, laundry basket
Heel-Toe Walking		•			•	•	•	•	•		•	•	•		•	•	•	None
Inchworm Races		•			•	•	•	•	•	•	•	•	•		•		•	Lively music
Magazine Tear Art	•		•	•		•	•	•	•	•	•	•	•	•		•	•	Magazines, glue, paper
Musical Hands	•		•	•		•		•			•	•	•	•		•	•	Lively music
Nose Circles		•				•	•	•			•	•	•			•		None
Perky Penguin		•	•	•	•	•	•	•	•	•	•	•	•		•		•	Lively music
Ping-Pong Bubble Bath	•		•	•		•		•			•	•	•	•	•		•	Fishnet, table tennis balls, bubble bath solution
Pop Goes the Pillowcase Pal	•	•	•	•	•	•		•		•	•	•	•	•	•	•	•	Pillowcase, stuffed animals
Power Pull Toys	•	•	•	•	•	•	•	•	•	•	•	•	•	•	•		•	Pull toy on a string
Quick Toy Grab	•	•	•	•	•	•	•	•		•	•	•	•	•		•	•	Three small toys
Rainbow Arms	•		•	•		•	•	•	•		•	•	•	•	•	•	•	None
Ready, Aim, Roll	•	•	•	•			•	•	•		•	•	•	•		•	•	Cardboard tube, plastic bowl, small wiffle balls

Athletic Activities for One, Two, and You	Fine Motor	Gross Motor	Arms & Shoulders	Hands & Fingers	Legs & Feet	Core Strength	Balance	Cognitive & Brain	Flexibility	Quickness	Visual	Spatial Awareness	Depth Perception	Eye-Hand	Eye-Foot	Midline Crossing	Bilateral Limb	Supplies
Ring-Around-the-Rosy: Sitting Cross-Legged		•	•	•	•	•	•	•	•	•	•	•		•	•	•	•	None
Roller Ball	•		•	•		•	•	•		•	•	•	•	•	•		•	Soft playground ball
Silky Swirling Kites	•	•	•	•	•	•	•	•	•	•	•	•	•	•		•	•	Two scarves, rulers, and duct tape
Squishy Snips	•	•	•	•		•		•	•	•	•	•	•	•		•	•	Modeling dough
Stringing Beads	•	•	•		•	•	•	•	•	•	•	•	•	•		•	•	Child-safe beads, string, tape
Super Snow Angels		•	•	•	•	•	•		•			•	•	•	•	•	•	None
Tasty Tongue Twisters	•					•	•	•	•		•	•	•			•		Small candy cake sprinkles
Ten Little Jumping Beans		•	•		•	•	•	•	•	•	•	•	•		•		•	None
Three-Legged Dog		•	•	•	•	•	•	•	•	•	•	•	•	•	•	•	•	None
Tissue Crunch 'n' Toss	•	•	•	•	•	•	•	•	•	•	•	•	•	•	•	•	•	Tissue paper
Up and Down	•	•	•	•	•	•	•	•	•	•	•	•	•	•	•		•	None
Wacky Waving	•		•	•		•		•	•	•	•	•		•			•	None

13

Building Blocks for Three-Year-Olds

Air Balloon Volleyball

Basketball Trash Pick-Up

Beach Ball Soccer

Beanbag Bombs

Beanbag Parade

Bicycling Babe

Big Bunny Hops:
    Standing Long Jumps

Body Parts: All About Me

Bottle Bowling

Broom Ball

Bubble Tennis

Colored Muffin Balls

Copy Me Clapping Body

Cutting Colorful Lines

Dog Dancing

Donkey Kicks

Dynamic Matchups

Edible ABCs

Eggroll-Overs

Elbows in Action

Fancy Flamingo

Fingerball Toss

Fingertip Dot Painting

Foam Ball Fun: Toss and Catch

Frog Hops

Giraffe Steps: Long Lunges

Heel and Toe: On the Line You Go

Ice Cube Basketball

Ice Skating, Ice Plating

Kangaroo Ball Taps

Kangaroo Jumps

Lots of Knots

Marshmallow Pops

Masterful Marching

Mirror, Mimes, and Super Shadows

Ping-Pong Up and Down

Pogo Pops:

    Two-Footed Jumping in Place

Ring-Around-the-Rosy:

    Walking and Hopping

Rockin' Sockin' Freeze Dance

Rolling Around the World

Skip with Me

Sticker Puppets

Tennis Hockey

Throw and Catch

Tiny Toe Art

Tiptoe Toddlers

Triangle Snippets

Tunnel Torpedoes

Twirly Birds

Two-Square Sidewalk Style

Wacky Ring Toss

Wheelbarrow Walks

GAME: Air Balloon Volleyball

   OBJECT: To develop fine and gross motor skills, eye-hand coordination, eye tracking, balance, quickness, volleyball fundamentals, depth perception, spatial awareness, and brain and visual stimulation.

   SUPPLIES: An inflated balloon about eight inches in diameter.

RULES OF PLAY: Pass the balloon back and forth with a partner using volleyball fundamentals. Your child should start in a balanced, ready position with his or her feet shoulder-width apart and the hands down at the sides. Extend your arms in front of the body. The palms of both hands are facing upward. Place the back of one hand onto the palm of the other. Keep them pressed together through the motion. Your arms will form the letter *V*. The key is to maintain straight arms to create a *platform*, which is the area above the wrist and below the elbow. Direct the balloon using the forearm platform back to your partner with a *bump pass*. For skill adaptation, place the balloon directly on your child's platform, and encourage him to hit the balloon. Also, decrease or increase the playing distance between you and your child.

LEVEL OF DIFFICULTY: Difficult.

GAME: Basketball Trash Pick-Up

OBJECT: To improve fine motor skills, eye-hand coordination, depth perception, spatial awareness, ball-throwing and eye-tracking development, and visual and brain stimulation.

SUPPLIES: An empty household trash can and paper, which will be scrunched into balls.

RULES OF PLAY: Shoot baskets with wads of paper into a regular trash can. Begin by gathering any type of paper and scrunch it into about a dozen palm-sized balls. At first your child should stand a few feet from the basket and try to toss the balls into the trash can. Repeat often and count the number of baskets. For skill adaptation, decrease or increase the tossing distance.

LEVEL OF DIFFICULTY: Easy.

GAME: Beach Ball Soccer

OBJECT: To improve gross motor skills, eye-foot coordination, kicking abilities, soccer fundamentals, bilateral leg use, depth perception, fitness, spatial awareness, and visual and brain stimulation.

SUPPLIES: A beach ball inflated to about eight inches in diameter.

RULES OF PLAY: Blow up the beach ball and kick or pass it back and forth with your child. Start a few feet apart and gradually increase the distance. Encourage your child to use both the right and left feet to direct the ball. The balance and support during this action is on the nonkicking leg. Make it a game by counting the number of successful kicks, or recite the alphabet while you play. For skill adaptation, decrease or increase the kicking distance to your child.

LEVEL OF DIFFICULTY: Easy.

GAME: Beanbag Bombs

OBJECT: To improve fine and gross motor skills, eye-hand coordination, hand grasping, arm strength, shoulder range of motion, target practice, bilateral limb use, eye tracking, spatial skills, depth perception, balance, flexibility, and brain development.

SUPPLIES: Six beanbags and one beach ball.

RULES OF PLAY: Begin in a balanced standing position. Place an inflated beach ball about two feet in front of your child in a hallway. Hand your child a beanbag and encourage him or her to use an overhand throwing motion to hit the beach ball. The goal is to move the ball forward a distance of about six to ten feet. For skill adaptation, decrease or increase the tossing distance to the beach ball.

LEVEL OF DIFFICULTY: Difficult.

GAME: Beanbag Parade

OBJECT: To develop gross motor skills, eye-hand and eye-foot coordination, good posture, balance, spatial awareness, depth perception, and visual and brain stimulation.

SUPPLIES: Several small beanbags, approximately four inches in size, and lively music.

RULES OF PLAY: March in a parade in which your child balances beanbags on his or her head, shoulders, and arms to teach balance and coordination. For skill adaptation, limit the number of beanbags to one on the head and one in each palm, or challenge your child by placing several on the shoulders, palms, or the backs of the hands.

LEVEL OF DIFFICULTY: Moderate.

GAME: Bicycling Babe

OBJECT: To improve gross motor development, eye-foot coordination, bilateral limb use, eye tracking, leg and hip range of motion, spatial awareness, strength, flexibility, auditory processing, language acquisition, and visual and brain stimulation.

SUPPLIES: Music.

RULES OF PLAY: Begin by placing your child on his back on a soft and safe surface. Sit in front of your child and turn on background music. Wrap your hands around your child's feet, one foot in each hand. The action is to pump the right leg and knee up to the belly button while you straighten the left leg. Then bring the left foot and knee up while you straighten the right leg. For skill adaptation, break the movement into several segments and slowly rotate the legs. Advanced levels can independently bicycle the legs as fast as possible.

LEVEL OF DIFFICULTY: Easy.

GAME: Big Bunny Hops: Standing Long Jumps

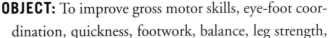

OBJECT: To improve gross motor skills, eye-foot coordination, quickness, footwork, balance, leg strength, jumping abilities, spatial awareness, and visual and brain stimulation.

SUPPLIES: None needed.

RULES OF PLAY: Pretend to be a bunny rabbit and leap forward in a very long jump using one or two-footed landing. Begin in a balanced, ready position with your feet close together. Bend your knees into a squat and bring both arms behind the body similar to a downhill skier. Now swing your arms to the front as you leap upward and forward. Repeat several times and measure your jumping distance. For skill adaptation, allow for a two-footed staggered landing. Other options are to decrease or increase your child's jumping goals.

LEVEL OF DIFFICULTY: Easy.

GAME: Body Parts: All About Me

OBJECT: To improve fine and gross motor skills, eye-hand coordination, balance, memory, auditory processing, and visual, spatial, and brain development.

SUPPLIES: None needed.

RULES OF PLAY: Recite the rhyme with your child and identify body parts as they are mentioned in the song. Begin in a balanced position facing your child. Your hands are down at your sides. Slowly sing the song and point to the corresponding body parts while your child follows your lead. For skill adaptation, guide your child's hand to tap body parts mentioned in the song. To increase the challenge, close your eyes as you play.

LEVEL OF DIFFICULTY: Easy.

RHYME: *All About Me*

>These are my hands, and this is my nose.
>Here are my knees, and I touch my toes.
>Look at my arms that stretch out wide.
>When I open my mouth, I see teeth inside.
>
>Here is my tongue that helps me eat.
>This is my bottom where I find my seat.
>Here are my fingers that help me play.
>I use my feet to walk each day.[1]

GAME: Bottle Bowling

OBJECT: To improve fine and gross motor development, balance, eye-hand and eye-foot coordination, depth perception, spatial awareness, underhand ball-rolling skills, and visual and brain stimulation.

SUPPLIES: Collect about ten empty two-liter soda bottles, sand or water, and a playground ball about four inches in diameter. The ball should be small enough for your child to hold with one hand.

RULES OF PLAY: Play a game of backyard bowling by knocking down soda bottles. Prepare the game by pouring about one inch of sand or water into each of the bottles for stability. Line them up in a triangular shape similar to bowling pins. Your child should stand a few feet away from the bottle pins. Use an underhand rolling motion to knock down the bottles. Keep rolling until all the pins fall down. Make a math game of counting the number of pins knocked down each turn. Keep track of the points. For skill adaptation, stand closer or farther away from the pins or increase the size of the ball.

LEVEL OF DIFFICULTY: Easy.

GAME: Broom Ball

OBJECT: To improve fine and gross motor skills, eye-hand and eye-foot coordination, hand strength, bilateral arm and leg use, midline crossing, quickness, footwork, balance, target practice, and visual and brain development.

SUPPLIES: One broom per person, a cardboard box, and a playground ball about six to eight inches in diameter.

RULES OF PLAY: Use the broom to sweep or strike the ball into a large open box resting on its side. Your child should hold the broom with two hands and stand sideways to the ball, which is located on the floor next to his or her feet. When making contact with the ball, keep the head down and have the eyes follow the ball's movement into the box. For skill adaptation, use a larger or smaller ball.

LEVEL OF DIFFICULTY: Easy.

GAME: Bubble Tennis

OBJECT: To develop fine and gross motor skills, eye-hand and eye-foot coordination, eye-tracking movement, spatial awareness, balance, quickness, depth perception, and brain development.

SUPPLIES: Bubble solution, a bubble wand, and a clean flyswatter.

RULES OF PLAY: Begin by blowing bubbles into the air and encourage your child to hit them with the flyswatter. Count the number of bubbles that make contact with the flyswatter. For skill adaptation, decrease or increase the number of bubbles. Other options are to thicken the flyswatter handle by wrapping it with paper and masking tape for easier hand grasping.

LEVEL OF DIFFICULTY: Easy.

GAME: Colored Muffin Balls

OBJECT: To improve fine motor skills; eye-hand coordination; finger dexterity; color identification; pincer grasping; memory; and visual, spatial, and brain development.

SUPPLIES: You will need several pieces of colored paper of any size and baking tins that hold a dozen muffins.

RULES OF PLAY: Tear up dozens of pieces of various colored paper using the thumbs and fingers of both hands. Wad them up. Take turns sorting them by color and size, and place them into the different muffin forms. This is a great visual game to teach your child about size and color. For skill adaptation, decrease or increase the colored paper choices and the sizes and shapes of the paper wads.

LEVEL OF DIFFICULTY: Easy.

GAME: Copy Me Clapping Body

OBJECT: To develop fine and gross motor skills; arm, shoulder, neck, and core strength; cross-crawling movement; memory; spatial awareness; flexibility; eye-hand and eye-foot coordination; and visual and brain development.

SUPPLIES: Lively music.

RULES OF PLAY: Create easy clapping rhythms with hands and different body parts. Start with a four-beat pattern such as clap, clap, pause, clap. Gradually add more elements including clapping, pausing and tapping other body parts, such as head, shoulders, and stomach. For example, clap, clap, pause, head tap, clap, clap. Be creative and design your own sets. For skill adaptation, decrease or increase the number of elements in a set. Two to four elements would be easy, six would be moderate, and more than eight would be a challenge.

LEVEL OF DIFFICULTY: Moderate.

GAME: Cutting Colorful Lines

OBJECT: To develop fine motor skills, eye-hand coordination, finger dexterity, cutting skills, hand and arm strength, muscle memory, eye-hand coordination, and visual and brain stimulation.

SUPPLIES: Construction paper and child-safe scissors. If your child is left-handed, make sure you have scissors that work for a southpaw.

RULES OF PLAY: Begin by drawing several straight, wavy, or crooked lines on a piece of paper that is small enough for your child to hold in his or her non-cutting hand. Provide child-safe scissors and allow plenty of time for your child to learn the skill of opening and closing the thumb and index and middle fingers of the cutting hand. For skill adaptation, draw simple or more complex cutting lines.

LEVEL OF DIFFICULTY: Difficult.

GAME: Dog Dancing

OBJECT: To develop gross motor skills; eye-hand and eye-foot coordination; shoulder range of motion; hand, leg, and core strength; cross-crawl movement; spatial awareness, depth perception, and brain stimulation.

SUPPLIES: Lively music.

RULES OF PLAY: Pretend to be a dog, and try to crawl, walk or dance to fun music while on all fours, using your hands and feet. Your knees are not touching the floor. Make wacky moves with the shoulders, buttocks, torso, arms, and legs while balancing the total body. When the music stops, freeze in place; play until the song is over. For skill adaptation, allow your child to place the knees on the floor. As upper body strength improves lift the knees off the floor for short periods of time.

LEVEL OF DIFFICULTY: Moderate.

GAME: Donkey Kicks

OBJECT: To develop gross motor skills, eye-hand and eye-foot coordination, balance, abdominal strength, body control, flexibility, spatial awareness, arm and shoulder stability, leg and calf control, and visual and brain stimulation.

SUPPLIES: None needed.

RULES OF PLAY: Begin in a balanced standing position with your arms extended up toward the sky. Step forward with your dominant foot. Bend forward and place your hands on the floor in front of your feet. Now kick your back leg up into the air as high as you can, followed by the front leg. Bring your legs together at the top and try to hold the position for three seconds. Finally, lower your front dominant leg back to the ground, immediately followed by your back leg. Your feet should land together. Be sure to look down at your hands while you kick up your legs. This activity builds the foundation for doing handstands. For skill adaptation, support your child's abdominals and legs during the donkey kick. Advanced levels can raise the height of the donkey kicks.

LEVEL OF DIFFICULTY: Difficult

GAME: Dynamic Matchups

OBJECT: To improve fine motor skills, eye-hand coordination, the tripod hand grasp, memory retention, visual awareness, depth perception, language development, and brain stimulation.

SUPPLIES: One shoebox per person, scissors, and a deck of cards.

RULES OF PLAY: In the top of the shoebox, cut a slot long enough to drop the cards through. Select from six to twenty matching pairs of playing cards, and put them in a pile face down. Shuffle and arrange the cards in random order on the floor. The goal is to turn over two cards per turn to find matching pairs. When two cards match, place them in the shoebox through the slotted id. When all pairs have been matched, remove your shoebox lid and count your pairs. The player with the most matches wins. For skill adaptation, decrease or increase the number of matching pairs.

LEVEL OF DIFFICULTY: Moderate.

GAME: Edible ABCs

OBJECT: To improve fine motor skills, eye-hand coordination, finger dexterity, pincer grasp, and visual, spatial, and brain development.

SUPPLIES: A bowl of any type of circular or ring-shaped cereal, a standard piece of paper, and a pen, pencil or marker.

RULES OF PLAY: Write a large upper- or lower-case letter at least six inches high on the paper, and encourage your child to place pieces of cereal on the lines, and watch the three dimensional letter appear. Your child should be seated at a table and use the thumb and index finger to manipulate the cereal. Encourage your child to complete the entire letter using the right and left hands. When finished, he or she can eat the cereal letter as a snack. For skill adaptation, decrease or increase the size of the letters.

LEVEL OF DIFFICULTY: Easy to moderate.

GAME: Eggroll-Overs

OBJECT: To improve gross motor skills, abdominal and core strength, eye-hand and eye-foot coordination, midline crossing, bilateral limb, balance, and visual, spatial, and brain development.

SUPPLIES: None needed.

RULES OF PLAY: Pretend to be an eggroll and rotate side-over-side in a large open area. To begin, your arms and legs are extended above your head. Hold your stomach muscles strong and tight. Rotate side-over-side. For skill adaptation, decrease the speed and slowly roll your child from front to back and then back to front. Advanced levels can increase rollover speed and try to race to a finish line.

LEVEL OF DIFFICULTY: Easy.

GAME: Elbows in Action

OBJECT: To develop gross motor skills, shoulder and arm strength, balance, range of motion, memory, eye tracking, eye-hand coordination, spatial awareness, and brain stimulation.

SUPPLIES: Lively music.

RULES OF PLAY: Bend your arm, and place your hand on the top of the corresponding shoulder. Pretend there is a crayon or marker extending from your elbow. Using your shoulder, draw with the imaginary elbow marker and make shapes in the air, such as circles, squares, ovals, or triangles. Use both arms. For skill adaptation, use simple shapes or draw complex letters and words.

LEVEL OF DIFFICULTY: Easy.

GAME: Fancy Flamingo

OBJECT: To develop gross motor skills, balance, coordination, leg strength, and bilateral leg and foot development.

SUPPLIES: None needed.

RULES OF PLAY: Pretend to be a flamingo and balance on one foot for as long as possible. Place one foot on the floor, and lift up the other foot. The knee of the lifted foot is at hip level. Extend your arms and hands out to the sides for balance. Switch legs and repeat. For skill adaptation, offer support by holding your child's hand or flamingo stand without help as you sing the alphabet song.

LEVEL OF DIFFICULTY: Difficult.

GAME: Fingerball Toss

OBJECT: To improve fine and gross motor skills, eye-hand coordination, hand grasping, manual dexterity, underhand throwing, bilateral limb use, eye tracking, spatial awareness, depth perception, and brain development.

SUPPLIES: A tennis ball.

RULES OF PLAY: Stand in a balanced position facing your child about three feet apart. To throw underhand, have your child hold the ball in his hand palmside up. The fingertips and thumb are around the ball. The action is to flick the forearm and wrist toward the target or person in an underhand motion. As you toss, step forward. For example, a right-handed toss needs a left-footed step. Catch the ball, and hand it back to your child. Toss with the right and left hands. For skill adaptation, decrease or increase the tossing distance.

LEVEL OF DIFFICULTY: Difficult.

GAME: Fingertip Dot Painting

OBJECT: To improve fine motor movements, eye-hand coordination, fingertip control, creativity, wrist and arm strength, spatial awareness, depth perception, and brain development.

SUPPLIES: Child-safe finger paint, a painting smock, newspapers, disposable plastic plates, paper towels, and a piece of large construction paper of any color.

RULES OF PLAY: Play on a flat surface that is lined with newspapers for easy clean up. Open the jars of washable finger paint and pour about a teaspoonful of each color on the plate. Place the plate and paper in front of both your child along with a clean paper towel. Show your child how to dip one fingertip into a color and create dot art. Encourage your child to paint with the fingers of both the right and left hands. Try to avoid smearing and dragging the fingers. This game develops finger control used in self-dressing, writing, typing, and playing musical instruments. For skill adaptation, allow your child to use one or more fingers or the whole hand.

LEVEL OF DIFFICULTY: Moderate.

GAME: Foam Ball Fun: Toss and Catch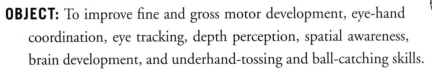

OBJECT: To improve fine and gross motor development, eye-hand coordination, eye tracking, depth perception, spatial awareness, brain development, and underhand-tossing and ball-catching skills.

SUPPLIES: A soft foam ball about four inches in diameter.

RULES OF PLAY: Play underhand toss and catch with your child. To begin, stand about three feet from your child, who has both hands pressed together as if to make a cup.

To catch a ball: Begin by pouring a little water into your child's hand-cup to promote the idea of keeping the hands together during play. After drying your child's hands, gently toss the ball into the hand-cup in a slow underhand motion. The toss should travel in an arch, like a small rainbow. Encourage your child to reach his hand-cup toward the ball and then back into the body.

To underhand toss a ball: see Fingerball Toss in this section. Try to alternate using the right and left hands. For skill adaptation, either decrease or increase the tossing distance.

LEVEL OF DIFFICULTY: Moderate.

GAME: Frog Hops

OBJECT: To develop gross motor skills; eye-hand and eye-foot coordination; quickness; flexibility; balance; jumping ability; and leg, calf, and abdominal strength.

SUPPLIES: None needed.

RULES OF PLAY: Your child should begin on all fours with the feet and the palms of his hands on the floor. The child's hands are on the outsides of the feet, and legs are bent, ready to spring up. Have your child stand up slightly while lifting the hands off the floor. Have the child swing his arms for momentum, lean forward, and jump upward for distance. Have the child land with feet first, quickly placing his palms on the ground. For skill adaptation, modify the frog jump to a half-knee bend where the hands do not have to touch the floor. Advanced levels include having the child try to jump as far and fast as possible.

LEVEL OF DIFFICULTY: Difficult.

GAME: Giraffe Steps: Long Lunges

OBJECT: To improve gross motor skills, eye-foot coordination, balance, posture, leg strength, flexibility, and cognitive development.

SUPPLIES: None needed.

RULES OF PLAY: Pretend to be a giraffe and walk with a tall neck and long, lunging steps. Hold each giraffe step or lunge for about two seconds. Have your child swing the right arm forward as he or she lunges with the left foot and vice versa when lunging with the right foot. For skill adaptation, take shorter or longer steps and vary the speed of play.

LEVEL OF DIFFICULTY: Easy.

GAME: Heel and Toe: On the Line You Go

OBJECT: To improve gross motor skills, eye-foot coordination, balance, flexibility, body control, visual and spatial awareness, and brain development.

SUPPLIES: Chalk or masking tape.

RULES OF PLAY: Begin by applying chalk or tape to the floor in a variety of patterns, such as a straight line, curved line, circle, square or triangle. Have your child start with one foot on the line while he or she places the heel of the second foot as close to or directly in front of and touching the toes of the first foot. Continue having the child walk along the lines in this heel-and-toe pattern. For skill adaptation, draw a thicker line, take longer steps, and make simple paths. For a greater challenge, draw complex patterns to follow.
LEVEL OF DIFFICULTY: Moderate.

GAME: Ice Cube Basketball
OBJECT: To improve fine and gross motor skills, eye-hand coordination, depth perception, target aim, spatial awareness, finger dexterity, hand grasping, quickness, and visual and brain stimulation.
SUPPLIES: Ice cubes and two to three mixing bowls or buckets.
RULES OF PLAY: Toss ice cubes into bowls or buckets to make baskets. Place the bowls or buckets about three to six feet away from your child. Have the child underhand toss the ice cubes into the containers as if he were shooting baskets. Award points for each basket scored. For skill adaptation, decrease or increase the tossing distance. Also, wear gloves if little hands get too cold.
LEVEL OF DIFFICULTY: Easy.

GAME: Ice Skating, Ice Plating
OBJECT: To improve gross motor skills, eye-foot coordination, spatial awareness, balance, depth perception, leg strength and flexibility, and brain stimulation.

SUPPLIES: Two paper plates per person and lively dance music.

RULES OF PLAY: Stand on paper plates, one foot for each, and pretend to ice skate on the floor. Have your child move or glide to the music without lifting the feet. For skill adaptation, shorten or lengthen the foot glide.

LEVEL OF DIFFICULTY: Easy.

GAME: Kangaroo Ball Taps

OBJECT: To develop gross motor skills, eye-foot coordination, leg and foot strength, balance, quickness, speed, footwork, depth perception, spatial skills, and visual and brain stimulation.

SUPPLIES: One soccer ball per person.

RULES OF PLAY: Your child should stand in a balanced position with the ball resting on the floor directly in front of and between his feet. Have your child try to tap the top of the ball starting with the dominant foot while balancing on the nondominant foot. Switch feet and repeat. For skill adaptation, play in slow step-and-tap motion. Advanced levels try hop-and-tap patterns.

LEVEL OF DIFFICULTY: Difficult.

GAME: Kangaroo Jumps

OBJECT: To develop gross motor skills, jumping ability, quickness, balance, flexibility, eye-foot coordination, leg and core strength, and brain stimulation.

SUPPLIES: None.

RULES OF PLAY: Begin in a balanced standing position. Have your child leap forward by raising one or both knees up to the chest, then land in an upright position with a one- or two-footed landing. For skill adaptation, lower or raise the height of the knee lift and decrease or increase the jumping distance.

LEVEL OF DIFFICULTY: Difficult.

RHYME: *Aussie Kangaroos*

>Aussie kangaroos, are oh so funny
>They hop in the air just like a bunny.
>Now lift your knees up to your chest.
>Jump like a kangaroo and do your best![2]

GAME: Lots of Knots

OBJECT: To improve fine motor skills, eye-hand coordination, finger dexterity, hand grasping, and visual, spatial, and cognitive skills.

SUPPLIES: An adult sports shoe with long laces.

RULES OF PLAY: Tie as many knots in the shoelaces as possible. Begin by placing your child's foot inside a large adult shoe with long laces. Show your child how to tie a single knot by using the thumb and index fingers. Repeat the action. For skill adaptation, hold your child's hands and help him or her through the motions. Advanced levels can tie multiple knots.

LEVEL OF DIFFICULTY: Moderate.

GAME: Marshmallow Pops

OBJECT: To improve fine motor development, eye-hand coordination, finger dexterity, pincer grasp, number sense, math challenges, visual and spatial awareness, and brain stimulation.

SUPPLIES: Tweezers, salad or ice tongs, a bag of larger marshmallows, and two empty bowls.

RULES OF PLAY: Your child should sit at a table with a flat surface. Place the supplies in front of your child. The challenge is to pick up the marshmallows with the tweezers, one at a time, and place them into the empty bowl using one hand. When all the marshmallows have been transferred, return them to the original bowl using the other hand. For skill adaptation, use larger marshmallows and connected salad tongs. Advanced levels can make it a contest and play for time.

LEVEL OF DIFFICULTY: Moderate.

GAME: Masterful Marching

OBJECT: To improve gross motor skills, cross-limb and bilateral coordination, fitness, eye-foot coordination, balance, flexibility, leg and ankle strength, spatial awareness, depth perception, and brain stimulation.

SUPPLIES: Lively music.

RULES OF PLAY: Begin in a standing balanced position. Your child should march forward with the left leg while pumping the right arm. Have him or her then step with the right leg while pumping the left arm. For skill adaptation, march slowly and exaggerate the opposite arm and leg action. Advanced levels include marching quickly to the beat of fast and lively music.

LEVEL OF DIFFICULTY: Easy.

GAME: Mirror, Mimes, and Super Shadows

OBJECT: To improve gross motor skills, visual tracking, balance, spatial awareness, depth perception, bilateral coordination, fitness, flexibility, arm and shoulder range of motion, leg strength, left and right orientation, and brain development.

SUPPLIES: Lively music.

RULES OF PLAY: Stand face-to-face with your child. Slowly move your arms, legs, feet, hands, or head, and encourage your child to copy your actions as if he were looking into a mirror. Reverse rolls. Then try the Super Shadow game where both players play facing the same direction. The person in front is the leader who initiates body movement, and the shadow is behind, copying the action. Reverse roles. For skill adaptation, move slower or faster and be sure your child is mirroring your actions.

LEVEL OF DIFFICULTY: Easy.

GAME: Ping-Pong Up and Down

OBJECT: To improve fine and gross motor and eye-hand coordination, hand grasping, depth perception, eye-tracking skills, spatial awareness, and visual, auditory, and brain stimulation.

SUPPLIES: A table tennis paddle and a soft foam ball approximately four inches in diameter.

RULES OF PLAY: Balance the ball on the paddle and then hit it into the air as many times as possible without letting the ball drop. Begin by having your child hold the paddle in one hand and the ball in the other. Have him or her place the ball directly on the center of the paddle and try to balance it without letting the ball drop. When this is easily accomplished,

have your child pop up the ball about twelve inches in the air and catch it with the free hand. For skill adaptation, retrieve the ball after it drops. Advanced levels can try to increase the number of pop-ups in a row without dropping the ball.

LEVEL OF DIFFICULTY: Difficult.

GAME: Pogo Pops: Two-Footed Jumping in Place

OBJECT: To improve gross motor and eye-foot skills; jumping ability; balance; flexibility; quickness; ankle strength; and visual, spatial, and cognitive awareness.

SUPPLIES: None needed.

RULES OF PLAY: Have your child jump straight up into the air with two feet as many times as possible. Strive for two-footed launches and landings, so the feet hit the ground at the same time. For skill adaptation, allow for the feet to finish with a staggered landing. Advance levels can play Pogo Pop follow-the-leader.

LEVEL OF DIFFICULTY: Easy.

GAME: Ring-Around-the-Rosy: Walking and Hopping

OBJECT: To improve gross motor skills; eye-foot coordination; balance; strength; flexibility; spatial awareness; and visual, auditory, and brain stimulation.

SUPPLIES: None needed.

RULES OF PLAY: Hold hands with your child and walk or hop in circles while you sing the traditional nursery rhyme "Ring-Around-the-Rosy." Begin in a balanced standing position and move to the rhyme. Take the cue and fall down with the last line, "We all fall down!" For skill adaptation, play slowly. Advanced challenges include skipping, walking backward or sideways, and heel-toe walking to the rhyme.

LEVEL OF DIFFICULTY: Easy to moderate.

LYRICS: *Ring-Around-the-Rosy*

> Ring around the rosy,
> A pocketful of posies,
> A-tishoo! A-tishoo!
> We all fall down!

GAME: Rockin' Sockin' Freeze Dance

OBJECT: To develop fine and gross motor skills, eye-hand coordination, finger strength and control, arm and shoulder range of motion, balance, strength, fitness, and visual, auditory, and cognitive awareness.

SUPPLIES: About a dozen pair of men's calf-length athletic socks, a variety of toys, a pillowcase, snacks, and fun music. The top of the socks must be long enough to tie into a loose knot.

RULES OF PLAY: Prepare the game by placing a small toy or favorite snacks inside each sock and tying a loose knot at the top. Place all of the filled socks into a pillowcase, and store it in a safe place near the game area. Then play freeze dance to upbeat music. When your child successfully freezes as the volume is turned down, he may pull out a toy-filled sock from the pillowcase. If still moving when the music stops, then return a filled sock to the pillowcase. The game is over when the pillowcase is empty. Finally, encourage your child to untie his filled socks and unveil the surprises. For skill adaptation, eliminate, reduce, or increase the number of knots in the socks.

LEVEL OF DIFFICULTY: Moderate.

GAME: Rolling Around the World

OBJECT: To improve fine and gross motor skills, eye-foot coordination, midline crossing, bilateral arm use, footwork, balance, fitness, quickness, visual awareness, depth perception, and brain development.

SUPPLIES: A tennis or soft foam ball.

RULES OF PLAY: Begin in a balanced standing position. Have your child hold the ball in one hand and rotate it around his or her body at waist height. When it gets to the other side, have your child transfer the ball to the free hand. Continue for several loops. For skill adaptation, use a larger ball and decrease or increase the speed of the rotations "around the world."

LEVEL OF DIFFICULTY: Moderate.

GAME: Skip with Me

OBJECT: To improve gross motor skills, cross-limb and eye-hand and eye-foot coordination, midline crossing, footwork, balance, fitness, quickness, leg and foot strength, visual awareness, depth perception, and brain development.

SUPPLIES: None needed.

RULES OF PLAY: Begin in a standing position. Have your child lift one knee and foot off the ground about waist height and balance on the other foot. Have him or her hop forward with the balanced standing leg. Now finish by stepping or walking forward with the raised bent leg. Repeat this alternating hop-and-walk motion. The arms should bend at the elbows. Try to have your child pump the arms in an opposite limb pattern. For example, when he or she hops forward on the right foot, pump the left arm. For skill adaptation, slowly perform the hop and step pattern. Advanced levels can skip for speed.

LEVEL OF DIFFICULTY: Difficult.

GAME: Sticker Puppets

OBJECT: To develop fine motor skills, eye-hand coordination, finger dexterity, tip-pinch hand grasp, and visual, auditory, and cognitive awareness.

SUPPLIES: A package of stickers.

RULES OF PLAY: Give your child a sheet of stickers of various types, shapes, and sizes. Have him peel the stickers off the paper using the thumb and index finger and apply them to the fingertips. Create little finger people, animals, and imaginary creatures for a finger-puppet show. Use both hands. For skill adaptation, use larger stickers and help your child peel them off the paper. Advanced levels can try tiny stickers and play independently without help.

LEVEL OF DIFFICULTY: Easy.

GAME: Tennis Hockey

OBJECT: To improve fine and gross motor skills, eye-hand and eye-foot development, spherical hand grasp on the racket handle, spatial awareness, arm and leg strength, and visual, auditory, and cognitive awareness.

SUPPLIES: One tennis racket per person, a foam, inflatable beach, or tennis ball, and chalk or a ten-foot length of rope. Your child should use a child-sized racket.

RULES OF PLAY: Begin by creating an imaginary net on the floor with chalk or a length of rope. Try to have your child guide, hit, or roll the ball on the floor past the center net line using a racket, similar to hockey. For skill adaptation, use larger balls such as beach or playground balls. Advanced levels can strike the ball with more power and speed.

LEVEL OF DIFFICULTY: Moderate.

GAME: Throw and Catch

OBJECT: To improve fine and gross motor skills, eye-hand and eye-foot coordination, hand grasping, throwing and catching fundamentals, midline crossing, arm and shoulder range of motion, footwork, spatial awareness, depth perception, balance, visual development, and brain stimulation.

SUPPLIES: A tennis ball.

RULES OF PLAY: Play toss and catch standing about four feet apart facing your child. To catch a ball, ask your child to press both hands together as if to make a cup with the center of the palms. At first, you can pour a little water into the cupped hand to promote the idea of keeping the hands together when catching a ball. Then gently toss the ball into your child's cupped hands in a slow underhand motion that is easy to track with the eyes. Encourage your child to reach the hands toward the ball, catch it, and then bring it back to the body.

To throw a ball, have your child hold it in the dominant hand with the palm facing up. The fingertips and thumb are around the ball. He or she should stand slightly sideways to the target: right-handers should position the left side of the body toward the target, and left-handers should position the right side of the body toward the target. The feet are balanced and shoulder-width apart. The front foot is turned slightly toward the target.

1. The arm position of throwing hand: right-handers should bring the ball above their right shoulder, neck, and ear (vice versa for a lefty). The throwing arm should form an *L*, with the elbow at shoulder height. The arm not throwing should be extended straight out, with the hand and fingers aiming toward the target.

2. The throw: The child should rotate at the waist away from the target while cocking the arm and wrist back. During the throw, the child should step toward the target with the front foot while push-

ing off with the back foot, releasing the ball when the arm is almost at full extension. The right shoulders of right-handers should finish in the front (vice versa for left-handers).

3. The follow-through: After the ball leaves the hand, the throwing arm should continue to wind down toward the side of the non-throwing arm.

For skill adaptation, increase or decrease the tossing distance.

LEVEL OF DIFFICULTY: Difficult.

GAME: Tiny Toe Art

OBJECT: To develop gross motor skills; eye-foot coordination; balance; leg, foot, and toe control; creativity; visual awareness; depth perception; and brain stimulation.

SUPPLIES: Child-safe paints, newspapers, paper towels, a painting smock or large T-shirt, foam or plastic dinner plates, and a large piece of art paper.

RULES OF PLAY: Prepare the painting area by lining the floor with newspapers. Place a child's chair in the middle of the protected area. Pour a few tablespoons of washable paint onto a plate and place it on the floor next to the chair. Have your child sit on the chair and use his toes to dip into the paint and create unique toe designs on the paper. Try toe-painting with both the right and left foot. For skill adaptation, guide your child's foot onto the paint and paper. Advanced levels can toe paint with both feet at the same time.

LEVEL OF DIFFICULTY: Moderate.

GAME: Tiptoe Toddlers

OBJECT: To develop gross motor skills, eye-foot coordination, quickness, balance, footwork, leg strength, flexibility, and visual, auditory, and brain stimulation.

SUPPLIES: Lively music.

RULES OF PLAY: Walk with small steps as if walking on tiptoes through a flower garden. Begin in a standing, balanced position. Shift your weight off your heels to the toes and the balls of your feet while you tiptoe-dance to music. Change the pace from slow to fast tiptoes. For skill adaptation, walk on tiptoes every other step or whenever possible. Advanced levels can add more tiptoe gross motor movement such as twirling, skipping, and hopping.

LEVEL OF DIFFICULTY: Easy.

GAME: Triangle Snippets

OBJECT: To improve fine motor skills, eye-hand coordination, finger dexterity, thumb and hand movements, and visual, cognitive, and spatial development.

SUPPLIES: A piece of strong craft paper and child-safe scissors.

RULES OF PLAY: Your child should be comfortably seated at a desk or table. Provide a small piece of craft paper and a pair of child-safe scissors. Your child should pick up the paper with the noncutting hand and the scissors with the dominant hand. Place the child's thumb in the top hole of the scissors and the index and middle fingers in the bottom hole. The action is to cut little triangles at the corners of the paper by opening and closing the hand with the scissors. For skill adaptation, make larger or smaller triangles.

LEVEL OF DIFFICULTY: Difficult.

GAME: Tunnel Torpedoes

OBJECT: To develop fine and gross motor skills, eye-hand coordination, finger dexterity, pincer or tripod grasp, visual and spatial awareness, and brain stimulation.

SUPPLIES: A cardboard paper towel or gift wrap roll, a bucket or small empty trash can, and a dozen unsharpened pencils.

RULES OF PLAY: Send the pencil torpedoes through the cardboard tube and into a bucket a few feet away. Your child should be in a standing position, with the bucket placed on the floor directly in front. Have the child place an unsharpened pencil into the cardboard tube and shoot it into the bucket. Load up and send more pencil torpedoes. For skill adaptation, decrease or increase the shooting distance.

LEVEL OF DIFFICULTY: Moderate.

GAME: Twirly Birds

OBJECT: To improve gross motor skills, eye-foot coordination, balance, quickness, visual stimulation, leg strength, brain development, and body control while spinning in circles.

SUPPLIES: None needed.

RULES OF PLAY: Start your child in a balanced, standing position with his arms outstretched to the sides about shoulder height. Have your child spin in circles while counting the rotations or reciting the alphabet. For skill adaptation, decrease or increase the spinning speed. Also, challenge your child to twirl on his tiptoes.

LEVEL OF DIFFICULTY: Easy.

GAME: Two-Square Sidewalk Style

OBJECT: To improve fine and gross motor development; eye-hand coordination; arm and shoulder strength; hand and finger flexibility; ball-passing and catching skills; and visual, cognitive, and spatial stimulation.

SUPPLIES: A playground ball about six to eight inches in diameter.

RULES OF PLAY: Find three sidewalk squares (or draw three squares on the driveway) approximately the same size. Each player stands in an end square, and the middle square is the bouncing zone. The goal is to use two hands to bounce the ball into the middle square to a partner, who will catch the ball and return the pass. Repeat the action. Your child should count the number of times the ball is passed and caught. For skill adaptation, use smaller or bigger balls and increase or decrease the pace of the game.

LEVEL OF DIFFICULTY: Moderate.

GAME: Wacky Ring Toss

OBJECT: To improve fine and gross motor skills, eye-hand coordination, finger and wrist dexterity, hand-grasping control, spatial awareness, depth perception, and brain stimulation.

SUPPLIES: A dozen paper plates with the centers cut out and about six empty plastic water bottles filled with about an inch of sand, water, or dirt.

RULES OF PLAY: Your child should begin in a balanced position about two feet away from a bottle target. Spread out the remaining bottles around this first bottle. Using the wrist, have your child try to flick the rings over the tops of the bottles—similar to throwing a flying disc—and ring the bottles' necks. For skill adaptation, decrease or increase the tossing distance to the bottle targets.

LEVEL OF DIFFICULTY: Difficult.

GAME: Wheelbarrow Walks

OBJECT: To improve gross motor skills, eye-hand coordination, shoulder control, neck and arm strength, balance, flexibility, spatial awareness, depth perception, and brain stimulation.

SUPPLIES: None needed.

RULES OF PLAY: Your child should begin in a crawling position on the hands and knees. Take careful hold of his ankles and help your young athlete walk around the house using hand, arm, and shoulder strength. For skill adaptation, support your child above the knees at the thighs as you support the lower legs. Advanced skills can wheelbarrow walk for speed.

LEVEL OF DIFFICULTY: Difficult.

Building Blocks for Three-Year-Olds	Fine Motor	Gross Motor	Arms & Shoulders	Hands & Fingers	Legs & Feet	Core Strength	Balance	Cognitive & Brain	Flexibility	Quickness	Visual	Spatial Awareness	Depth Perception	Eye-Hand	Eye-Foot	Midline Crossing	Bilateral Limb	Supplies
Air Balloon Volleyball	•	•	•	•	•	•	•	•	•	•	•	•	•	•	•	•	•	Balloon
Basketball Trash Pick-Up	•	•	•	•	•	•	•	•	•		•	•	•	•		•	•	Paper, trash can
Beach Ball Soccer		•			•	•	•	•	•	•	•	•	•	•	•		•	Inflated beach ball
Beanbag Bomb	•		•	•							•	•		•	•		•	Beanbags
Beanbag Parade	•	•	•	•	•	•	•	•	•		•	•		•	•	•	•	Beanbags, music
Bicycling Babe		•			•	•	•	•	•			•	•			•	•	Music
Big Bunny Hops: Standing Long Jumps		•	•		•	•	•	•	•	•	•	•	•	•		•	•	None
Body Parts: All About Me	•	•	•	•	•	•	•	•	•	•	•	•		•	•	•	•	None
Bottle Bowling	•	•	•	•	•	•	•	•	•	•	•	•	•	•	•		•	Empty two-liter soda bottles, water, playground ball
Broom Ball	•	•	•	•	•	•	•	•	•	•	•	•	•	•	•	•	•	Broom, box, ball
Bubble Tennis	•	•	•	•	•	•	•	•	•	•	•	•	•	•	•	•	•	Bubbles, flyswatter
Colored Muffin Balls	•		•	•				•			•	•	•	•			•	Paper, muffin tins
Copy Me Clapping Body	•	•	•				•	•		•	•			•	•	•	•	Music
Cutting Colorful Lines	•	•	•	•			•	•	•	•	•	•	•	•			•	Paper, child's scissors
Dog Dancing	•	•	•		•	•	•	•	•	•	•	•	•	•	•	•	•	Music
Donkey Kicks	•	•	•	•	•	•	•	•	•	•	•	•	•	•	•	•	•	None
Dynamic Match Ups	•		•	•		•		•	•	•	•	•	•	•		•	•	Shoebox, cards, child's scissors
Edible ABC's	•		•	•			•	•	•	•	•	•	•	•		•	•	Cereal, paper, marker

Building Blocks for Three-Year-Olds	Fine Motor	Gross Motor	Arms & Shoulders	Hands & Fingers	Legs & Feet	Core Strength	Balance	Cognitive & Brain	Flexibility	Quickness	Visual	Spatial Awareness	Depth Perception	Eye-Hand	Eye-Foot	Midline Crossing	Bilateral Limb	Supplies
Eggroll-Overs		•	•		•	•	•	•	•	•	•	•	•	•	•	•	•	None
Elbows in Action		•	•			•	•	•	•	•	•	•	•	•		•	•	Music
Fancy Flamingo		•				•	•	•			•	•	•	•	•		•	None
Fingerball Toss	•	•	•	•	•	•	•	•	•	•	•	•	•	•		•	•	Tennis ball
Fingertip Dot Painting	•		•	•		•										•	•	Paint, plate, newspaper, paper towels, smock, art paper
Foam Ball Fun: Toss and Catch	•	•	•	•	•	•	•	•	•	•	•	•	•	•	•	•	•	Foam ball
Frog Hops	•	•	•	•	•	•	•	•		•	•	•	•	•	•		•	None
Giraffe Steps: Long Lunges		•	•		•	•	•	•	•	•	•	•	•		•	•	•	None
Heel and Toe: On the Line You Go		•			•	•	•	•		•	•	•	•		•	•	•	Chalk, masking tape
Ice Cube Basketball	•	•	•	•	•			•	•	•	•	•	•	•	•		•	•	Ice cubes, buckets or bowls
Ice Skating, Ice Plating		•			•	•	•	•	•	•	•	•	•		•		•	Paper plates, music
Kangaroo Ball Taps		•		•	•	•	•	•	•	•	•	•	•		•		•	Soccer ball
Kangaroo Jumps		•			•	•	•	•		•	•	•	•		•		•	None
Lots of Knots	•		•	•				•	•	•	•			•		•	•	Adult sports shoe with laces
Marshmallow Pops	•		•	•			•	•			•			•		•	•	Tweezers or tongs, marshmallows and two bowls
Masterful Marching		•	•		•	•	•	•			•	•	•	•	•		•	Music
Mirror, Mimes, and Super Shadows		•	•	•	•	•	•	•			•	•	•	•	•		•	Music

Building Blocks for Three-Year-Olds	Fine Motor	Gross Motor	Arms & Shoulders	Hands & Fingers	Legs & Feet	Core Strength	Balance	Cognitive & Brain	Flexibility	Quickness	Visual	Spatial Awareness	Depth Perception	Eye-Hand	Eye-Foot	Midline Crossing	Bilateral Limb	Supplies
Ping-Pong Pop-Ups	•	•	•	•	•	•	•	•	•	•	•	•	•	•	•	•	•	Small paddle, foam ball
Pogo Pops: Two Footed Jimping in Place		•	•		•	•	•	•	•	•	•	•	•	•			•	None
Ring-Around-the- Rosy: Walking and Hopping		•	•		•	•	•	•	•		•	•	•	•			•	None
Rockin' Sockin' Freeze Dance	•	•	•	•	•	•	•	•	•	•	•	•	•	•	•	•	•	Men's socks, toys or snacks, pillowcase
Rolling Around the World	•	•	•	•		•	•	•	•		•	•	•	•		•	•	Tennis ball
Skip With Me		•	•		•	•	•	•	•	•	•	•	•	•	•	•	•	None
Sticker Puppets	•		•	•			•				•	•	•	•		•	•	Stickers
Tennis Hockey	•	•	•		•	•	•	•	•	•	•	•	•	•	•	•	•	Child's racket, ball, chalk or rope
Throw and Catch	•													•	•	•	•	Small foam ball
Tiny Toe Art		•			•	•	•	•	•		•	•	•		•	•	•	Paint, newspaper, paper towels, smock, art paper
Tiptoe Toddlers		•			•	•	•	•			•	•	•		•		•	Music
Triangle Snippets	•	•	•	•			•	•	•		•	•	•	•	•		•	Child's scissors, craft paper
Tunnel Torpedos	•	•	•	•	•			•			•	•	•	•		•	•	Cardboard roll, unsharpened pencils, trash can
Twirly Birds		•	•		•	•	•	•	•	•	•	•	•		•	•	•	None

Building Blocks for Three-Year-Olds	Fine Motor	Gross Motor	Arms & Shoulders	Hands & Fingers	Legs & Feet	Core Strength	Balance	Cognitive & Brain	Flexibility	Quickness	Visual	Spatial Awareness	Depth Perception	Eye-Hand	Eye-Foot	Midline Crossing	Bilateral Limb	Supplies
Two-Square Sidewalk Style	•	•	•	•	•	•	•	•	•	•	•	•	•	•		•	•	Playground ball
Wacky Ring Toss	•	•	•	•	•	•	•	•	•	•	•	•	•	•		•	•	Paper plates, empty water bottles
Wheel-barrow Walks	•	•	•	•	•	•	•	•	•			•	•	•	•	•	•	None

14

The Golden Years:
Four- to Six-Year-Olds

Awesome Alphabet Stretches

Backward Running and Jumping

Backyard T-Ball

Badminton Boogie

Balance Beam

Beanbag Bowling

Beanbag Flapjacks

Bountiful Broad Jump

Cat Stretch

Criss-Cross Legs Across

Cutting by Design

Doggie Races

Dribbling Obstacle Course

Feet on Fire

Finger ABCs

Fingertip Push-Ups

Fishnet Golf

Five Little Piggies

Flying Saucer Toss

Follow-the-Leader

Forward Rolls

Go Fish Snack Time

Golf Ball Races

Hallway Beanbag Bombs

Handstands

Head, Shoulders, Knees, and Toes

Hopscotch

Hot Potato

Hula Beanbag Basketball

Hula-Hoop Skip Around

Jumping Rope

Kickin' It

Laundry Hoops

Limbo Stick

Magic Pan

Magic Wand

Mixing Bowl Toss and Catch

Moving Targets

Musical Bouncing Balls

Musical Fingers

Nifty Number Stretches

Orchestral Delights

Over-and-Under Zoo Hunt

Paper Plate Tennis

Pegleg Pirate Races

Putting Around the World

Secret Sign Language

Soccer Bowling

Tee for Two

Volleyball Beach Style

GAME: Awesome Alphabet Stretches

OBJECT: To develop fine and gross motor skills, eye-hand and eye-foot coordination, overall strength, flexibility, balance, quickness, auditory processing, midline crossing, bilateral limb use, spatial awareness, depth perception, and brain stimulation.

SUPPLIES: None needed.

RULES OF PLAY: Stretch the body into the shapes of the letters of the alphabet by moving, twisting, and turning the arms, legs, and torso into uppercase letters. Begin by demonstrating for your child how to form the letter *A* by standing with straightened legs in a wide stance. Then have your child do the same, bending at the waist and reaching the right hand across to the left knee to form the crossbar of the letter *A*. Be creative and continue on with the rest of the alphabet. For skill adaptation, use just hands and arms to make the letters. Advanced challenges include finding several ways to make each letter.

LEVEL OF DIFFICULTY: Moderate.

GAME: Backward Running and Jumping

OBJECT: To develop gross motor skills, eye-hand and eye-foot coordination, leg strength and flexibility, balance, quickness, vertical leaps, midline crossing, spatial awareness, depth perception, and brain stimulation.

SUPPLIES: None needed.

RULES OF PLAY: Walk, run or jump backward at various speeds and paces. Have your child begin with his back toward the desired direction. Have your child look over his shoulder for visual guidance. Have your child lift up the knees as he or she moves backward in a straight line or in circles. Pump the arms in a cross-limb motion. For skill adaptation, move and jump backward slower or faster.

LEVEL OF DIFFICULTY: Difficult.

GAME: Backyard T-Ball

OBJECT: To develop fine and gross motor skills, eye-hand and eye-foot coordination, hand grasping, shoulder and arm range of motion, leg strength, spatial awareness, depth perception, balance, eye tracking, and brain stimulation.

SUPPLIES: A plastic or lightweight bat, a T-ball stand, and a ball designed for the stand.

RULES OF PLAY: Use a child-sized bat to hit a ball resting on a T-ball stand.

The stance: Put the ball on the stand and place your child next to it. The T-ball stand should be about two feet away from your child, and in line with the arch of the front foot. For right-handed hitters, the left foot is in front and vice versa for left-handed players.

The grip: If your child is right-handed, place the left hand on the bottom of the grip near the butt of the bat. The right hand is above, and the hands are gently touching but not overlapping. The reverse holds true for left-handers. Have your child lift the bat above the right shoulder so it is parallel to the ground.

The swing: Have your child bring the thickest part of the bat, or the barrel, around to meet the ball on the tee. After making contact with the ball, allow the bat to follow through around the outside of the left shoulder (vice versa for left-handers).

As the ball is hit, right-handers should take a small step forward with the left foot toward the direction of an imaginary pitcher. Left-handers should step forward with the right foot.

For skill adaptation, begin the swing at the point of contact between the bat and ball, more like a bunt. Advanced levels can move on to live underhand pitches.

LEVEL OF DIFFICULTY: Moderate to difficult.

GAME: Badminton Boogie

OBJECT: To improve fine and gross motor skills; eye-hand and eye-foot coordination; spherical hand grasp on racket handle; arm, hand, and shoulder strength; balance; footwork; flexibility; quickness; and visual and brain stimulation.

SUPPLIES: Badminton rackets and a shuttlecock or birdie.

RULES OF PLAY: Draw a line on cement or lay a piece of rope on a lawn to create a center or net line in the middle of the play area. Hit the birdie on the rounded bottom side with an underhand motion up and over the line. Try to rally with your child. For skill adaptation, allow your child to pick up a dropped birdie to continue the rally.

LEVEL OF DIFFICULTY: Difficult.

GAME: Balance Beam

OBJECT: To develop gross motor skills, eye-hand and eye-foot coordination, balance, footwork, flexibility, spatial awareness, depth perception, leg and core strength, and visual and brain stimulation.

SUPPLIES: A balance beam, which can be made from a two-inch by four-inch by eight-foot piece of wood (found at home improvement stores or lumberyards). You will also need sandpaper, nails, and clear varnish.

RULES OF PLAY: Walk forward, backward, and sideways on the balance beam in a heel-toe fashion. Other options include walking on a chalk line, length of rope, sidewalk curb or on top of a low brick retaining wall. Have your child stretch his arms out to the sides for balance as he moves. To build the balance beam, cut three twelve-inch sections, and leave a five-foot length of wood. Sand the surface of the wood on all sides to protect small feet from splinters. Nail one twelve-inch section in a perpendicular direction on the bottom of each end and one in the middle to become a base for the beam. Varnish all exposed areas of wood for added protection.

For skill adaptation, draw a chalk line on the floor to use as a balance beam. Advanced levels can walk backward, forward on tiptoes, sideways, hop with two feet, and balance on one foot.

LEVEL OF DIFFICULTY: Difficult.

GAME: Beanbag Bowling

OBJECT: To develop fine and gross motor skills, eye-hand and eye-foot coordination, finger dexterity, hand grasping, underhand throwing skills, balance, depth perception, spatial awareness, eye tracking, and auditory and brain stimulation.

SUPPLIES: Several beanbags and six to ten empty two-liter soda bottles.

RULES OF PLAY: Throw the beanbags in an underhand motion at the soda bottles and knock them down to score points. To prepare the empty bottles, fill them with about one inch of water and tightly twist on the caps. The water will stabilize the bottles when upright.

To play the game, line up the bottles on a level floor in a triangular shape or a form of your choice. Have your child stand about four to six feet away from the bottles. Award points for each fallen bottle to make it a fun competition. For skill adaptation, decrease or increase the tossing distance.

LEVEL OF DIFFICULTY: Moderate.

GAME: Beanbag Flapjacks

OBJECT: To improve fine and gross motor skills, eye-hand coordination, manual dexterity, hand grasping, arm and shoulder strength, balance, fitness, footwork, spatial awareness, eye tracking, language development, and brain stimulation.

SUPPLIES: One beanbag and one tennis racket per person, and lively music.

RULES OF PLAY: All players should have a tennis racket. (Be sure your child is using kid-sized equipment.) Pass a beanbag back and forth on a tennis racket without letting it fall to the floor. Place the racket in your child's dominant hand and a beanbag on the strings. Have him or her move around the room to the music while balancing the beanbag on the strings.

Then flip the beanbag from one person to another using only the head of the racket. For skill adaptation, have the child use two hands to hold the racket. Advanced levels can toss the beanbag up into the air and catch it using only the head and strings of the racket.

LEVEL OF DIFFICULTY: Difficult.

GAME: Bountiful Broad Jump

OBJECT: To improve gross motor skills, eye-hand and eye-foot coordination, vertical leaps, balance, footwork, quickness, leg strength, spatial awareness, depth perception, and brain development.

SUPPLIES: Masking tape and chalk.

RULES OF PLAY: Your child should begin in a balanced, standing position and jump forward as far as possible with both feet. Press the arches of the feet together while jumping, and use the momentum of the legs and from the torso, arms, and upper body for more power. Strive for the feet to land together. For skill adaptation, allow for staggered foot landings. Advanced levels can mark jumps with chalk or tape and try to improve on previous attempts.

LEVEL OF DIFFICULTY: Moderate.

GAME: Cat Stretch

OBJECT: To improve gross motor skills, eye-hand and eye-foot coordination, flexibility, balance, depth perception, total body strength, and visual awareness.

SUPPLIES: Lively music.

RULES OF PLAY: Start in the cat position on all fours with the palms of the hands and the knees and toes on the floor. Pretend to be a cat and walk on all fours for a total body warm-up. While still on hands and knees, have your child arch his back upward like a rainbow in the sky, then return to the basic cat position. For the reverse stretch, have your child keep the knees stationary and walk the hands forward in front of the body as far as possible. Your child's back will curve downward. Repeat several times. For skill adaptation, stretch slowly and guide your child's back through the movement.

LEVEL OF DIFFICULTY: Easy.

GAME: Criss-Cross Legs Across

OBJECT: To improve gross motor skills, eye-foot coordination, midline crossing, hip range of motion, abdominal and leg strength, ankle flexibility, bilateral limb use, quickness, balance, and brain development.

SUPPLIES: Chalk or rope.

RULES OF PLAY: Draw a chalk line about six to ten feet long on concrete, or use rope. Straddle the line with one foot on each side of it. Have your child jump in a forward direction as he or she criss-crosses both feet over the line. For example, the right foot should cross over to the left side of the line while the left foot jumps over to the right. Keep moving forward. For skill adaptation, have your child slowly walk or hop through the motion. Advanced levels can play for speed and quickness.

LEVEL OF DIFFICULTY: Difficult.

GAME: Cutting by Design

OBJECT: To improve fine motor skills; eye-hand coordination; finger dexterity; hand grasping; paper cutting abilities; hand, arm, and finger strength; spatial awareness; and visual and brain stimulation.

SUPPLIES: Several pieces of colored art paper, child-safe scissors, a glue stick, and a sheet of craft paper.

RULES OF PLAY: Create geometric lines, shapes, and designs on the colored craft paper for your child to cut out. Later, glue the cut-outs into a collage on a larger piece of paper. For skill adaptation, draw simple lines for your child to cut. Advanced levels include challenging shapes such as squares, triangles, circles, and ovals.

LEVEL OF DIFFICULTY: Moderate.

GAME: Doggie Races

OBJECT: To improve gross motor skills; eye-hand and eye-foot coordination; cross-crawl development; arm, hand, core, and shoulder strength; fitness; spatial awareness; and visual and brain stimulation.

SUPPLIES: None needed.

RULES OF PLAY: Pretend to be a dog on all fours and play games while moving with hands and feet. Have your child start on all fours with his or her hands and feet only (no knees) on the floor. Create start and finish lines. Participants should line up at the starting line and move like a dog as fast as possible to reach the finish. For skill adaptation, allow the knees to rest on the floor.

LEVEL OF DIFFICULTY: Easy.

GAME: Dribbling Obstacle Course

OBJECT: To improve fine and gross motor skills, eye-hand coordination, finger dexterity, ball control, arm and shoulder strength, balance, flexibility, quickness, eye tracking, spatial awareness, and brain development.

SUPPLIES: Sports cones, a basketball or playground ball about ten-inches in diameter, and chalk.

RULES OF PLAY: Dribble a ball with one hand through an obstacle course. Design a zigzag path with about ten sports cones or chalk. The technique for dribbling is to softly use the thumb and the fingerpads of the hands to push the ball down to the ground. Have your child flex the wrist to control the bounce. Have him or her use the left and right hands to develop total coordination. For skill adaptation, have your child use two hands at the same time to dribble and dribble slowly. Advanced levels can dribble one-handed without looking at the hands. Your child should try to "see" or "feel" the ball with the fingertips.

LEVEL OF DIFFICULTY: Difficult.

GAME: Feet on Fire

OBJECT: To improve gross motor skills; eye-foot coordination; balance; speed; quickness; agility; leg, calf, and ankle strength; spatial awareness, and brain stimulation.

SUPPLIES: None needed.

RULES OF PLAY: Have your child begin in a balanced standing position. Your child should run in place as fast as possible while moving on the balls of the feet, pumping the arms and lifting the knees to improve quickness. For skill adaptation, decrease or increase the foot speed.

LEVEL OF DIFFICULTY: Moderate.

GAME: Finger ABCs

OBJECT: To improve fine motor skills, eye-hand coordination, arm and upper-back strength, finger dexterity, shoulder range of motion, memory, and visual, spatial, and cognitive development.

SUPPLIES: None needed.

RULES OF PLAY: Have your child use his dominant hand, placing the index finger in the air. Then imagine there is a pencil, crayon, or marker on the tip of his finger. "Write" in the air or on a wall while using the dominant hand. Follow up with the nondominant hand. Have your child spell out his name or play guessing games. For skill adaptation, manipulate your child's finger to learn the letters and movement. Advanced levels can try to write the alphabet.

LEVEL OF DIFFICULTY: Moderate.

GAME: Fingertip Push-Ups

OBJECT: To improve fine motor skills, eye-hand coordination, hand and arm strength, finger dexterity, joint flexibility, isometric finger movements, spatial awareness, depth perception, and visual and brain stimulation.

SUPPLIES: None needed.

RULES OF PLAY: Face the palms of the hands together with only the fingertips and thumbs touching. Have your child press the fingertips together to provide resistance. Have your child try to bend only the top knuckle near the fingernail, then only the second knuckle, and finally only the largest knuckle. Repeat. For skill adaptation, guide your child's fingers to bend at each joint.

LEVEL OF DIFFICULTY: Moderate.

GAME: Fishnet Golf

OBJECT: To improve fine motor skills; eye-hand coordination; hand grasping; finger dexterity; spatial awareness; depth perception; midline crossing; and visual; auditory; and brain stimulation.

SUPPLIES: One fishnet and about four golf balls.

RULES OF PLAY: Catch golf balls in the air using a fishnet. Stand about three feet away from your child, who is holding a small- to moderate-sized fishnet in his or her dominant hand. The other hand is behind the back. Toss a golf ball toward your child in a slow and gentle underhand motion, and encourage him to catch it with the net. To include midline crossing, toss the ball to the right and left sides of your child's body. For skill adaptation, use a larger fishnet and decrease or increase the tossing distance.

LEVEL OF DIFFICULTY: Difficult.

GAME: Five Little Piggies

OBJECT: To increase fine motor skills, finger dexterity, eye-hand coordination, depth perception, spatial awareness, language development, eye tracking, and auditory and brain stimulation.

SUPPLIES: None needed.

RULES OF PLAY: Use the thumb and fingers of one hand to tap the fingertips of the other as fast as possible. To begin, have your child hold the left hand up and spread the fingers apart. Begin by using the thumb of the right hand to quickly tap the fingertip of the left thumb, then the left index, middle, ring, and pinky fingers. Now reverse the direction and have him retap the ring, middle, and index fingertips and back to the thumb. Repeat using the right index finger as the tapper and continue the progression. Switch hands. For skill adaptation, decrease or increase the tapping speed.

LEVEL OF DIFFICULTY: Difficult.

GAME: Flying Saucer Toss

OBJECT: To improve fine and gross motor development, eye-hand coordination, finger dexterity, hand grasping, hand and wrist flexibility, depth perception, midline crossing, bilateral hand use, eye tracking, spatial awareness, disk throwing and aiming, catching skills, and brain development.

SUPPLIES: A flying disk.

RULES OF PLAY: Try to throw and catch a flying disk with your child. There are three aspects:

The hold: Grasp the disk arched-side down and parallel to the ground in the dominant hand. Have your child put the thumb on the top of the disk and the index finger on the outside edge. Curl the middle, ring, and pinkie fingers under the inside rim of the disk.

The throw: Stand sideways to the target. For a right-hander, have him or her face the right shoulder toward the target and vice versa for lefties. Have your child pull the disk across the body toward his nonthrowing side and step toward the target. Right-handers step with the right foot and opposite for lefties. Have your child bring the throwing arm across the body as he prepares to release the disk. Then snap the elbow and wrist to release it.

The catch: The child's dominant hand should be placed palm-side down above the path of the incoming flying disk, with the nondominant hand palm-side up below the path of the disk. The catch is like a hand clap with the disk being caught in the middle of the clap. For skill adaptation, guide your child's hand through the tossing action. Other modifications are decreasing or increasing the tossing distance.

LEVEL OF DIFFICULTY: Difficult.

GAME: Follow-the-Leader

OBJECT: To improve gross motor skills, eye-foot coordination, footwork, quickness, agility, fitness, balance, cross-limb movement, visual and spatial awareness, and brain development.

SUPPLIES: Lively music.

RULES OF PLAY: Play follow-the-leader and teach your child how to skip, gallop, run, and perform other physical actions as a way of strengthening gross motor movement. Also try backward walking, sideways walking, marching, and heel-toe walking. When your child feels confident, encourage him or her to take charge as the leader. For skill adaptation, move slowly and start with walking and marching. Advance to skipping, galloping, and running.

LEVEL OF DIFFICULTY: Moderate.

GAME: Forward Rolls

OBJECT: To develop gross motor skills; eye-foot and eye-hand-coordination; balance; flexibility; total body strength; depth perception; spatial awareness; bilateral limb use; and visual, auditory, and brain stimulation.

SUPPLIES: None needed.

RULES OF PLAY: Have your child curl his body into a ball and perform a forward roll. Have him or her begin in a squat position with the hands and feet on the floor on a soft surface such as carpet or grass. The hands are in front of the body. Have your child tuck his chin to the chest to form a ball and maintain the rolled-up position as the head and shoulders make contact with the ground. Have the child stay rolled up like a ball as the spine meets the floor as he leans forward, finishing on the feet. Finally, have your child reach the arms out in front of the body for balance. For skill adaptation, place your hand on top of your child's head to hold his chin on the chest. Keep it there until the head touches the ground. Help your child regain balance after the roll. Advanced levels can try to do several forward rolls in a row. If there is any doubt as to how this game is played, err on the side of caution.

LEVEL OF DIFFICULTY: Difficult.

GAME: Go Fish Snack Time

OBJECT: To improve fine motor skills, eye-hand coordination, pincer grasp, finger dexterity, spatial awareness, math and counting skills, visual and spatial awareness, and brain development.

SUPPLIES: A pair of dice, a plastic jar with a screw-on lid for each person, and a bowl of fish-shaped crackers.

RULES OF PLAY: Each player chooses a special number from two to twelve, and takes a turn rolling the dice. When the child rolls his special number, he or she should pick up that number of crackers from the bowl using the pincer grasp, unscrew the lid from a jar, drop the crackers into the jar, and close the lid. When the adult's number is rolled, he or she should pick up that many crackers and do the same. After about twenty rolls each, players count their fish crackers to see who has the most. Eat some as a reward. For skill adaptation, lightly twist the lid on the jar for easy opening.

LEVEL OF DIFFICULTY: Easy.

GAME: Golf Ball Races

OBJECT: To teach fine and gross motor skills, eye-hand and eye-foot coordination, spatial skills, balance, depth perception, bilateral hand use, concentration, midline crossing, and visual and brain development.

SUPPLIES: Each person needs one large spoon, two large empty bowls, and four to six golf balls.

RULES OF PLAY: Create a start and finish line. Fill a bowl with four to six golf balls and place it near the start. The empty bowl is at the finish. Have your child carry a golf ball on a spoon and walk about five to ten feet as he transfers the ball from one bowl to the other. Have your child return and pick up another ball. Repeat until the bowl is empty. If the ball is dropped, pick it up and keep playing. The first person to empty his bowl wins the game. Play again and have your child use the nondominant hand to hold the spoon and ball. For skill adaptation, use a larger spoon and allow your child to use two hands to hold it. Advanced levels can include various movements such as twirling in a circle or walking heel-toe.

LEVEL OF DIFFICULTY: Difficult.

GAME: Hallway Beanbag Bombs

OBJECT: To improve fine and gross motor skills; eye-hand coordination; hand grasping; throwing skills; balance; depth perception; arm and shoulder range of motion; spatial awareness; midline crossing; and visual, auditory, and brain stimulation.

SUPPLIES: A dozen beanbags and a large inflatable beach ball at least twelve inches in diameter.

RULES OF PLAY: Use an overhand motion to throw beanbags at a beach ball to push it several feet toward a partner. Stand facing your child about six feet apart. Each person has about four to six beanbags. Place the ball at a point midway between you and your child. Take turns throwing the beanbag at the ball and sending it away from you. The person who sends the ball into the opponent's start area wins the game. For skill adaptation, decrease or increase the throwing distance.

LEVEL OF DIFFICULTY: Difficult.

GAME: Handstands

OBJECT: To develop gross motor skills, eye-hand and eye-foot coordination, balance, abdominal strength, body control, flexibility, spatial awareness, arm and shoulder stability, depth perception, midline crossing, leg and calf control, and visual and brain stimulation.

SUPPLIES: None needed.

RULES OF PLAY: Your child should stand in a balanced position with arms raised up straight over the head. Then step forward with the dominant foot, then bend forward, placing the hands on the floor in front of the feet. Now your child should kick his or her nondominant leg up into the air as high as possible, followed by the dominant leg. The toes should be pointed up as the legs are brought together. The pose should be held for three to five seconds. Parents can support by holding the legs. Finally, the child should lower the dominant leg back to the ground, immediately followed by the nondominant leg. The feet should land together. Stand up again. Repeat two to four times. For skill adaptation, place one hand on your child's stomach and one hand on the back as he or she pushes the legs into the air. Maintain assistance for body balance. Advanced levels can try and hold the handstand for as long as possible.

LEVEL OF DIFFICULTY: Difficult.

GAME: Head, Shoulders, Knees, and Toes

OBJECT: To improve fine and gross motor skills, body awareness, flexibility, balance, eye-hand coordination, auditory processing, language development, agility, fitness, and brain development.

SUPPLIES: None needed.

RULES OF PLAY: Point to specific body parts while singing the song "Head, Shoulders, Knees, and Toes," and encourage your child to imitate your movements. For skill adaptation, play slowly and have your child mirror your actions. Advanced levels can play for speed and in foreign languages.

LEVEL OF DIFFICULTY: Easy.

LYRICS: *Head, Shoulders, Knees, and Toes*

Head, shoulders, knees, and toes, knees and toes,

Head, shoulders, knees, and toes,

Eyes and ears and mouth and nose.

GAME: Hopscotch

OBJECT: To improve fine and gross motor skills, one- and two-footed hopping, balance, footwork, quickness, eye-hand and eye-foot coordination, depth perception, spatial awareness, and visual, cognitive, and auditory development.

SUPPLIES: Sidewalk chalk or masking tape to mark the hopscotch grid. Use any small object like a small chain, rock, or shell for a marker.

RULES OF PLAY: Hop on one foot through the hopscotch squares from numbers one to eight while, inside the lines. Start by drawing a hopscotch grid with squares that are at least twice as big as your child's feet. Have your child toss a marker into square one, hop over it and land in square two. Continue hopping on one foot while landing in squares three through eight.

When reaching the last square, your child should turn around and hop back through the grid, from squares seven through two. When reaching square two, have your child bend down and pick up the marker from square one without touching the ground with the non-hopping foot. Then he or she should hop onto square one and past the starting line. On the next turn, have your child toss the marker into square two, and repeat the action. The basic rule is to not step into the square that contains a marker. Take turns. For skill adaptation, jump with two feet in each square and draw very large hopscotch squares.

LEVEL OF DIFFICULTY: Moderate.

GAME: Hot Potato

OBJECT: To improve fine motor skills, visual acuity, eye-hand coordination, bilateral hand use, quickness, balance, spatial awareness, depth perception, tossing and catching skills, and brain development.

SUPPLIES: A small stuffed animal, a beanbag or a tennis ball.

RULES OF PLAY: Stand in a balanced position about three to five feet from your child. Toss an object back and forth with your child, and imagine it is a hot potato. Toss the object in a gentle underhand motion with a high arch to allow time for your child to catch the object. Pretend you cannot hold the "potato" for too long because it is hot and will burn your fingers. Use both hands for tossing. Teach two-handed catching skills by having your child cup his hands together as if holding water. When the object makes contact with the hands, have your child bring his hands into the body to absorb the catch. See how many times in a row you and your child can catch and quickly toss the object without dropping it. For skill adaptation, use larger objects and increase or decrease the tossing distance.

LEVEL OF DIFFICULTY: Moderate.

GAME: Hula Beanbag Basketball

OBJECT: To increase fine and gross motor skills, eye-hand coordination, finger dexterity, hand grasping, spatial awareness, depth perception, under- and overhand throwing motions, balance, shoulder range of motion, midline crossing, and visual, auditory, and brain development.

SUPPLIES: One large hula hoop and five to ten beanbags.

RULES OF PLAY: Your child should stand about four to six feet away from the hula hoop, which is placed on the floor. The object of the game is to throw the beanbag using an overhand motion into the hoop to make a basket. Count the baskets made. For skill adaptation, increase or decrease the tossing distance.

LEVEL OF DIFFICULTY: Moderate.

GAME: Hula-Hoop Skip Around

OBJECT: To improve fine and gross motor skills, eye-hand and eye-foot coordination, quickness, footwork, balance, leg and ankle strength, spatial awareness, depth perception, and visual and cognitive development.

SUPPLIES: One hula hoop per person.

RULES OF PLAY: Begin in a balanced standing position with one foot inside the hoop and the other outside. Have your child try to swing the hoop around the ankle area of the foot. As the hoop rotates around, your child should lift his outside foot to give the hoop room to turn. Then your child should place the outside foot down again. Repeat. For skill adaptation, move the hoop as slow as possible and have your child walk or step over it. Advanced levels can play for speed.

LEVEL OF DIFFICULTY: Difficult.

GAME: Jumping Rope

OBJECT: To improve fine and gross motor skills; eye-hand and eye-foot coordination; footwork; quickness; balance; conditioning; depth perception; spatial awareness; hand and wrist strength; and visual, auditory, and brain stimulation.

SUPPLIES: A jump rope and lively music.

RULES OF PLAY: Your child should hold the handles of the jump rope and place the rope behind the heels of his feet. Try to flip the rope over the head in a forward direction. Use the wrists, not the shoulders, to turn the rope. As the rope approaches the feet, your child should jump off the ground a few inches, using the balls or padded portion, of his or her feet. This clears a path for the rope to pass under the body. Repeat. For skill adaptation, have your child flip the rope over the head and walk over it when it hits the ground. Gradually pick up speed. Advanced levels can try the one-footed or skipping technique, which is when you use alternate feet to skip or jump.

LEVEL OF DIFFICULTY: Difficult.

GAME: Kickin' It

OBJECT: To improve gross motor skills, eye-foot coordination, foot-work, bilateral foot development, balance, quickness, spatial awareness, depth perception, and visual and brain stimulation.

SUPPLIES: One balloon per participant.

RULES OF PLAY: Blow up the balloon to the size of a soccer ball. Have your child tap the balloon into the air as many times as possible with his feet without letting it hit the ground. Other options include passing or kicking the ball back and forth to a partner using only the feet. Use left and right feet. For skill adaptation, allow the ball to fall to the floor between kicks.

LEVEL OF DIFFICULTY: Moderate.

GAME: Laundry Hoops

OBJECT: To improve fine and gross motor skills; eye-hand coordination; hand grasping; throwing motion; spatial awareness; depth perception; shooting skills; and visual, auditory, and brain stimulation.

SUPPLIES: A laundry basket and about five to ten foam or tennis balls or a midsize playground ball.

RULES OF PLAY: Place the laundry basket about four to eight feet away from your child. Have your child toss a ball into the basket in either an underhand or overhand throwing motion, or use the two-handed shooting motion used in basketball. Award points for each basket scored. For skill adaptation, use larger balls and decrease or increase the tossing distance.

LEVEL OF DIFFICULTY: Moderate.

GAME: Limbo Stick

OBJECT: To improve gross motor skills; flexibility; balance; core and back strength; spatial awareness; depth perception; and visual, auditory, and brain stimulation.

SUPPLIES: A rounded stick, such as a broom handle, and lively music.

RULES OF PLAY: Hold the limbo stick parallel to the floor a few inches shorter than your child to make it easy for him or her to pass under the stick with minimal back bend. Have your child lean his head back, pushing the chin toward the sky as he or she moves under the stick. With each successful pass, lower the stick a fraction of an inch until your child can no longer walk under it. For skill adaptation, raise or lower the height of the stick.

LEVEL OF DIFFICULTY: Difficult.

GAME: Magic Pan

OBJECT: To improve fine motor skills, eye-hand coordination, finger dexterity, language and writing acquisition, letter identification, spatial awareness, visual and auditory stimulation, and brain development.

SUPPLIES: A rectangular baking pan and uncooked rice or small beans.

RULES OF PLAY: Fill a pan with rice or beans to a depth of about one-quarter inch, covering the entire bottom of the pan. Have your child use the index finger to draw lines, shapes, and letters in the magic pan. When done with each letter or shape, shake the pan gently and make the image disappear. For skill adaptation, use a larger pan and guide your child's finger through the rice to make shapes. Advanced levels can draw mini pictures or write words.

LEVEL OF DIFFICULTY: Easy.

GAME: Magic Wand

OBJECT: To improve fine and gross motor skills; eye-hand coordination; finger dexterity; eye tracking; hand grasping; balance; quickness; footwork; fitness; spatial awareness; depth perception; and visual, auditory, and brain stimulation.

SUPPLIES: A bottle of bubbles and enough wands for each participant. (A battery-operated bubble toy works well for this game.)

RULES OF PLAY: Have your child blow a mass of bubbles into the air and catch them on the tip of the wand. The key is for your child to hold the bubble wand using the thumb and index finger during play. Count the number of bubble catches, and alternate using the left and right hands. For skill adaptation, use a wand with a thicker handle. Advanced levels include using both hands simultaneously with a wand in each hand.

LEVEL OF DIFFICULTY: Moderate.

GAME: Mixing Bowl Toss and Catch

OBJECT: To improve fine and gross motor skills, eye-hand coordination, finger dexterity, balance, eye tracking, footwork, quickness, depth perception, spatial awareness, and visual and brain stimulation.

SUPPLIES: One large, plastic mixing bowl and a small- to moderate-sized playground ball that is approximately four to eight inches in diameter. The ball must fit into the bowl.

RULES OF PLAY: Stand four to six feet away from and facing your child, who is holding the mixing bowl. Toss the ball toward your child in an underhand motion so he or she can catch it using the bowl. Take turns and switch roles. For skill adaptation, decrease or increase the tossing distance. Advanced levels can toss the ball to the right and left of the child to encourage lateral or side-to-side movement.

LEVEL OF DIFFICULTY: Moderate.

GAME: Moving Targets

OBJECT: To improve fine and gross motor skills, eye-hand coordination, hand grasping, finger dexterity, balance, footwork, agility, depth perception, spatial awareness, and throwing and catching fundamentals.

SUPPLIES: A tennis ball or a small foam football.

RULES OF PLAY: Face your child five to ten feet apart in standing positions. Encourage him to throw a ball directly to you. Then move your location and repeat the action. Continue to play catch from different locations and angles to help your child judge distances, develop eye-tracking skills, improve depth perception, and increase arm strength. For skill adaptation, decrease or increase the throwing distance.

LEVEL OF DIFFICULTY: Moderate.

GAME: Musical Bouncing Balls

OBJECT: To improve fine and gross motor skills; eye-hand coordination; finger dexterity; arm and shoulder strength; fitness; balance; spatial skills; and visual, auditory, and brain stimulation.

SUPPLIES: Lively music and a medium-sized playground ball.

RULES OF PLAY: Have your child bounce or dribble the ball with one hand to the beat of the music. Use the pads of the fingertips and the thumb to make

the ball bounce on the floor. (Do not palm or slap at the ball.) To begin, have your child dribble the ball in place to develop hand control. Advance to walking while dribbling, then to running. Try to use the left and right hands. For skill adaptation, dribble the ball slowly with two hands.
LEVEL OF DIFFICULTY: Difficult.

GAME: Musical Fingers

OBJECT: To improve fine motor skills, eye-hand coordination, finger joint flexibility, hand control, arm movement, spatial awareness, depth perception, visual stimulation, and brain development.

SUPPLIES: Favorite classical music.

RULES OF PLAY: Have your child move his fingers in clockwise and counterclockwise circles simultaneously around each other to the rhythm of classical music. Have him or her start with the index fingers of both hands, repeat with the middle, ring, pinkie, and thumb. For skill adaptation, have your child isolate one hand and finger at a time and rotate it in circles. Continue with the other fingers and thumb. Switch hands and repeat. Gradually try to have your child coordinate the fingers moving together. Advanced levels can play for speed and quickly reverse spinning directions.

LEVEL OF DIFFICULTY: Difficult.

GAME: Nifty Number Stretches

OBJECT: To improve gross motor skills, eye-hand and eye-foot coordination, overall strength, flexibility, balance, quickness, auditory processing, midline crossing, bilateral limb use, spatial awareness, and visual and brain stimulation.

SUPPLIES: None needed.

RULES OF PLAY: Along with your child, create number shapes using just your bodies. The number zero can be formed by standing with your feet together and bending forward at your waist until your hands touch your toes. The oval space between your arms and legs creates the shape. Number one is formed by standing tall with your feet touching and your arms are raised to the sky. Be creative and continue with more numbers. For skill adaptation, provide a number chart to help with visualization. Advanced levels can turn it into a guessing game.

LEVEL OF DIFFICULTY: Moderate.

GAME: Orchestral Delights

OBJECT: To improve fine motor skills, eye-hand coordination, manual dexterity, hand and forearm strength, flexibility, eye tracking, depth perception, spatial awareness, and brain development.

SUPPLIES: A short stick or unsharpened pencil and classical music.

RULES OF PLAY: Try to move a short stick or unsharpened pencil to the beat of music like an orchestra conductor. Stand or sit on the floor next to your child. Lead by example and move the stick to the rhythm of the music. Try lines, waves, circles, squares, angles, hoops, and figure eights. Have your child move his hands to make different shapes and motions. Also have your child try moving the stick similar to an orchestra conductor with a baton, in ¼ or ¾ signature time (see illustration). For skill adaptation, move your hand slowly for your child to copy your actions, or move your child's hand to the music. Advanced levels can play independently.

LEVEL OF DIFFICULTY: Easy.

GAME: Over-and-Under Zoo Hunt

OBJECT: To develop fine and gross motor skills, cross-limb crawling, eye-hand and eye-foot coordination, core strength, fitness, balance, quickness, midline crossing, arm and leg strength, spatial awareness, depth perception, and visual and brain stimulation.

SUPPLIES: Pillows, chairs, furniture, small stools, and a collection of toys such as military men, stuffed animals, or dolls, and a child-sized backpack.

RULES OF PLAY: Set up a fun and challenging obstacle course using chairs, pillows, couches, tables, and other household items. Design several stations for your child to crawl over and under objects. At each station, hide a toy for your child to find. For example, your child can crawl under and over kitchen chairs, stand on couches, crawl over a pile of pillows, hop over a pile of books, crawl under living room tables, twirl around inside doorways, or step on small footstools. Also include stations where your child hops in place on one foot or both feet, stretches like a cat, or stands on one leg for thirty seconds. For skill adaptation, decrease or increase the number of stations or vary the level of difficulty.

LEVEL OF DIFFICULTY: Moderate.

GAME: Paper Plate Tennis

OBJECT: To develop fine and gross motor skills, eye-hand and eye-foot coordination, hand grasping, eye-tracking, depth perception, spatial awareness, balance, quickness, footwork, fitness, leg and ankle strength, and visual and brain stimulation.

SUPPLIES: Each person needs a balloon, chalk, and a tennis racket that is made from a large paper plate stapled or duct-taped to a wooden paint stick. (Paint sticks are usually available at home improvement stores.)

RULES OF PLAY: Stand in a balanced position facing your child a few feet apart. Create an imaginary net with a length of rope or chalk. Have your child hit the balloon back and forth with you, using the paper plate racket. For skill adaptation, decrease or increase the rally distance. Also try a solo game of hitting the balloon up into the air to oneself as many times as possible. Advance levels can play to a rally game.

LEVEL OF DIFFICULTY: Difficult.

GAME: Pegleg Pirate Races

OBJECT: To improve fine and gross motor skills, eye-foot coordination, one-legged hopping abilities, bilateral foot development, balance, footwork, quickness, flexibility, spatial awareness, and visual and brain stimulation.

SUPPLIES: A cardboard box or plastic toy tub to serve as a treasure chest, a dozen of your child's favorite toys, markers, stickers, magazine cutouts, and nontoxic glue.

RULES OF PLAY: Decorate a cardboard box with markers,

stickers, or magazine cutouts to serve as a treasure chest. Select about a dozen of your child's favorite toys and place them in the chest. Create start and finish lines about eight feet apart. Place the treasure chest at the finish line. Your child should begin at the starting line, hop on his dominant foot to the treasure chest, pull out a toy, and hop back. Play until the chest is empty. The winner is the person who can pull out the most toys. Play again using your nondominant foot for hopping. Other variations include using the dominant foot to hop *to* the chest and the nondominant foot on the return trip. For skill adaptation, decrease or increase the hopping distance and allow for two-footed hopping on the return to the start line.

LEVEL OF DIFFICULTY: Difficult.

GAME: Putting Around the World

OBJECT: To improve fine and gross motor skills, eye-hand coordination, hand grasping, eye tracking, spatial skills, depth perception, balance, arm and shoulder strength, flexibility, and visual and brain stimulation.

SUPPLIES: A child's golf club (a putter), about six to eight clean and empty food cans of various sizes (larger is better), and several plastic golf balls or tennis balls. Number the cans one through eight with a permanent marker. Adults can play with a regulation putter.

RULES OF PLAY: Putt a golf ball into a series of empty food cans to play a round of miniature golf. To create a putting circuit for your child, line up the empty cans on their sides, spaced four to six feet apart along a path. Arrange the cans according to their numbers. Start with can number one and have your child putt the ball into that can. Once successful, putt toward can number two.

Follow the course and have your child count his strokes. Demonstrate for your child how to hold the golf club with both hands on the grip. The right hand should be at the bottom of the grip for a right-hander and vice versa for a left-hander. Avoid placing one hand directly over the other. To putt, place the head of the club behind the ball near the floor, and gently tap it into the opening of the can. For skill adaptation, use larger cans. Also decrease or increase the distance between the cans.

LEVEL OF DIFFICULTY: Difficult.

GAME: Secret Sign Language

OBJECT: To develop fine motor skills, eye-hand coordination, finger dexterity, language acquisition, auditory processing, and visual and cognitive development.

SUPPLIES: The American Sign Language chart (see appendix).

RULES OF PLAY: Teach your child how to communicate through sign language, using the American Sign Language chart. Spell out the letters of the alphabet. For skill adaptation, sign slowly and help your child move his fingers to make letters. Advanced challenges can spell out names and words. For fun, make it a guessing game.

LEVEL OF DIFFICULTY: Difficult.

GAME: Soccer Bowling

OBJECT: To develop fine and gross motor skills, eye-foot coordination, kicking fundamentals, leg and hip strength, depth perception, spatial awareness, and visual and brain stimulation.

SUPPLIES: A size three soccer ball or small playground ball, about a dozen empty two-liter soda bottles, and sand or water.

RULES OF PLAY: Prepare the bottles by pouring about an inch of sand or water into them for stability. Tighten the cap. Place the bottles about six to ten feet away from your child. Either line them up like bowling pins or scatter them at varying distances. Demonstrate for your child how to kick a ball using the instep (or arch) of the foot. Place the ball on the floor and try to kick down the bottle pins, using both the right and left feet to develop eye-foot spatial judgment. Award points for each successful attempt. For skill adaptation, decrease or increase the kicking distance.

LEVEL OF DIFFICULTY: Moderate.

GAME: Tee for Two

OBJECT: To improve fine motor skills; eye-hand coordination; pincer grasping; finger dexterity; hand, arm, and shoulder strength; spatial skills; midline crossing and visual and brain stimulation.

SUPPLIES: Modeling dough, plastic place mats, and a bag of golf tees.

RULES OF PLAY: Poke golf tees into balls of dough using the pincer grasp, and create interesting designs, objects, and animals. (Tees can be purchased at sports, toy, or department stores or at golfing facilities. Be aware that tees can be a choking hazard for young children.) Protect the tabletop with a plastic place mat. Demonstrate for your child how to make a ball of dough about three to five inches in diameter by rubbing the dough between the palms of your hands in a circular motion. Place a bowl of golf tees in front of your child. Have your child pick up one tee at a time from the bowl using the tripod grasp with the thumb and index and middle fingers. Then push the tees into the dough ball, using just the index finger. Make faces or objects with the dough and tees. To make animals, create smaller dough balls for the head, torso, and limbs. Once one creation is made, roll out another dough ball and start over. For skill adaptation, start a basic dough ball for your child and allow him to finish it. Offer help with hand grasping and finger control.

LEVEL OF DIFFICULTY: Moderate.

GAME: Volleyball Beach Style

OBJECT: To develop fine and gross motor skills; eye-hand and eye-foot coordination; arm, shoulder, and hand strength; spatial awareness; language development; fitness; balance; footwork; quickness; volleyball fundamentals; and auditory, visual, and brain stimulation.

SUPPLIES: An inflatable beach ball and chalk.

RULES OF PLAY: Begin in a standing, ready position, facing your child a few feet away. Your child's feet should be shoulder-width apart and the arms relaxed in front of the body. The knees should be slightly bent and the upper body leaning forward.

To pass the ball: Your child should open the palms of both hands and face them upward. He or she should place the back of the top hand onto the palm of the bottom. The child should keep the hands pressed together during the bump pass; arms are extended straight in front of the body. The child should use the platform area of his forearms—the padded area between the wrist and elbow—to pass the ball to a partner.

To underhand serve: A right-hander should stand sideways with the left shoulder directed toward the net line or target and vice versa for a left-hander. The ball should be held waist high in the nonserving hand. A fist should be made with the serving hand. Be sure your child's thumb is straight up and snuggles into the curve of his bent index finger. It should look like the letter *A* in sign language. Your child's serving hand should strike the ball in an upward arch or rainbow to lift it up into the air and toward the target. They should serve the ball with the palm side up.

LEVEL OF DIFFICULTY: Difficult.

The Golden Years: Four-to-Six-Year-Olds	Fine Motor	Gross Motor	Arms & Shoulders	Hands & Fingers	Legs & Feet	Core Strength	Balance	Cognitive & Brain	Flexibility	Quickness	Visual	Spatial Awareness	Depth Perception	Eye-Hand	Eye-Foot	Midline Crossing	Bilateral Limb	Supplies
Awesome Alphabet Stretches	•	•	•	•	•	•	•	•	•	•	•	•	•	•	•	•	•	None
Backward Running and Jumping		•	•	•	•	•	•	•	•	•	•		•				•	None
Backyard T-Ball	•	•	•	•	•	•	•	•	•	•	•	•	•	•		•	•	Plastic bat, wiffle ball, T-ball stand
Badminton Boogie	•	•	•	•	•	•	•	•	•	•	•		•	•	•	•	•	Child's badminton rackets, shuttlecock or birdie
Balance Beam		•	•		•	•	•	•	•	•	•	•	•	•	•		•	Wood, nails, varnish, sandpaper
Beanbag Bowling	•	•	•	•	•		•	•	•	•	•	•	•	•	•	•	•	Beanbags, two-liter soda bottles
Beanbag Flapjacks	•	•	•	•	•	•	•	•	•	•	•	•	•	•		•	•	Beanbags, child's tennis racket
Bountiful Broad Jump		•	•		•	•	•	•	•	•	•	•	•		•		•	Masking tape or chalk
Cat Stretch		•	•	•	•	•	•		•		•		•	•	•		•	Music
Criss-Cross Legs Across		•			•	•	•	•	•	•	•	•	•		•	•	•	Chalk or rope
Cutting by Design	•		•	•			•		•	•	•	•	•	•		•	•	Paper, glue, child's scissors
Doggie Races		•	•	•	•	•	•	•	•	•	•	•	•	•	•		•	None
Dribbling Obstacle Course	•	•	•	•	•	•	•	•	•	•	•	•	•	•	•		•	Sport cones, basketball, chalk
Feet on Fire		•			•	•	•	•	•	•	•	•	•	•	•		•	None
Finger ABCs	•		•	•			•	•	•	•	•	•	•	•		•	•	None
Fingertip Push-Ups	•	•	•	•		•	•	•	•	•	•	•	•	•		•	•	None
Fishnet Golf	•			•	•		•		•	•	•	•	•	•		•	•	Fishnet, golf balls
Five Little Piggies	•		•	•		•	•	•	•	•	•	•	•				•	None

The Golden Years: Four-to-Six-Year-Olds	Fine Motor	Gross Motor	Arms & Shoulders	Hands & Fingers	Legs & Feet	Core Strength	Balance	Cognitive & Brain	Flexibility	Quickness	Visual	Spatial Awareness	Depth Perception	Eye-Hand	Eye-Foot	Midline Crossing	Bilateral Limb	Supplies
Flying Saucer Toss	•	•	•	•		•	•	•	•	•	•	•	•	•		•	•	Flying disc
Follow-the-Leader	•	•	•	•	•	•	•	•	•	•	•	•	•	•	•	•	•	Music
Forward Rolls		•	•		•	•	•	•			•	•	•	•	•		•	None
Go Fish Snack Time	•	•	•	•		•		•		•	•	•	•	•		•	•	Dice, jar with lid, fish-shaped crackers
Golf Ball Races	•	•	•	•	•	•	•	•	•	•	•	•	•	•	•	•	•	Golf balls, empty bowls, tablespoons
Hallway Beanbag Bombs	•	•	•	•		•	•	•	•	•	•	•	•	•	•	•	•	Beanbags, beach ball
Handstands	•	•	•	•	•	•	•	•	•	•	•	•	•	•	•	•	•	None
Head, Shoulders, Knees, and Toes	•	•	•	•	•	•	•	•	•	•	•	•	•	•	•	•	•	None
Hopscotch	•	•	•	•	•	•	•	•	•	•	•	•	•	•	•	•	•	Chalk, small chain
Hot Potato	•	•	•	•			•	•	•	•	•	•	•	•		•	•	Stuffed animal, ball or beanbag
Hula Beanbag Basketball	•	•	•	•		•	•	•	•	•	•	•	•	•		•	•	Hula Hoop, beanbags
Hula-Hoop Skip Around	•	•	•	•	•	•	•	•	•	•	•	•	•	•	•		•	Hula-Hoop,
Jumping Rope	•	•	•	•	•	•	•	•	•	•	•	•	•	•	•		•	Jump rope, music
Kickin' It		•	•		•	•	•	•	•	•	•	•	•		•	•	•	Balloons
Laundry Hoops	•	•	•	•	•	•	•	•	•	•	•	•	•	•		•	•	Balls, laundry basket
Limbo Stick		•	•		•	•	•	•	•	•	•	•	•		•		•	Rounded stick or broom
Magic Pan	•		•	•				•		•		•	•	•	•		•	Baking pan, uncooked rice
Magic Wand	•	•	•	•		•		•		•		•	•	•		•	•	Bubble solution with wand
Mixing Bowl Toss and Catch	•	•	•	•	•	•	•	•	•	•	•	•	•	•	•			Large mixing bowls, playground ball

The Golden Years: Four-to-Six-Year-Olds	Fine Motor	Gross Motor	Arms & Shoulders	Hands & Fingers	Legs & Feet	Core Strength	Balance	Cognitive & Brain	Flexibility	Quickness	Visual	Spatial Awareness	Depth Perception	Eye-Hand	Eye-Foot	Midline Crossing	Bilateral Limb	Supplies
Moving Targets	•	•	•	•	•	•	•	•	•	•	•	•	•	•	•	•	•	Tennis ball or foamball
Musical Bouncing Balls	•	•	•	•	•	•	•	•	•	•	•	•	•	•	•	•	•	Playground ball, music
Musical Fingers	•		•	•			•	•	•	•	•	•	•	•			•	Music
Nifty Number Stretches		•	•		•	•	•	•	•		•	•	•				•	None
Orchestral Delights	•	•	•	•												•	•	Classical music, unsharpened pencil or stick
Over-and-Under Zoo Hunt	•	•	•	•	•	•	•	•	•	•	•	•	•	•	•	•	•	Pillows, chairs, cushions, furniture, toys, backpack
Paper Plate Tennis	•	•	•	•	•	•	•	•	•	•	•	•	•	•	•	•	•	Balloon, paper plate, duct tape, ruler or paint stick, chalk
Pegleg Pirate Races	•	•	•		•		•		•	•	•	•	•	•	•	•	•	Box, toys, markers, stickers, glue
Putting Around the World	•	•	•	•	•	•	•	•	•	•	•	•	•	•	•	•	•	Child's golf club, ball, empty tin cans
Secret Sign Language	•	•	•	•			•	•	•	•	•	•	•	•		•	•	Sign language chart in appendix
Soccer Bowling	•	•	•	•	•	•	•	•	•	•	•	•	•	•	•		•	Soccer ball, empty two-liter soda bottles
Tee for Two	•	•	•	•		•	•	•	•		•	•	•	•			•	Modeling dough, plastic place mats, golf tees
Volleyball Beach Style	•	•	•	•	•	•	•	•	•	•	•	•	•	•	•	•	•	Inflatable beach ball, chalk

15

Warm-Up and Stretch
for Four- to Six-Year-Olds

A good warm-up consists of a slow and easy physical activity like jogging to prepare the body to play a vigorous sport. The goal is to increase blood flow, circulation, and heart rate in an athlete's body. A light warm-up also raises a person's core temperature and cuts down on injuries. Kids might jog, skip, or hop for about two minutes in an open area outside or warm up indoors by running in place.

After a light warm-up, it is important to do a simple yet safe stretching routine. A good program should start with the head, neck, and shoulder areas, and work down to the legs, feet, and toes. Begin in a balanced standing position for these stretches. Your feet should be shoulder-width apart. Your back should be straight and tall. Try to hold each stretch for about ten seconds, and perform about two to four repetitions per stretch. Be sure to avoid bouncing of any kind since it could cause injury. Here is a condensed list of stretches, followed by detailed explanations.

THE PROUD PARENTS' STRETCHING ROUTINES

Giraffe Stretch: For the Head and Neck

Begin in a balanced standing position. Your hands are resting down at your sides. Lift your right arm and hand up toward the sky, and wrap it around your head to gently hold the left side of your head near your ear. Urge your head to lean toward the right shoulder. Feel the stretch on the left side of the neck. Next, lift your left hand up to the sky and hold your head on the right side near the ear. Pull the head toward the left shoulder. Now hold your chin on your chest, and then your nose to the sky.

Leaning Towers: Lateral Side Stretch

Begin in a balanced standing position. Place both arms and hands straight up toward the sky. Your palms are facing upward. The stretch is to lean slowly your arms to the side a little bit. Now lean toward the other side.

I Don't Know: Shoulder Shrugs

Stand in a balanced position with your arms down by your sides. Shrug your shoulders up and down, and then roll them forward and backward as if to express "I don't know."

Elbow Up: Arm and Triceps Stretch

Begin in a balanced standing position. Now point your right hand up to the sky, and then gently lower it so your right palm is on your right shoulder blade. Place your left hand on the right pointed elbow to hold it securely. Maintain the stretch for ten seconds. Switch sides.

Airplane: Arm Circles

Begin in a balanced standing position. Lift your arms shoulder-height out to your sides with your palms facing upward. Move your arms in small and then larger circles, forward and backward like the wings of a plane.

Helicopter: Torso Twists

Begin in a balanced standing position. Your arms are straight out shoulder-height to the sides. Your palms are facing upward. Now gently twist right and left like a helicopter propeller.

The Diver: Standing Hamstring Stretch

Begin in a standing balanced position. Bend your knees in a squat position to place your hands on the floor directly next to your feet. Your heels are flat in the floor, and your chest is resting on top of your thighs. Slowly try to straighten out your legs. Stop when you feel too much tension. Bend back down into the starting squat position and repeat two to four times.

Sitting Toe Touches: Hamstring Stretch

Sit on the ground with your legs extended straight out in front. With a straight back, bend forward at the hips and reach for your toes. Your stomach should be over your thighs. Hold the stretch for ten seconds and repeat two to four times.

Quiet Butterfly: Sitting Groin Stretch

Sit on the floor with a very straight back. If you are indoors, press your back against a wall. Bend your legs and knees out to the sides. Your heels are pressed together as they meet in the middle of your body. Pretend your legs are like the wings of a very still butterfly remaining quiet and motionless. Do not bounce your legs up and down. Finally, gently press your elbows on your inner thighs and slightly press your legs to the floor. Hold for ten seconds. Repeat two to four times.

Knee Hugs: Lower Back Stretch

Lie on your back with your face up to the sky. Gently bring your knees up to your chest and hug them with both arms. Try to lift your hips off the floor. Hold the hug for ten seconds. Repeat twice.

Awesome Abdominal Crunches: Abdomen and Torso

Lie on your back with your face up to the sky. Now place your hands next to your ears (not behind your head). Lift and bend your knees so that your feet are flat on the floor. The action is to lift your head, neck, upper shoulders, and arms only six inches upward in the direction of the sky. Hold for a second and slowly lower your body with control to the floor. Repeat four to ten times.

Quacky Quadriceps: Legs, Thighs, and Quadriceps

Lie facedown on the floor. Now bend your right knee, and lift your right heel directly toward your buttocks. Grab the right ankle and gently pull the right heel in for the stretch to your buttocks. Be very careful not to overpull the motion or push the feet out to the sides. Stop when you feel tension and hold it for ten seconds. Switch feet. Repeat two times.

Traditional Push-Ups: Arms, Shoulders, and Torso Strength

Begin by lying facedown on the floor with your legs out straight. Place your palms on the ground, about head and shoulder level. Your toes are supporting your lower torso. The action is to use your arms to push up your entire body in one motion. Using control, gently lower your body into the starting position. For a variation, you can bend at the knees and place them on the ground for mini push-ups.

Push the Wall Down: Lower Leg and Achilles Tendon Stretch

Begin in a standing position a few feet from a fence or wall. Lean forward and place your hands and forearms against the vertical surface. One leg is bent, and the other is straight out with the heel raised. Shift your weight forward against the wall while you try to press the back of your heel to the floor. Hold it for ten seconds and switch leg positions. Repeat two to four times.

Notes

Chapter 1: What Is Physical Fitness?

1. Medical College of Georgia, "Exercise Improves Thinking, Reduces Diabetes Risk In Overweight Children," *ScienceDaily*, October 23, 2007. Retrieved October 30, 2007, from www.sciencedaily.com /releases/2007/10/071022120209.htm.
2. John Ratey, "Exercise Helps Students in the Classroom," interview by Patricia Neighmond, *Morning Edition* with Patricia Neighmond, National Public Radio, August 31, 2006, www.npr.org/templates/story/story.php?storyId=5742152.

Chapter 2: Positive Child's Play

1. Kurt Badenhausen, "The World's Top-Earning Athletes," Forbes.com, October 26, 2007, www.forbes.com.

Chapter 4: Building Better Brains

1. A. Gopnic, A. Meltzoff, P. Kuhl, *The Scientist in the Crib: What Early Learning Tells Us About the Mind* (New York: HarperCollins, 1999).
2. Jack Fincher, *The Brain: Mystery of Matter and Mind* (New York: Torstar, 1984).
3. Diane Luckow, "Tracking the Progress of Romanian Orphans," SFU News Online, vol. 28. no. 4, October 16, 2003, www.sfu.ca/sfunews/sfu_news/archives_2003/sfunews10160317.htm.

Chapter 6: Right- or Left-Handed

1. Neuroscience for Kids, "One Brain . . . or Two?: Handedness," www.faculty.washington.edu/chudler/split.html/.
2. Texas Child Care, www.childcarequarterly.com/spring07_sroty3.htm
3. For more information, visit Answers.com, www.answers.com/topic/handedness?cat=health.
4. Special thanks to Tammy Shaffer, occupational and sensory therapist, for her insights in helping me write this chapter.

Chapter 7: Gross Motor Development

1. J. Herbert, J. Gross, H. Hayne, "Crawling Is Associated with More Flexible Memory Retrieval by 9-Month-Old Infants," *Developmental Science*, vol, 10, no. 2 (March 2007): 183–89.
2. M.H. McEwan, R.E. Dihoff, G.M. Brosvic, "Early Infant Crawling Experience Is Reflected in Later Motor Skill Development," *Perceptual and Motor Skills*, vol. 72, no. 1 (February 1991): 75–79.

3. M.S. Hempel, "Neurological Development During Toddling Age in Normal Children and Children at Risk for Developmental Disorders," *Early Human Development,* September 1993, 47–57.

Chapter 8: Coordination and Sidedness
1. Stanley Coren, *The Left-Hander Syndrome: The Causes and Consequences of Left-Handedness* (New York: Free Press, 1992).
2. C. Porac and S. Coren, *Lateral Preferences and Human Behavior* (New York: Springer-Verlag, 1981).
3. Stanley Coren, *The Left-Hander Syndrome.*
4. C. Porac and S. Coren, *Lateral Preferences and Human Behavior.*

Chapter 10: Rules of Play and Praise
1. Deborah Norville, *Thank You Power: Making the Science of Gratitude Work for You* (Nashville, TN: Thomas Nelson, 2007).

Chapter 11: Crib Capers in the First Twelve Months
1. "The Bubble Song" rhyme by K. Ronney, 2008.

Chapter 12: Athletic Activities for One, Two, and You
1. Adaptation by K. Ronney, 2008.
2. "Up and Down" rhyme by K. Ronney, 2008.

Chapter 13: Building Blocks for Three-Year-Olds
1. "All About Me" rhyme by K. Ronney, 2008.
2. "Aussie Kangaroos" rhyme by K. Ronney, 2008.

Recommended Resources

Web Sites

National Center for Biotechnology Information, www.pubmed.gov.

Anything Left-Handed, www.anythingleft-handed.co.uk/fam_history.html#philosophers.

Simon Fraser University, www.sfu.ca/sfunews/sfu_news/archives_2003/sfunews10160317.htm.

wikipedia.org/wiki/American_Sign_Language_alphabet.

Learning Success Institute, www.learning successcoach.com.

American Academy of Pediatrics Ages and Stages, www.aap.org/healthtopics/stages.cfm.

Books & Magazines

Linda Acredolo and Susan Goodwyn, *Baby Signs: How to Talk with Your Baby Before Your Baby Can Talk* (New York: McGraw-Hill, 2002).

Thomas Armstrong, *In Their Own Way: Discovering and Encouraging Your Child's Personal Learning Style* (New York: Tarcher/Putnam, 1987).

Thomas Armstrong, *You're Smarter Than You Think: A Kid's Guide to Multiple Intelligences* (Minneapolis, MN: Free Spirit Publishing, 2003).

Kurt Badenhausen, "The World's Top-Earning Athletes," Forbes.com, October 26, 2007, www.forbes.com.

Jenn Berman, *The A to Z Guide to Raising Happy*, Confident Kids, CA: New World Library, 2007.

D. Ross Campbell, MD, *How to Really Parent Your Child*, CO: David C. Cook, 1992.

Don Campbell, *The Mozart Effect for Children* (New York: HarperCollins Inc., 1995).

Christine D'Amico, *The Pregnant Woman's Companion*, MN: Attitude Press, Inc., 2004.

Susan Linn, *The Case for Make Believe: Saving Play in a Commercialized World* (New York: The New Press, 2008).

Mariaemma Willis, M.S., *Discover Your Child's Learning Style*, Crown Publishing Group, 1999.

Appendix

BLACK DOT (SEE P. 142)

RECIPE FOR HOMEMADE PLAYING DOUGH

Ingredients: 1 cup of flour, ½ cup salt, 2 teaspoons of cream of tartar, 2 teaspoons of vegetable oil, 1 cup of water. Optional: add a package of Kool-Aid drink mix to the water for color and scent.

Directions: Boil water. In a separate bowl, mix the dry ingredients together, then add them to the water. Lower the heat and stir until the dough leaves the sides of the pan and sticks together. Remove dough from pan, let it cool slightly, and knead it into a ball. Store the dough in an airtight bag or container. The recipe can be doubled or tripled.

Date	Proud Parents' Guide Game	Age Group	Fine Motor Skill	Gross Motor Skill	Total Body (Fine and Gross)	Observation

STRETCHING CHART FOR FOUR- TO SIX-YEAR-OLDS

Name	Body Part	How To Do the Stretch
Giraffe Stretch	Head and neck	Begin in a balanced standing position. Your hands are resting down at your sides. Lift your right arm and hand up toward the sky, and wrap it around your head to gently hold the left side of your head near your ear. Urge your head to lean toward the right shoulder. Feel the stretch on the left side of the neck. Next, lift your left hand up to the sky and hold your head on the right side near the ear. Pull the head gently toward the left shoulder. Now hold your chin on your chest, and then your nose to the sky.
Leaning Towers	Lateral Side Stretch	Begin in a balanced standing position. Your palms are facing upward. Place both arms and hands straight up toward the sky. The stretch is to lean your arms to the side a little bit. Now lean toward the other side.
I Don't Know	Shoulder Shrugs	Stand in a balanced position with your arms down by your sides. Shrug your shoulders up and down, and then roll them forward and backward as if to express "I don't know."
Elbow Up	Arm Circles Triceps Stretch	Begin in a balanced standing position. Now point your right hand up to the sky, and then gently lower it so your right palm is on your right shoulder blade. Place your left hand on the right pointed elbow to hold it securely. Maintain the stretch for 10 seconds. Switch sides.
Airplane	Arms Circles	Begin in a balanced standing position. Lift your arms shoulder-height out to your sides with your palms facing upward. Move your arms in small and then larger circles, forward and backward like the wings of a plane.

Helicopter	Torso or Trunk Twists	Begin in a balanced standing position. Your arms are straight out shoulder-height to the sides. Now gently twist right and left like a helicopter propeller.
The Diver	Standing Hamstring Stretch	Begin in a standing balanced position. Bend your knees in a squat position to place your hands on the floor directly next to your feet. Your heels are flat on the floor, and your chest is resting on top of your thighs. Slowly try to straighten out your legs. Stop when you feel too much tension. Bend back down into the starting squat position and repeat 2 to 4 times.
Sitting Toe Touches	Hamstring Stretch	Sit on the ground with your legs extended straight out in front. With a straight back, bend forward at the hips and reach for your toes. Your stomach should be over your thighs. Hold the stretch for 10 seconds and repeat 2 to 4 times.
Quiet Butterfly	Sitting Groin Stretch	Sit on the floor with a very straight back. If you are indoors, press your back against a wall. Bend your legs and knees out to the sides. Your heels are pressed together as they meet in the middle of your body. Pretend your legs are like the wings of a very still butterfly remaining quiet and motionless. Do not bounce your legs up and down. Finally, gently press your elbows on your inner thighs and slightly press your legs to the floor. Hold for 10 seconds. Repeat 2 to 4 times.
Knee Hugs	Lower Back Stretch	Lie on your back with your face up to the sky. Gently bring your knees up to your chest and hug them with both arms. Try to lift your hips off the floor. Hold the hug for 10 seconds. Repeat twice.

Awesome Abdominal Crunches	Abdomen and Torso	Lie on your back with your face up to the sky. Now place your hands next to your ears (not behind your head). Lift and bend your knees so that your feet are flat on the floor. The action is to lift your head, neck, upper shoulders, and arms only six inches upward in the direction of the sky. Hold for a second and slowly lower your body with control to the floor. Repeat 4 to 10 times.
Quacky Quadriceps	Legs, Thighs, and Quadriceps	Lie face down on the floor. Now bend your right knee, and lift your right heel directly toward your buttocks. Grab the right ankle and gently pull the right heel in for the stretch to your buttocks. Be very careful not to over-pull the motion or push the feet out to the sides. Stop when you feel tension and hold it for 10 seconds. Switch feet. Repeat 2 times.
Traditional Push Ups	Arms, Shoulders, Torso Strength	Begin by lying facedown on the floor with your legs out straight. Place your palms on the ground, about head and shoulder level. Your toes are supporting your lower torso. The action is to use your arms to push up your entire body in one motion. Using control, gently lower your body into the starting position. For a variation: bend at the knees and place them on the ground for mini push-ups.
Push the Wall Down	Lower Leg and Achilles Tendon Stretch	Begin in a standing position a few feet from a fence or wall. Lean forward and place your hands and forearms against the vertical surface. One leg is bent, and the other is straight out with the heel raised. Shift your weight forward against the wall while you try to press the back of your heel to the floor. Hold it for 10 seconds and switch leg positions. Repeat 2 to 4 times.

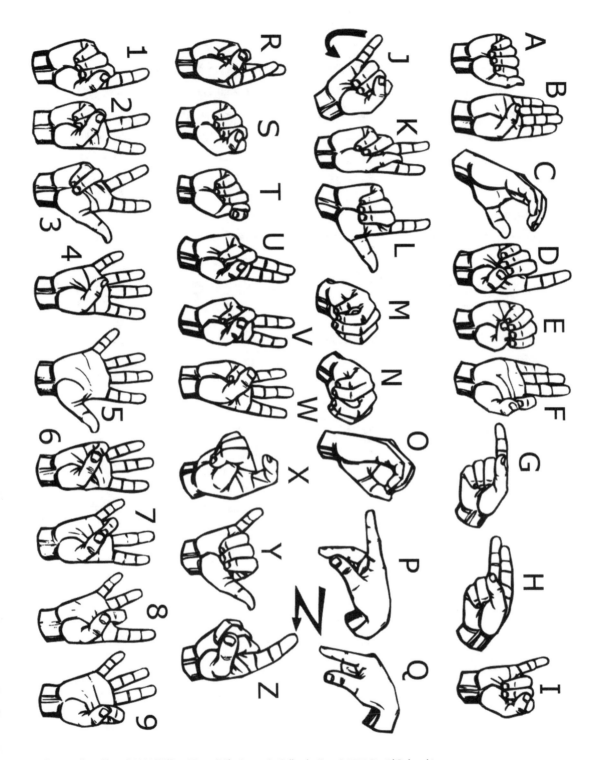

Acknowledgments

Writing this book was a team effort. Special thanks to my husband, who became Mr. Mom, and my three girls for their patience and inspiration. Gratitude goes to Marilyn and Phil Ronney, my proofreader and media expert; Irene and Bob Frawley; and Mae and Marvin Goodson—all who supported this dream.

Thanks also to my agent, Paul Levine; and editor, Debbie Wickwire, who believed in this project from the start. It's a privilege to work with you. Heartfelt thanks to artist Jorge Pacheco and my editing posse of Karen Pearlman, Rose Leenerts, and the Thomas Nelson staff.

Friends played a crucial role. Thanks to the Katz and Quick families for the soccer rides, the Freibergs for the kind words, and my preschool moms for the coffee chats. To friends Heather Hafner, Jackie Hall, and Suzie Aulicino—thanks for listening. To my Lake Murray and Patrick Henry High tennis families— you're the best.

My medical and technical experts were awesome. Thanks to Whitney Edwards, MD, for writing the foreword, and appreciation to Alan Schwartz, MD; Janet Crow, MD; physician assistant Linda Schwartz; occupational therapist Tammy Shaffer; physical therapist Dara Hunt; and biologist Michelle Mardahl-Dumesnil, PhD.

My appreciation also goes to educators Eldora Winter, Marina Monta, Pete Saccone, LaDreda Lewis and the Language Academy teachers. Thanks also to USTA's Kirk Anderson and Melanie Bischoff (and all of the folks in the NY and LA offices), Craig Pippert from Special Olympics, Wayne Wilson at the LA84 Foundation, Dan Santorum at the PTR and artist Joe Nyiri.

Finally, thanks to all for your support and my gratitude to those who wrote endorsements for this book. God bless you all!

About the Author

Karen Ronney, an accomplished NCAA tennis player and a world touring pro, used her bachelor degrees in journalism and public relations to become a seasoned staff writer for several prestigious publications, including the *Los Angeles Times*, *San Diego Union-Tribune*, *Los Angeles Daily News*, and *Chicago Tribune*. A professional journalist for more than twenty years, Ronney has also spent fifteen years as a public speaker and twenty-five years as a professional coach.

Karen has worked with coaches and athletes in a variety of sports including tennis, soccer, volleyball, track, golf, basketball, baseball, softball, and football. As a licensed United States Professional Tennis Association instructor, she is also the director of the Mission Trails Tennis and Golf Academy for kids ages five to fifteen. A master coaching instructor, Ronney has led hundreds of seminars as a representative of the LA84 Foundation. She is also a national coach for the Special Olympics, and is affiliated with the Professional Tennis Registry.

She travels nationwide for the United States Tennis Association as a Regional Coaching Workshop Trainer. Karen is a dynamic speaker on the mental, philosophical, psychological, and emotional aspects of working with children. She educates youth coaches and parents on sportsmanship issues, health and safety, and the technical side of sports.